STATE
OF THE
GAME

A Look at Baseball as it Enters the 21st Century

Thomas U. Tuttle

Beaver's Pond Press

Edina, Minnesota

ISBN: 1-890676-58-6

Library of Congress Catalog Card Number: 00-101612

First Printing: March 2000
Printed in the Unites States of America

04   03   02   01   00   6   5   4   3   2   1

Cover design by Jack Caravela and John K. Tuttle
Interior design by Mori Studio

Address orders to:

Beaver's Pond Press

5125 Danen's Drive
Edina, Minnesota 55439-1465
(952) 829-8818

This book is dedicated to my father,
Robert D. Tuttle,
who has been a good friend,
a great coach
and a wonderful Dad.
Thank you for your love,
patience
and support.

CONTENTS

ACKNOWLEDGMENTS

This book is the result of a two-year effort to gather a variety of information related to baseball, and thus includes conversations with players, coaches, writers, vendors, scouts, and grounds people and numerous fans. I would like to express my appreciation to all of those who contributed their time to this effort.

There are a number of people who should be thanked for their skilled efforts on behalf of this project. Jeff Lucast provided a valuable extra set of eyes and hands, as did Carolyn Cesario and Gretchen Logan. Thank you for your tireless work on my behalf.

Some people who helped to fire my passion for the game through the years should be recognized: coaches Dave Williams and Dave Keefe, along with a variety of players including Dave Brown, Bill Reynolds, Kevin McPhillamy, Frank Goldak, Bill Dierberger and many others. To my many teammates throughout the years, I say thank you.

To Melissa Scott and Corky Tuttle, bless you both.

To Greg Wagner of Wagner Photography in Fort Myers, Florida, thank you.

I am obliged to Jack Caravela of Mori Studio for his extraordinarily high-quality design work and creativity.

This project became a shared vision with Doug Benson, former managing editor of *Twin Cities Business Monthly,* who was the managing editor of this book. My heartfelt gratitude for your steady hand.

Finally, I would be remiss not to thank my publisher Milt Adams of Beaver's Pond Press, for providing clarity of purpose to my writing efforts. It's finally your turn to buy breakfast, Milton.

INTRODUCTION

I moved to Minnesota in the winter of 1990-1991. Within the following twelve months or so, my new home state played host to the Final Four in college basketball's NCAA Division I tournament, placed a team in the Stanley Cup Finals (the former Minnesota North Stars), hosted the Special Olympics, held the U.S. Open National Golf Tournament (played at Hazeltine National and won by the late Payne Stewart), hosted Super Bowl XXVI and saw the Minnesota Twins defeat the Atlanta Braves four games to three in one of the most dramatic World Series finishes ever.

Given my sports-spectacular introduction to Minnesota, I was certain that I had moved into a sports-lover's Nirvana. A few short years later, however, professional sports in the land of 10,000 lakes had undergone a series of major changes. The North Stars hockey team had left Minnesota for Texas, leaving Minnesota Timberwolves basketball as the only professional sports entertainment option during the winter months.

Ownership of the Wolves changed hands (which some observers believe propelled the team from being a perpetual doormat to near-contender status), as did ownership of the Minnesota Vikings football franchise (though with little apparent effect on the team's reputation as a solid contender fated not to win a Super Bowl). And the once-beloved baseball team, the Minnesota Twins, had descended from the giddy heights of a World Series championship to the disheartening status of a franchise under the gun, driven by baseball's bizarre economics to a point where the likelihood of leaving town vastly exceeded the odds of winning another championship.

My, how the times do change.

Beyond the profusion of major sports events that greeted me my first year in Minnesota, I've come to realize that the traditions of sport, both professional and amateur, run deep in my adopted state and are in many ways independent of the vagaries afflicting professional franchises. And not just competitive sport. For a lot of folks, physical fitness is a big part of being a Minnesotan, and I have never seen health club systems like those I've found here. It must have something to do with the winter weather. When I went to the gym that first winter of '90–'91 to play pick-up basketball, I always found an extraordinarily good game to participate in, and the players were top notch.

The same thing happened when I played recreational tennis. The quality of competition surprised me; it seemed like any match that I played involved players who could really play the game. The athleticism in the state of Minnesota, I decided, is of great quality.

It took me a couple of years to learn about town team baseball. (I refer to it as town ball, and you will hear a lot more about it as you read on.)

What I found when I discovered town ball was a wonderful world of baseball played in towns throughout the state of Minnesota. Not just casual, "toss-the-ball-around-let's-have-a-game" baseball, but high-quality competition in some of the most surprisingly quaint and quirky ballparks that I had ever seen. Being from Chicago I didn't know such a thing existed. I have always been something of a big-city guy.

Many of these town parks are superior examples of rural design

accomplishment that also serve as a reminder of the timelessness of the game of baseball. They are things of quiet elegance and beauty.

Since I have been in Minnesota, I have played in a couple dozen of these parks. I feel blessed to have had the opportunity to share in the tradition that is Minnesota town baseball.

That's because Minnesota is a place where good baseball is played and where baseball history is made. The Minnesota Twins won two world titles within five years and have a tradition that includes some of the greatest names in the game; Allison, Killebrew, Carew, Puckett, Hrbek, Molitor, and Steinbach, to name just a few. The University of Minnesota has won three national titles over the years and competes annually for the Big 10 Title. The program has designs on larger accomplishments. Small-college baseball flourishes in the state, as do the high school game and all manner of youth competition.

Baseball is alive and well in Minnesota.

In the past few years I have often heard the Commissioner of Baseball speak of "Baseball leaving the state of Minnesota" when he refers to a possible move by the Minnesota Twins to another state. If the Twins were to leave, Major League Baseball would indeed be gone, but baseball itself would not depart. The St. Paul Saints would continue to play their high-level independent minor league ball-games. The Golden Gophers would continue to challenge the finest teams in the nation, as would St. Thomas University and their Division Three championship-quality squad. Cretin-Derham Hall, owners of a recent 66-game winning streak and the high school home of Paul Molitor, will long endure. Town ball will continue to go on everywhere in the state during Minnesota's beautiful springs and summers.

The state even welcomes older players; I eventually found a 35-and-over league in which I could continue to practice my skills on various "fields of dreams."

Minnesota is a state that knows the game. Minnesotans are not foolish enough to accept any blame for the failures of its big league franchise, nor for the actions of the powers that be in Major League Baseball. Minnesotans are coming to realize that the game is over for small market major league teams if something isn't done to reduce or eliminate the current economic disparity those teams face in comparison with their large market counterparts. In many ways, the citizens have decided that any talk about building stadiums is putting the facilities cart ahead of the economic horse.

Despite the problems facing Major League Baseball, most Minnesota baseball fans have not given up. I am a fan of big league base-ball. I love to watch the best players in the game participate in their craft almost as much as I enjoy playing the game myself. All of us who are fans are concerned about Major League Baseball and in particular about salaries that continue to escalate into the stratosphere, to the ultimate detriment of the game.

Financial issues are threatening the wonderful game of Major League Baseball. The sad reality is that a team with a Twins-like $17 million payroll is really on equal footing with one sporting a $50 million payroll; neither of them will be able to compete against the $100 million budgets of the big-market super clubs.

Sitting in the bleachers at Wrigley Field one day in 1999, enjoying the blue sky and the smell of the grass, the warm breeze and the sunshine, remembering how peanuts and Cracker Jacks and hot dogs taste twice as good as they do at home, I was reminded that the highest level of the game of baseball has been warmly embraced by generations, by my father and his father, and his father's father. Generations have loved the game, but the major league game today is suffering some real pain. How can it not, when many Major League Baseball franchises have no realistic chance of competing to be the best?

After that game ended, I stayed in the stands just gazing at the ballpark for a full half hour, letting my mind wander back to my many happy memories of golden afternoons spent at Wrigley Field. My reverie was finally interrupted when I was asked to leave by a member of the clean-up crew.

As I took a last look at the ballpark, I was struck by the stark contrast between beautiful Wrigley's "friendly confines" and the "lonely confines" of the Metrodome. At Wrigley, the field may be empty when the Cubs are not playing, but the dreams remain. When the Twins ballpark, the Hubert H. Humphrey Metrodome, is empty, the feeling is that of the desolation of a bare stage in an empty theater. It sounds different, it smells different. It feels different. For me, baseball is not the same without the sunshine. The dreams are different.

There certainly are stadium issues that should be considered.

I don't think most Minnesotans could abide losing the Minnesota Twins. I may be wrong, and it may happen, but it would be a great loss. I remember what Dan Wilson, the former Gopher and current Seattle star said: "I think that, if you lose a major league franchise, it has effects that people don't anticipate. There are costs associated with a city suffering the loss of a baseball team, and with

my fond memories of Minnesota, I really hope that things can work out there. But I know the game itself needs to address some issues."

Yes it does.

Mark McGwire told me at the 1998 All Star game "nobody is worth the money that is being paid today. And it could get worse." Mark McGwire is a great ballplayer and a tremendous hitter, as well as a good human being who brings a lot to the game of baseball. I believe McGwire was quite sincere in his comment on the outrageous amount of money that is being paid out in baseball salaries. As he said to me, "I'm not worth the money I'm making. But the free market has decreed what players are worth. It's a tough issue."

To be sure, too much money is being paid to the so-called superstars of the game; but there is a ridiculous amount of money being spent on players who are less than outstanding at the major league level. What's more, although other, less well-compensated players can hit better, throw faster, scratch harder, and even spit farther, some of these overpaid galoots are perceived as ingrates as well. For example, when Derek Bell lost his starting job with the Houston Astros after hitting .236 with 12 home runs and 66 RBI's in 1999, he ripped Manager Larry Dierker, saying, "For the first time in my career I've struggled, and they've turned their backs on me.

I'm going to turn it around on them." Bell, who was traded, will be paid $5 million in 2000 despite his anemic performance in '99. Perhaps baseball can find a way to tie payment more closely to performance.

The Los Angeles Dodgers, in their rush to spend Rupert Murdoch's money, signed a pitcher, Carlos Perez, for over $16 million and sent him to the minor leagues in the middle of the 1999 season when he had produced only 2 wins and 10 losses. The Minnesota Twins cannot, and should not, try to compete with such idiocy.

Of course, the L.A. Dodgers (also known as the Rupert Murdoch Dodgers) doubled their payroll after being acquired by Murdoch's Fox corporation. The game may be going this direction, with corporate conglomerates owning the national pastime.

There is much talk of the new power that has been vested in Bud Selig, the Commissioner of Baseball. Selig will possess new autonomy in his decision-making and will have an opportunity to change the way revenue is distributed in the big leagues. Twins president Jerry Bell calls this "the most significant development I have seen," in 14 years in the job.

Remember, Bud Selig is the man who oversaw the strike of 1994 and called off the '94 World Series.

Selig has to do something, and his actions need to consist of more than peddling stadiums to an unwilling

populous. Options that he could pursue will be discussed in the book.

Selig's duties and powers have increased as owners have begun dissolving the American and National Leagues as legal entities. In Selig's favor, especially from the perspective of small-market teams like the Twins, is the fact that he is a former owner of the Milwaukee Brewers, itself a smaller market team, and he's been involved in the game for thirty years.

The challenges Selig faces in trying to preserve the game's status as the national pastime are enormous. For starters, the Minnesota Twins have a market value similar to the new contract signed by Cincinatti Reds outfielder Ken Griffey.

Additionally, even if the Twins had a new ballpark that was used to its maximum potential, the Twins would probably be able to sustain a payroll only about half that of the New York Yankees or the Los Angeles Dodgers. How much can baseball redistribute revenue without wholesale subsidization of franchises?

Maybe some teams are destined to fail.

It would be heartbreaking for many if there were no Twins in Minnesota. I never saw a game at the old Metropolitan Stadium, but I hear it had its charms. When I was growing up in Chicago, the Minnesota Twins were a respected opponent whose battles with the Chicago White Sox I frequently captured on radio. Harmon Killebrew and Tony Oliva are two of my all-time favorite players, and the legacy that they left would be sorely missed.

The 1987 and 1991 World Series Champions provided a tremendous adventure for all Minnesotans. Kirby, Herbie and company.

But if they were gone tomorrow, *baseball* would go on. The globe-trotting Tommies of the University of St. Thomas still would use their experience playing in Cuba in January 2000 to try to win a national title. The Minnesota Gophers, with the expected return of ace left hander Ben Birk, still will be favored to win the Big 10 championship. The St. Paul Saints will look to win another Northern League championship.

Dundas, Minnesota will try to win a third consecutive town ball state title, and my 35-and-over senior team will try to challenge for our league title.

Thousands of children will play baseball no matter how the issues threatening the top levels of the game are resolved. Baseball is bigger than agents and lawyers and commissioners and superstars.

Baseball will survive.

THE FANS SPEAK

Memories of the Met

Doug Addison

D oug Addison is the Vice President of Field of Dreams, a thriving sports memorabilia store at the Mall of America, where home plate is in its original Met Stadium location (though today that location is in the middle of Camp Snoopy, an amusement park in the center of the largest shopping mall in the United States).

"My favorite memories of Met Stadium involve Rod Carew's pursuit of a .400 batting average in 1977. It was a big deal all over baseball, and doubly big for a young baseball fan who already adored him" Addison said.

"I recall that Ted Williams made a trip to Minneapolis as Carew stayed hot during the late summer. Carew's closing in on a .400 average was a big national story, with Carew on the cover not only of *Sport Magazine* but also on the cover of *Time Magazine*.

He really had it going. He would hit the ball all over the field, which made it very tough for pitchers to figure out how to pitch to him. Yes, he hit a lot of balls that had eyes, but he hit a lot of line drives too.

"That whole team could hit a baseball. They were a great hitting ballclub, with Larry Hisle and Lyman Bostock and Butch Wynegar, who had a good year. So it wasn't real easy to pitch around Rod and he kept the .400 average looking like a possibility until September.

"That team was coached by Gene Mauch; they could score a lot of runs, but they didn't have strong pitching. There were a lot of exciting games though, and I saw a bunch of them. That was one of the best summers I can remember."

Larry McMahon

Larry McMahon's first memories of Major League Baseball are of the old Met Stadium in summertime when, as a young boy, he would come up from

New Ulm with his family to catch a ballgame. "We used to look forward to making that trip to the old Met," he said. "I don't remember exactly how much it cost to get into the park—I think it was two bucks, but I never was the one paying—and let me tell you it was a joy to be there. I remember what it was like to come up the ramp and get that first sight of the grass. I can remember the smell very distinctly. You'd come into that place and it would bombard your senses.

"It was really the place to be, and it tells you how much of baseball is really about the environment it's played in. Today, it's baseball in a laboratory in the Metrodome; a laboratory that needs more mice in the seats."

Larry is a resident of St. Paul, and he was able to vote in the November 2, 1999 referendum that asked whether public funds should be used to build a stadium in his city. He was sorry, but not surprised, to see the ballot measure go down to defeat.

"In St. Paul, you don't know what might happen if a ballpark were built downtown, or near downtown. You don't know what the benefits might be. It could be a tremendous thing for the city of St. Paul, and a new baseball facility would certainly be a complement to the new hockey arena [for the Minnesota Wild]. I don't think the rallies that were held were that effective; the crowd that was gathering at places like Mancini's (a popular downtown restaurant frequented by business people and sports fans), you're pretty much preaching to the choir when you're addressing a lot of those people."

Marty Hansen

Marty Hansen, who now resides south of the Twin Cities in suburban Burnsville, Minnesota, tells of hitchhiking to Twins games as a teenager.

"I grew up in Savage, Minnesota, and I was a big Twins fan as a boy. Some friends and I used to hitchhike out of Savage on Highway 13 to Cedar Avenue and then head north to Metropolitan Stadium. Sometimes we would get lucky and go the whole distance with one ride, but more frequently it might be two rides or three rides or more to get to the Met."

"As a matter of fact I used to go to Twins games at the old ballpark so often that my mother told me she was going to forward my mail to the Met. I think she was kidding."

Marty was in attendance at the classic sixth game of the 1965 World Series, when Bob Allison made his famous sliding catch in left field. He was underneath the left field pavilion, pressed up against a screen as Allison made his spectacular grab.

"I remember the rain; it was raining on and off most of the day. They were using helicopters to try to dry the field, but I can recall the spray when Allison went sliding. I should have had a camera, because from my vantage point I was level with Allison as he made the catch. In fact, when they show World Series highlights and they inevitably show Allison's grab, you can see me in the background. That's me, the young kid in the white jeans pressed up against the screen."

Marty still has great affection for the old Met and what it stood for. "We used to call it the Erector Set Stadium because that's kind of what it looked like. Those were real ballplayers who played in those days: Allison, Tony Oliva, Harmon Killebrew, Earl Battey and the rest. They could really play the game and those were some excellent baseball teams. I sure appreciate them now."

Hansen's favorite memory may be of the weekend that Bill Rigney brought the old Los Angeles Angels into town to face the Twins. During the weekend series Harmon Killebrew launched a couple of prodigious home runs that landed near where Hansen was sitting in the left field stands. "I saw a lot of Killebrew home runs at the Met. I'll tell you what; he hit a couple of monster homers that weekend against the Angels. That Harmon could sure drive a baseball."

Stadium Issues—the Present and the Future

Brad Larson

My friend Brad Larson believes that user fees are the best way to finance a new baseball stadium. Other major league teams have found a way to recycle ticket and concession revenues into paying off debt. That way, the fans pay for the ballpark when they use the ballpark, and taxpayers are off the hook. Just going to the games creates a natural, dare I say painless, type of debt relief.

Brad's other thought is that Carl Pohlad is going to die a tremendously wealthy man. His sons Jim, Bob and Bill are going to become very wealthy men when Carl Pohlad passes from this earth, even if he leaves them only a portion of his estate. So why wouldn't Carl want to devote some of his vast wealth to leaving a legacy to the Twin Cities, which he no doubt loves? A small-footprint urban ballpark called "Pohlad Field," financed by Carl, would doubtless leave a markedly different and much more positive impression on a lot of people than the one they currently have.

This remark drew laughter when I brought it up at lunch with some other journalists. The general impression is that it would be a cold day in the nether world before Carl would make such a grand gesture. I don't know. The man is worth well over a billion dollars. You don't see any armored cars at a funeral service. He is not taking it with him. How, and with whom, he decides to leave it behind is up to him.

Sara Powers

Sara Powers has worked in the Twin Cities for the past ten years, since moving to the area from New York City. She is a baseball fan who enjoys the intensity and excitement of a well-played major league game. "I go to ballgames because I love the game of baseball and it's part of summer tradition for me. I don't go to a lot of games at the Metrodome in the summertime if the weather is good. I like to be outside in the summer, so I find myself going to Twins games when the weather is lousy."

Sara thinks that more could be done to market baseball to women in the Twin Cities, although she does believe that the Metrodome is limiting. "Women are a lot more involved in sports today than they ever have been. You even have someone like Ila Borders pitching in professional baseball up north (in Duluth for the Duluth-Superior Dukes). Baseball should market to women so that they can create more of a fan base.

"I think women do react badly to the big money that is paid to athletes today. Talk about skyrocketing salaries! There's way too much money being tossed around in professional sports, and baseball seems to bear the most guilt in terms of the big money, Kevin Garnett not withstanding." (Garnett, of the basketball Timberwolves, signed a $120 million contract a few years ago).

I asked Sara about the idea of bringing baseball to St. Paul.

"I think it would be a great thing for St. Paul to pick up the Twins. When you think about it, they don't really do that much for Minneapolis. I think it's important to bring some action to the city of St. Paul. It's a great city, and a new ballpark, especially one that would fit in the city, would have great entertainment value. I've been reading about some new ideas in ballpark construction, smaller parks that might be workable in St. Paul." Sara is referring to the ideas of Chicago architect Philip Bess and his "Small Footprint" stadium design.

"St. Paul has a lot of government activity and insurance companies and banks, but it would be nice to feel like St. Paul had a larger identity. I'm very much in favor of what's going on with the new hockey team, the Minnesota Wild.

"And one more thing. The new stadium, if it's built, has to have a lot of women's bathrooms. I heard the Wild is accommodating women in a new way. That's important. Going to the bathroom at the Metrodome has always been an issue, although not so much recently with the Twins when the crowds are down."

The Money Game

Dan Mills

My friend Dan Mills has had it with the big money that has flooded into big league baseball. Dan is more than a little bit cynical about the money, and it doesn't bother him at all that some of the teams with enormous payrolls have ended up with decidedly mediocre results.

"Look at some of the teams that have spent a pile of money," Mills said. "I like the fact that you can't guarantee results when you spend the money that some of those guys did. How about the Dodgers? What a mess! All of those millions of dollars and they're just terrible! I know during the off season they'll spend even more money and bring in some guys who may or may not work out."

"So you don't like the Rupert Murdoch Dodgers?" I asked.

"They're a joke. And so were the Anaheim Angels. They spent a lot of money and look where they ended up: 70 wins and 92 losses in 1999. And the Colorado Rockies did nothing despite spending millions and playing all their home games at a mile-high altitude. They thought they had a shot at doing some good. They didn't."

Mills continued his tirade: "The Baltimore Orioles are lucky they play in that beautiful ballpark. They've got only one guy who plays hard all the time, B. J. Surhoff (a Joe Girardi-era All American catcher at North Carolina), and I'll bet he wants to get the heck out of there. Albert Belle and Brady Anderson are worthless—Belle's a cancer wherever he goes and money doesn't seem to change that. The Orioles spent all that money and can't get anything done, to the point where I don't know whether to laugh or cry when they're eliminated from the pennant race in late May," said Mills.

"I can't quite figure out the Cubs, except that I don't think that they need to win and management doesn't feel too much pressure. Cubs General Manager Andy McPhail has one of the best jobs in baseball. The Cubs make the playoffs in '98 and look like they're going in the right direction, and then the whole outfit takes a big step backward in 1999. It looks like they just don't know their talent on the north side of Chicago. You'd think they could put together a supporting cast for Sammy Sosa," Mills concluded, nearly breathless.

I firmly believe that if Tom Kelly and Terry Ryan had Chicago Tribune Company dough to work with, the Twins would challenge the best in baseball year in and year out. They're good baseball men, and with a positive environment we might see wonderful new things from Kelly and Ryan, things that would warm the

Sammy Sosa

hearts and maybe even open the wallets of Twins fans. I think T.K., for all the frustrations of managing untried talent, has fun working with the kids and would love an opportunity to manage a winner again. I'm not so cynical that I believe the Twins management, as baseball men, don't care about winning. The trouble is, they just don't have the resources, the tools if you will, to be competitive. There is, in fact, a semblance of sanity in the leadership and decision-making of the Minnesota Twins. They're not foolishly throwing money after overpriced, overstuffed free agents. But we want to compete, so another catch-22 arises: We want to act sanely,

we in fact pride ourselves on our common sense, and like any sane person we'd rather win than lose, but we can't be sane and be competitive at the same time. So if we're going to be competitive, if we're going to win, we have to act insanely, and I don't see that happening.

The State of the Game

John Hunter

John Hunter is a baseball fan who, like a few others, is in danger of becoming a cynic as he regards the big league game. John has attended major league ballgames for decades at some of the great ballparks around the country. He is especially fond of Yankee stadium.

"That place is haunted with so many great baseball spirits," he said.

John is a fan of pitching battles that have meaning, and he recalls the great Bob Gibson with fondness. "I saw Gibson face Tom Seaver in St. Louis and, as I recall, Gibson won the ballgame 2-1. It was something I will never forget. Those guys were athletes."

"One thing that bothers me about the game today is when a starting pitcher has thrown his heart out and maybe has a small lead. With the relief pitchers today, the starter is pulled regardless of whether he might be able to pitch another inning. I don't like the way relief pitching has become so essential a part of the game.

"I guess I'm an old-timer. I don't like the DH. I don't really like the idea of interleague play, although I liked seeing McGwire. The game has changed.

"I'm happy that baseball feels revitalized. I believe the home run race was of benefit to the game. I certainly hope that kids, who I think are increasingly uninterested in playing baseball, justify baseball's feeling of resurgence. Kids need to play the game. It's tough to get my grandchildren outside anymore."

The fact that players are able to move freely from team to team without the bond that was in the game before free agency is another element

that Hunter dislikes. "These guys just ramble from team to team, without any regard whatsoever for the fans. Those guys owe a debt to the fans! Whenever they are questioned about things like loyalty or commitment to a city, all you ever hear is that baseball is a business and that no one should take it personally.

"Well, I don't buy that."

John doesn't get to the Metrodome much anymore, but he was a witness to the '87 and '91 World Series games played in Minnesota. "I've got the tickets right here," he says, reaching for a scrapbook with hundreds of old pictures in it.

"It's not the price of tickets that keeps me away. It's a bunch of things. I'm becoming an old guy. The Metrodome doesn't do that much for me anymore, though the weather is guaranteed. When the Dome was brand new, there was a fascination with it, and when the Twins were winning their titles you had to go to the Metrodome to watch them play. It was special then.

"It's not a special place to watch a game, anymore. The team can't compete for a title the way things are going. There aren't many people in the seats, not even for the Yankees. That's the last game I saw, Mike Lincoln beat the Yankees. Come to think of it, that was fun!

"I watch the team on TV sometimes. I was happy when they picked up Paul Molitor; I saw him play at the University of Minnesota and also with the Brewers. I saw him in Milwaukee in 1982. He's a beautiful ballplayer.

"I like seeing Harmon Killebrew when they feature him once in a while. He doesn't look all that different than he did 35 years ago. He looks like he could still swing a bat, so I guess he's aging pretty well."

Roger Johnson, town ball coach, Minnetonka Cavaliers

I had to ask Roger Johnson about the state of the Minnesota Twins, on the field and otherwise.

"They're playing a lot of young guys, and it's certainly tough for them to compete given the limitations of youth in Major League Baseball. I understand that the team is limited financially, but they've got to improve on the field. It's a good question how they're going to do that with such a small budget, compared to a team like the Yankees.

"I mean, I love the Yankees, but I want to see good competition throughout the American League. The Yankees have been a dominant team for 75 years, but they've always had to battle for their championships. I didn't feel last year was a great test.

"The Minnesota Twins need a new playing facility; there is no doubt in my mind that the Metrodome has outlived its usefulness. I say that in full awareness of the joy of 1987 and 1991. It was the humanity, so full of enthusiasm, that created the good atmosphere in the dome at that time.

"Currently, the dome offers little ambiance or warmth and, for me, is an uninviting experience in general. There's no freshness to the experience of watching a big league game at the Metrodome. It's the basic things that are missing.

"Baseball is about the senses, about sounds and smells as much as sights. The dome doesn't sound right and it doesn't smell right. I don't enjoy experiencing baseball at the Hump-Dome."

PEOPLE AND PERSONALITIES: BEHIND THE SCENES

Ken Griffey-Tiger Woods

One late summer day during the 1999 season, my journalist friend and golf buddy Larry Fitzgerald gave me a tip that Tiger Woods was coming to town to play some charity golf and work with some inner city kids in a golf program well known to Fitzgerald.

I think Woods timed his visit to coincide with the Seattle Mariners being in town to play the Twins, because that's how it worked out. Woods' friend Ken Griffey, Jr. was launching rockets at the Metrodome, and Tiger stopped by to try his hand at a little batting practice and to entertain his adoring fans by leaning on a bat near the batting cage.

When Junior gets it going in BP, there are not too many who can put on as impressive a show. He typically starts out by ripping a few line drives around the park to loosen up a bit. Then, as if on command, he starts depositing American League baseballs in the right-field upper-deck seats. He

does this on all of his visits to the Metrodome, but he seemed to be taking particular glee on this day, enjoying a few laughs with Woods as he pummeled one ball after another. Junior twirls his bat as he exits the cage after banging one off the football press box façade in right center. One gets the distinct impression, as he puts charge after charge into the batting practice servings, that Griffey's okay with the Hump-dome.

Griffey talked a little about Seattle's new ballpark, Safeco Field, a facility whose construction was burdened by cost overruns that eventually became a burden to Griffey. When Safeco went $100 million over budget, there was talk that the extra costs of the stadium would make it difficult for the team to come up with the money to retain both Junior and Alex Rodriguez. Griffey's discomfort was made clear when he turned down a $17 million a year offer from the Mariners in October of 1999, substantially more than the contract he signed with the Cincinatti Reds in early 2000.

On Tiger's day at the dome, Griffey was still optimistic about the future of Safeco field. He was enjoying himself in the new park, he said, and things were looking up for Mariner baseball in the new environs.

"There's a real difference, a big difference, between playing in front of 30,000 or 40,000 fans at Safeco, and the 10 or 15 thousand we've been drawing at the Kingdome. Man, sometimes it just felt like a burden to play in Seattle, like no one cared."

But Griffey does not want to continue to be a part of Safeco. Safeco field is a beauty, with its retractable top revealing a natural roof—the sky—and its infield a natural carpet of grass. At $517 million to build, including the cost overrun, the ballpark is the most expensive in history. It has all the bells and whistles one might imagine a ballpark could have, but it was not enough to keep Griffey. Griffey made a final decision, he says, to move closer to his family with the Reds.

The irony is striking. The money turned down by Griffey ($17 million) is roughly equal to the entire Twins payroll for the 2000 season. As Dick Enberg would say about a spectacular Junior moonshot: "Oh, my."

Changing the subject, Griffey laughed when he talked about his golf games with Tiger Woods. "I love to play with Tiger; he's just a great guy to golf with any time of the year. And he's a great guy to hang with, period. We're like neighbors, you know."

"But it's hard to hang with him when it comes to hitting golf shots. Lots of times I'll hit one way out in the trees, and Tiger will put one right on the flag, from the same lie as mine.

"He's a phenomenal golfer, best in the game."

Tiger will certainly keep his day job and leave the hitting to Junior. Stepping into the cage late in the Mariner's batting session, Woods never looked comfortable at the plate, lofting one fly ball to the warning track with his best rip. He looked rather mortal pounding a number of grounders to shortstop and third base. Like a regular Joe (but with a huge entourage), hitting into some easy outs.

I don't know about the rest of the crowd that day, but it made me feel good.

Bob Casey,
Twins P.A. Announcer

Bob Casey is the long-time Minnesota Twins Public Address announcer, and he has been with the team for both World Series victories. Bob is a fascinating guy with an especially interesting look on this late August day. He is wearing some wild looking Converse All-Stars tennis shoes.

I tell him that he looks sharp.

"Thanks," he mutters, as he heads across the field.

Bob is a gruff but softhearted man whose grandson became one of my better friends down in the little closet where Casey does his P.A. work. Bob Casey knows his baseball and has a treasure chest of good memories; after all, he's had the privilege of being the announcer for two World Series championship teams. He has some affection for the dome, or as he puts it "the dome has been berry, berry good to me."

The Killer B's: Biggio and Bagwell

When Houston came to town I made an effort to keep an eye on the Killer B's. The Killer B's, Craig Biggio and Jeff Bagwell, are tough guys and winners who play hard and get the most out of their ability despite the big dough they're paid. They're my type of players.

Looking at them from up close, one recognizes the amount of weight training that has gone into their bodies. They're both powerfully built, although of different dimensions. "We've got a good team and everybody's been playing hard without exception," said Biggio. "We play as a unit because that's the only way we're going to win."

As Biggio repeats the time-honored cliché, he somehow gives it more meaning by spitting and giving a slight snarl as he speaks. For a guy who's not that big, Biggio has huge, old-looking gnarly hands, like an old-time blacksmith.

"The Twins always play us hard" said the former first round pick from Seton Hall, class of 1987. "The Twins are really serving youth with what they're doing now, and they've got some good players."

When Biggio was drafted back in '87 he was selected as a catcher. Now he carries about 190 pounds on a short but powerful frame. Biggio has a thing about playing in bad weather: He has a tremendous fear of lightning as a result of a bad experience as a young man. I am reminded of a storm that came in to Burnsville, Minnesota in the fourth inning of a game that I was pitching. It was one of those monster storms that speeds across the plains and arrives relatively unannounced. We kept trying to get the game in (as we always do—we're paying the umpire after all!), but eventually we were pinned down and couldn't get out to our cars very easily. The lightning was striking in the park and I heard a tree crack during my exit. Any child would have known that the game should have been called earlier than it was. Winds were over 50 mph and the afternoon went pitch black. Our slow departure could have been costly. The last thing I remember seeing in my rear view mirror was a tree falling down where cars had been parked seconds earlier.

Jose Canseco

Jose Canseco had an outstanding year in 1999. If he had stayed healthy the entire season, he would have been a factor in the league home run race. Jose jumped out of the gate for the Tampa Bay Devil Rays hitting the ball hard and far.

When I caught up to Canseco at the Metrodome in June, the lesser-known of the Bash Brothers was in a jovial mood as he ripped balls into the Metrodome outfield seats. Jose launched a high fly that just touched a speaker attached to the roof on its way down. I laughed with the big man as he contemplated the oddity of such interference.

"Hey, we've got one too (at domed Tropicana Field)! You know, the baseball can get caught up there and I think the hitter should get to take as many bases as he can. Maybe it should be a couple of home runs if it never comes down."

I asked Jose if he likes the Metrodome. "I'm more of an outdoor baseball guy," said Jose. "But this is a good hitter's park and I've always had a lot of success in here. I see the ball pretty well in the Thunderdome."

That's great. A big home run slugger likes the Metrodome because he can hit the balls out and has done so since he was doing it with McGwire and Steinbach back in Oakland. He doesn't really like the park, he says laughingly as his ball nearly gets stuck in the speaker system in the sky, but he can hit a lot of baseballs into the dome seats. The Teflon Tent is OK with him. I'm not real crazy about that.

Larry "Moose" Stubing

Larry "Moose" Stubing is built like a football player—he looks like he might have been a great linebacker not that long ago. The fact is, Moose is 60 years old and has been around the game of baseball for most all of his life. With his clear blue eyes and bald pate he looks like a man you could trust, and in fact, in addition to his duties as an Anaheim Angel talent scout, he has had a 30-year career as a college basketball referee.

"I don't do anything for the money" says Moose. "I'm around sports for the people. And I'm around basketball for the towns and the young people and for the travel."

Moose Stubing was a great minor league baseball player who once hit 33 home runs down in El Paso, Texas. They've even named a street after Moose in El Paso. Moose received the proverbial "cup of coffee" in the major leagues, but he never had a base hit in any of his pinch-hit at bats. That's right—the Moose has a lifetime batting average of .000 in his Major League Baseball career.

To make matters more interesting, Moose was also a Major League Baseball field manager. He became interim manager of the Anaheim Angels in 1988, after Cookie Rojas was fired. Moose quickly re-established the level of play that the Angels were comfortable with; after going 0-8 Moose hung up his spikes forever and became a scout. That's right; Moose Stubing is the only player/manager in Major League Baseball history to never record a hit in an official at-bat and never record a victory while managing.

Even Moose acknowledges that this was a pretty neat trick. "I'm not sure exactly how that happened. I guess I'm just one of a kind because that's a one-of-a-kind accomplishment" Moose said.

It occurs to me that Moose is in the brotherhood of Major League Baseball; he's in the fraternity, perhaps not high up the pecking order (not that he ever wanted to be) but he's one of the guys. Moose seems to be universally well-liked and is quick with a joke and a kind gesture that belies a man of his gruff demeanor.

And Moose Stubing loves the game. "I'd like to go until I'm 70" says Moose. "But I'll be around the game as long as I live."

Omar Vizquel

I keep catching Omar Vizquel acting strangely at the Metrodome. It started before a Twins vs. Cleveland Indians contest during the 1998 season, when I found him in the Indians' dugout bouncing a ball off the dugout steps and trying to catch it on the top of his baseball shoe. He succeeded more often than he missed. Ballplayers do a lot of things to pass the time, and I suppose this was just one of them, but the intensity with which he was playing this solo game was intriguing. Maybe he was thinking about hitting a home run.

In 1998 Vizquel went the better part of the season without a home run. It took over five hundred at bats for Vizquel to "go deep." Later in the year, I found him bouncing a ball against the grate that covers the ventilation shaft behind home plate at the Dome. He was just bouncing the ball off of the screen that protects the shaft. These are the shafts that were rumored to be blowing out toward right field during the Twins victories in 1987 and 1991. Unproven, of course. Anyway, I had to ask Omar what he was doing bouncing the ball off the ventilation shaft screens continuously for over five minutes. He moved closer to the wall and put his ear flush with the screen. "I'm listening to the ball echo," he said.

Okay, I was just asking....

I'm thinking to myself, here's the All Star shortstop, with his ear pinned to the wall, listening to echoes in an air duct. Like Charlie Brown. But now sometimes, when a ball gets away from the Twins batting cage, I'll bounce it against the ventilation shaft to see if I can figure out what Omar's fascination was.

Maybe he's looking for that friendly breeze that's supposed to blow out beneficially from the duct. Unlike his homer-deficient 1998 season, the 1999 season saw Vizquel hit a home run in his second at-bat of the year. Vizquel, a .270 lifetime hitter entering the season, went on to hit .333 during another All Star caliber campaign.

Omar said hello to me at the All Star game. He may be a little bit different, but I like him.

John McDonald, Vizquel's Backup

Backing up Omar Vizquel at shortstop for the Indians at this time was John McDonald, a nice-looking, somewhat smallish shortstop who had played his college ball at Providence College in Rhode Island. Not exactly a baseball hot-bed. I couldn't help but notice that he was originally from Lyme, Connecticut, which is where my maternal grandfather, Tom, had died before I was born.

We got to talking as he was hitting off the tee into the net behind the batting cage. It was obvious how excited he was to be in the big leagues; he had been called up from AAA Buffalo just the previous week.

So what's it like to be backing up Omar Vizquel in the major leagues? "This is very satisfying," McDonald said. "I think I'm up here because my offense has come along pretty well and they're not afraid to see me do some hitting. I'm hoping I can hold my own.

"I started 1998 at AA Akron, and in '99 I moved from Akron to Buffalo early in the season. I think they've always liked my defense, but this year my offense seems to be coming around."

With that, the little-big man from Providence strolled into the batting cage to rattle some line drives around the Metrodome. He's a solid looking ballplayer who didn't appear to be rattled climbing into the cage after big Jim Thome got done blasting them out.

I watched as he pulled a couple of balls into the left-field seats. He looked over at me and smiled, and I smiled back.

My world is OK, but I'm happy for John McDonald. He's in the big league world, at least for now. He's earned every bit of the joy that I know he is feeling.

Dennis Denning

A story from St. Thomas coach Dennis Denning relates to former Twins prospect Jim Eisenreich, whom the Twins gave up on during the 1984 season, but who went on to have a long and distinguished career in the major leagues.

One day, as I was telling my radio audience about Bryce Pleschcourt and his MVP season in Dundas, Denning chimed in with an interesting piece of trivia. "Jim Eisenreich, during his year off from organized baseball in 1985, was a town ball MVP as well. He spent that summer in St. Cloud playing with the locals, and they must have had a heck of a team."

That's pretty interesting considering that the town ball MVP, Eisenreich, would go on to hit World Series home runs for the Philadelphia Phillies in 1992 and the Florida Marlins in 1997.

"I've got to tell you something else about Eisenreich," Denning said. "As you know, it was Tourette's Syndrome that drove Jim out of the game for a period of time, and he's as well known for his courageous battle with Tourette's as for his big World Series home runs."

"I had a player at St. Thomas who also suffered from that ailment. He had originally gone to a big school in a nearby state, but it wasn't working out for him. I remember when I asked the coach how he performed, the coach said, 'he didn't hit. I don't think that he can hit at this level' ".

"Well, with Tourette's you might not sleep at night, or you might be sick, or you might lose control of your eye movement. The thing is tough. But I thought I'd try something."

"I dialed the number for the Marlins, the team Eisenreich was playing for at the time, and told whoever picked up the phone that I was Jimmy Weisner, the clubhouse manager for the Twins."

I laughed pretty hard as what Denning was telling me sank in. Denning continued.

"Yeah, so I'm Jimmy Weisner and I somehow get through to the locker room of the Florida Marlins and Eisenreich comes on the phone. I say, 'Jim, this is Dennis Denning, the coach at St. Thomas University in St. Paul. Would it be okay if I had a ballplayer get hold of you regarding Tourette's, because he's got a [problem] similar to what you had.'"

"My ballplayer called Eisenreich and they talked and Eisenreich gave my guy the phone number of his doctor; this guy is the best doctor in the world for Tourette's Syndrome."

That player, Matt Faulken, went on to become a two-time All American for the Tommies.

Harmon Killebrew

One day late in the 1998 baseball season I had a chance to talk to Baseball Hall of Fame member Harmon Killebrew at the Metrodome, where the Twins were about to take on the Boston Red Sox.

Harmon, who retired as a player in 1974, was elected to the Hall on his fourth try in 1984, which makes one wonder about the Hall of Fame voters. True, his career batting average of .256 was less than spectacular, but his on-base-average of .379 is higher than

Roberto Clemente's, and his 500-plus home runs came in the era of solid pitching and few "nutritional supplements."

With his navy blue blazer and clear blue eyes, signing autographs with a smile, Harmon is a picture of contentment today. Life at his year-round home in Arizona must be good.

Killebrew played in the era of Roger Maris and knew Maris personally. His recollections of the man are spoken in quiet, reflective tones, as though he is placing himself back in time.

"I thought Roger Maris was a great guy; I really did. But he was a very misunderstood individual. His good qualities were never brought across. New York was a tough place for him to play baseball. The New York media considered Roger to be an out-sider—not a true Yankee—and they always gave Mickey Mantle more positive coverage because he was a Yankee through and through.

"Roger was his own worst enemy, too. He always gave very short answers to the reporters' questions. He wasn't happy being in that constant spotlight, and he had a nervous problem that compounded things. I'm impressed that McGwire seems to thrive on the attention."

McGwire, of course, plays his baseball in St. Louis. Maris spent time in St. Louis as well. Killebrew thinks that Maris was happiest in the smaller major league towns. Would he have been happy in Minnesota?

"Kansas City and St. Louis were good places for Roger to play. He was from Fargo and that's not far from here (Minnesota). I think he would have liked it in the Twin Cities."

Returning to the present, Killebrew took a look at the Twins team that was loosening up in front of him. "This team just doesn't have any power," he said. "They're desperately in need of somebody to drive in some runs. It's tough to win these days without the power."

Killebrew had some years where his power drew big notice at the All Star game, to the tune of 30 home runs and 78 RBI at the break.

"Yeah, I had a couple of years where I was on track to hit a few more than I did," he said. "The key is to be consistent, and that's what I respect about McGwire; he has no weak months. He keeps on hitting 'em.

"I said earlier this year that he might hit 80," Killebrew said with a twinkle in his eye, "but now he's had a little slowdown, so maybe he'll only hit 70."

Yes, Harmon, he will. He will hit exactly 70 by the end of the 1998 season.

Although Killebrew never played in the Metrodome, with the exception of some old-timers ballgames, he had some thoughts on the dome as a place to watch baseball.

"The Metrodome has never been a great place to play baseball and I think that translates to the fans. It never quite fit.

"World Series excitement is one thing; day-to-day baseball in Minnesota seems to be another."

Killebrew worked to generate fan support for a new ballpark, making appearances in and around St. Paul as the stadium referendum grew closer.

He believes the Twins need a new outdoor ballpark and he views a retractable roof as something of a necessity.

"I think it's important to have the retractable roof on a new facility," said Killebrew. "It's necessary because of the weather situation up here in Minnesota. I can tell you we played a lot of games when we shouldn't have out at the old Met, because of the location of this ballclub. It's awfully cold early in the year. We had people coming from Iowa, Wyoming, South and North Dakota, Canada, so we did our best to get the games in."

KEEPING THE TOOLS IN REPAIR
JOHN MARQUISS, THE GLOVE MAN

I fell in love with the glove man down in Fort Myers.

The baseball glove repair man, that is. His name is John Marquiss, and his forte is relacing gloves at the work table in his home in Bradenton, Florida. He works the senior tournaments because he knows the old guys tend to let their equipment get pretty worn before they look for help.

"Some players will think about getting rid of their gloves rather then fixing them up," John says. "They don't realize that all their gloves need are new laces and some TLC."

For thirty bucks, John has restored my ancient Wilson A-2000 to good working order, and in the process has taught me a good deal about a part of a ballplayer's gear that is often taken for granted. For example, John has seen brand-new gloves fall apart at the seams for no apparent reason, which, he explained, indicates that the leather lacing for those damaged gloves came from a part of the animal that had been bruised; all leather from a bruised location on the animal is weakened.

Ever seen a ball go directly through a glove, perhaps beaning a player in the head?

"Happens more than you would think," John says.

Another potential problem emerges when players run their gloves over to the "shoe repair man." Most players have used a shoe repairman at one point or another, but that's a mistake, John says. "Glove leather tends to stretch. Shoe leather doesn't, so it tends to break, sometimes unexpectedly. And that, too, can land a ball on your noggin."

John counts Andy Van Slyke and Bobby Bonilla as friends from the big leagues, and although he spends a lot of time around the minor league facilities working with young people, he maintains a special affection for older players as well as "fantasy campers." Bill Mazeroski was a star for the Pittsburg Pirates and participates in fantasy camps for the organization. (A fantasy camp is a recreational baseball experience intended for those who desire the atmosphere of a big league baseball camp.) It seems that Mazeroski's famous home run for the Pirates against the Yankees in 1961 won a young soldier in New Mexico, John Marquiss, a small pile of money. When John ran into Mazeroski many years later at a fantasy camp, he returned the favor with a couple of neatly laced gloves for the Pirate hero, on the house.

"I have learned some tricks from the players too, some of their techniques for taking care of baseball gloves," Marquiss said. "Bobby Bonilla told me about using Avon Skin-so-Soft®, both inside and outside the glove, for general conditioning and softening of the leather." (Does it leave a healthy glow, too, John?)

"Barry Bonds likes to use Edge® shaving gel on his gloves (for close shaves with the outfield wall?); the lanolin in Edge® provides the desired conditioning effect."

I sat for a time with John at his table, watching him work so gracefully with his hands, while waiting for an Over-30 game at the Lee County complex in Fort Myers. It was a perfect Florida day, and it was clear that John Marquiss was in his element as he worked. As some players from the Russian team walked by, big fellows who looked like they missed the bus for the Red Army hockey team, John said, "I love to see the friendship here with all the boys. It's a gorgeous atmosphere for a ballgame, just a gorgeous atmosphere." John was right about the feel of that lovely day and the grand baseball atmosphere surrounding the Roy Hobbs tournament taking place at Lee County. As much as any ballplayer, he was a part of it.

To communicate with John Marquiss, write to him at:
7104 41st Ave. East
Bradenton, Florida 34208

- 1 glove, $30.00 + shipping and handling
- 5 gloves, $120.00 + shipping
- 1st Baseman's glove add $5; catcher's mitt add $10

MEDIA

National Media

Scott Taylor,
Winnipeg *Free Press*

Scott Taylor is a highly respected writer for the Winnipeg *Free Press* and a radio personality as well. The 40-something Taylor sees a lot of baseball games and covered the Twins' championship runs in 1987 and 1991. Having watched Winnipeg lose the Jets, the city's National Hockey League franchise, in the early 90's, he is concerned about what the future holds for other small market professional sports franchises such as the Twins.

"You've already started to see the elimination in professional sports of the old money guys, guys who like to run a sports operation as a business. Those are not the guys who are happy leaking money away for an extended period of time. It helps to be a software mogul or an Internet big shot so that you can afford to throw money down the drain as nec-

essary. It's not pretty, and we've moved a long way away from Calvin Griffith.

"I think there's also a question as to whether the Twin Cities have the necessary fan base to support four major league sports franchises. When the Vikings are 15 and 1 or even 10 and 6 you're going to load the place up with fans, but I remember being in the Metrodome when the Vikings were playing at the .500 level and seeing a lot of empty seats. You had a tremendous outpouring of support for the baseball franchise in '87 and pretty much through '92 or '93. Now they're not competitive and that makes the problem that much more challenging.

"Pro football has its house in much better order, not perfect, but in much better order. Pro football has parity. Say what you want, but having teams with 8-8 won-lost records going to the playoffs means that those teams have a shot. There's interest and the way you get into the play-

The author with Scott Taylor of the Winnipeg *Free Press* at All Star Game, Fenway Park, 1999.

offs in football is to spend your 60 million dollars (the salary cap ceiling) as best you can. You have to handle your money well, so in many ways you are on an even footing with your competition.

"Baseball has to have a salary cap. Nobody was surprised to see the Yankees in the World Series last year, to see the Yankees winning the World Series. George Steinbrenner can afford the best players in the game, the best pitchers, and a lot of it has to do with his local TV revenue.

"Steinbrenner has a lot of money to work with in New York City that isn't available in the Twin Cities. Despite their new ballparks, Baltimore and Cleveland and a few of the others still don't have a license to print money. Having a salary cap and some equitable revenue distribution is the only way to restore the game to healthy competition."

Al Pinder, Grinnell *Herald Register*

A 79-year-old Al Pinder, of the Grinnell, Iowa *Herald Register*, attended the 1999 All Star Game, where I was treated to his comments on pitching in the big leagues today. "I can't tell whether the pitchers are getting worse or the hitters are getting stronger. It seems as though the pitchers are taking more of a beating these days than I can ever remember. I've got a feeling it may have something to do with the Creatine and muscle building."

Al is huge fan of Sammy Sosa and of the type of player and person that Sosa is. "I'm not sure Sammy would know what some of this stuff is. Sammy's got the magic. I think he frightens the pitcher when he cocks that bat. When he stands next to McGwire, he's about half his size, but boy can Sammy hit."

Al loves to travel to Wrigley Field to see the Cubs and has done so many times over the years. He thinks that Wrigley is both boon and bane for Sosa. "Wrigley helps him when the wind is blowing out, there's no doubt about that, but remember the wind blows in as well. Wrigley's the most beautiful park I've ever seen; I've been to them all, but Wrigley is my favorite. I'm at home there."

Chris Berman, ESPN

ESPN sportscaster Chris Berman was very active at the '99 All Star game, as befits a man who's involved heavily with all the big sporting events. "Boomer," as he's called, was watching the home run derby when I caught up with him.

"The home run derby is a lot of fun. I think it's fun not just for the fans, but for the players as well. They get a chance to ride each other a little bit and I think it helps to break the ice. Of course, the fans get to see McGwire hit one 800 feet or so. I thought Jim Thome put on a great show, and I'm so pleased that Ken Griffey, Jr. listened to the fans and decided to participate. I think it's important that "Junior" listened to his audience. He's so important to the whole game of baseball, not just the home run derby."

I asked Berman what he thought about the situation with baseball in Minnesota, and in the smaller markets in general. "I'm not tuned in to the situation up there; I've been doing my homework but I'm not close to the Twin Cities deal. I know that baseball has done a better job than football at keeping teams where they are. I'd hate to see the Twins have to move. The Minnesota Twins moving—oh no!"

Berman's mood turned serious as he continued. "The big teams need to do more to help out the smaller ones. Otherwise, you're going to have ten Harlem Globetrotters and twenty Washington Generals. No one wants that—I certainly don't. We're in a situation where the Minnesotas and the Montreals of the world don't have a chance, and that's wrong. It's a tough one. Baseball needs to do more to remedy the situation."

Mike Eisenbach, St. Louis *Post Dispatch*

Mike Eisenbach is a baseball writer for the St. Louis *Post Dispatch* who has seen Mark McGwire in batting practice many times over the past few years. After McGwire's stunning display before the 1999 All Star Game, however, Eisenbach said, "I've seen that show before—I watch Mark take batting practice every day—but never in that arena or in such a spectacular a fashion.

"I've watched McGwire draw 15,000 fans just for batting practice, including some occasions when he's managed to hit only a few out of the ballpark," Eisenbach continued. "When that happens, he really feels like he's letting people down, and he doesn't like that. In previous home run contests, especially in 1998, I think Mark was really trying too hard. But this year Tim Flannery was putting the ball right where Mark wanted it. He hit some monster shots, that's for sure."

Mike Eisenbach went on record predicting that McGwire would break Roger Maris' home run record by hitting 66 home runs in 1998. (You can look it up in the sports section of the March 31, 1998 *Post Dispatch*.) In making that prediction, Eisenbach must have confused McGwire with Sammy Sosa, for it was Sosa who finished the '98 season with 66 home runs.

One still has to give credit to Eisenbach and his crystal ball for predicting that McGwire would indeed break the home run record. I

asked Mike if he thought McGwire's record of 70 home runs would be broken in our lifetime. "I'm 38 and I don't believe it's breakable in my lifetime," he replied. "There were a lot of factors that came together [fortuitously] in 1998. Expansion required the addition of pitchers, and I really believe it thinned out the quality of pitching in the league. Also, Mark had such a strong finish heading into the end of his 70-homer season. I think we're going to see more guys in the next couple of decades with home run totals in the 60's. But remember, a player needs to be close to 60 by the first of September and then keep hitting them out. That's going to be tough.

"With the excitement of the last couple years, people have forgotten that Mark hit 58 home runs in 1997, and I think expansion and the way Mark really connected with the St. Louis Cardinals was a big factor. He had good protection behind him in the order with Ray Langford and Brian Jordan supporting him.

"And people underestimate the kind of hitter Mark McGwire is, with great form and the beautiful swing that he can put on the ball. There are other players more powerfully built than McGwire, but a lot of these players don't put as good a swing on the baseball as Mark McGwire does."

I asked Mike how he thought

McGwire handled the pressure of the home run race in 1998. "I think he handled it as well as any human being possibly could," Eisenbach said. "He got a little cranky once in a while—just human nature stuff, like when his back was hurting or he wasn't feeling well. Sometimes the media would be all over him if he hit a home run and the team lost. Mark is team player, and if the team failed, he didn't want to talk about his home runs. For those of us who followed him all year, he was always terrific. But I do remember when the AP writer was poking in his locker and how angry that made him. That was when the [Androstendione] story broke."

I asked Eisenbach if he thought the Andro controversy taints McGwire's home run record.

"No, I don't think so, I think a lot of that stuff is hogwash. Mark is incredibly dedicated to baseball. If you want to look at a major change in the game, look at the strength training. McGwire lifts weights after almost every game. Lifting today is as much a part of baseball as locker room BS. There's no doubt that the power in the game has increased all over. But nobody else has hit 70 home runs. That says it all."

Mike Austin, Arizona Radio

At the all star game I met a man named Mike Austin, a radio guy from Arizona. Mike had some insights into baseball at the new Bank One ballpark in Phoenix. I was a bit jealous of his excitement about his city's new team. He hadn't been to the Metrodome, but he wasn't much of a fan. "My friends say you've got a garbage bag in the outfield. What's up with that?"

I tried to explain to my new friend that he's picturing a literal garbage bag in his mind, and that's not quite right. It's plastic and it's blue, but it's not a garbage bag. He's picturing a big old Hefty bag. I tried to improve the visual connection he is failing to make. Our right field wall isn't the trash bag, isn't a big Hefty bag. It's more like…

It's more like… Okay, a giant Glad bag.

The Young Turks View the State of the Game

LaVelle Neal, Minneapolis *StarTribune*

I was sitting with Eric Nelson before a game against the Oakland Athletics talking Twins stuff, when LaVelle Neal (a beat baseball writer for the Minneapolis *StarTribune*) walked up and said with a smile, "The fans hold the gavel," referring to the stadium referendum that was to be held in St. Paul.

LaVelle is a young Turk in the baseball business, with a great smile and an attentiveness to detail. He caused a controversy by his unwillingness to vote for a pitcher for MVP of the American League. Some in the game were upset that LaVelle would not write the name of Pedro Martinez, who LaVelle believes to be the best pitcher in the American League, but who is not a position player and thus is not eligible in LaVelle's mind. It caused a little brouhaha.

I asked LaVelle for some of his observations on the Twins, particularly the pitchers. "The Twins have a tall order this year and probably for the foreseeable future. I firmly believe that too many rookies spoil any big-league broth. The Twins have 15 rookies! And they're all seeing some action.

"There are going to be good days and bad days; there will be days when they play aggressive baseball, bunch some hits and maybe hit the ball over the fence."

We laughed and agreed that there were not a whole lot of those days that we had witnessed. There had been a few, but not enough.

"The big key is pitching. Having two or three rookies in the starting rotation is going to haunt you. With expansion, the major leagues are calling up players who are not polished, players who probably need more seasoning in the minor leagues. Mike Lincoln should be in the minor leagues. So should a couple of others.

They have talent, but that talent needs to be refined."

I had to ask LaVelle about a player who has become a pet peeve of mine. Why doesn't LaTroy Hawkins pitch better? "LaTroy has tremendous talent, a real live arm with great stuff. He has a good work ethic, he works out all the time. But I think he tries to do too much.

"LaTroy should focus on two or three pitches and master those. [Bob] Tewksbury taught him a new curve, and he's trying to work it in [to his repertoire]. The staff of the Twins loves the curve ball.

"I think an argument could be made for LaTroy staying with the fastball, slider and change-up. LaTroy is always evolving during the season. He needs to stop evolving during the regular season. That's no time to try and perfect new pitches."

What bothers me about LaTroy Hawkins is that he looks like he's got the best stuff on the staff. He throws heat! He has good control when you watch him work in the bullpen. I asked LaVelle why he hasn't won a lot of games with a much lower ERA than he's had the past few years.

"You're right, it's a good question. He's throwing 95 mph and yet it takes him 80-85 pitches to get through four or five innings. That tells me that he doesn't have a feel, that he needs to simplify. LaTroy needs to work with what he has, change speeds and hit his spots."

Ah yes. My favorite pitching commentary. "Work fast, change speeds, throw strikes." It doesn't change at any level of the game. "Work fast, change speeds, throw strikes." You will be okay if you can just do that.

"Yes, there are a lot of coaches and scouts who believe that if you can change speeds and hit your spots you can be a dominant pitcher. Young pitchers want to strike everybody out, they want to make the hitter hit their pitch, the pitch they want to throw, instead of the pitch the batter has trouble with. That's the key. When Radke has it going there are a lot of taps to shortstop and pop-ups. Sometimes LaTroy will throw four innings and look like he spent eight hours in the sauna."

Our talk reminds me of my town ball friend, pitcher Jim Wheeler. Nobody hits Wheeler. He moves the ball around, has nice stuff, and makes the batter hit his pitch. And he gets a lot of outs.

Of course, it's never that easy when I go out to the mound.

On another occasion, LaVelle was telling me a great story about New York Mets Manager Bobby Valentine's ejection from a game in early June for arguing an interference call. Valentine was upset about being tossed out,

and decided that he was going to continue to hang out in the dugout anyway. So after being ejected, he left the dugout briefly, then returned, sporting big goofy glasses and a fake mustache.

Although the TV cameras closed in on the Groucho-like figure wearing a Mets T-shirt in the New York dugout, hunched over but clearly a presence, the umpires never seemed to catch on to the ruse.

Valentine stayed and managed the entire game, a game the Mets went on to win. He was fined and suspended, but not before he burst out of the dugout at the end of the game and celebrated, in costume, with his players.

Bill Robertson, Communications Director, Minnesota Wild

Bill Robertson is the Director of Communications for the newly formed Minnesota Wild hockey team of the National Hockey League. Previously, "Billy Rob" was the Executive Director of Communications for the Anaheim Angels, where he was vital in the transformation of Anaheim Stadium to Edison Field when Disney bought the club from the Gene Autry family.

"It was a tremendously valuable experience," said Robertson. "To this day, I treasure my sports business opportunity with the Angels. It was my job to reshape the image of that franchise at a time when it was changing a lot of things—from the Anaheim Angels' uniforms to the team's logo."

"Of course, our department was the source of team information as well, and developing proactive public relations tactics was a large part of the job."

I know Billy was pulling for the ballpark referendum to pass in St. Paul. Robertson and the Wild believe that combining the introduction of the new NHL club with a Twins move to St. Paul could have produced a relationship that would benefit both teams. Alas, the referendum failed by a good percentage. "As a son of St. Paul," he said, "I thought the people of this city missed an opportunity on November 2 (the date of the referendum). It would have been nice for St. Paul to further develop its reputation as a big league city."

Billy Rob is an avid baseball fan who strongly favors the outdoor version of the national pastime. "Baseball was meant for summertime, for blue sky and a warm breeze. Some of my fondest childhood memories are of going to the old Met with my father and watching the great ones play: Carew, Oliva and Killebrew. Harmon Killebrew was my idol as a young boy, and I would go to the games hoping to catch a Killebrew home run ball. Those are great memories for me."

Robertson believes that Major League Baseball must develop a comprehensive revenue sharing plan to ensure its future. "Baseball appears to be in danger of becoming an organization of 'have' and 'have-not' ballclubs, with only six or seven 'haves.' You may see an occasional club sneak in to the top echelon, but for long term success baseball must put in place an operative revenue-sharing plan. I believe the long-term health of the game requires this."

Changing the subject from baseball's future to events and players that have reinforced his affection for and excitement about the game, Robertson said, "It's a wonderful game. I wasn't here in 1987 for the Twins' first World Series title, but I was here in '91 and had a spectacular experience at game six. I took my wife to that game and after Kirby homered to seal the deal, I told her that there was no way that I could ever recapture that feeling. I chose not to go to game seven. That may sound kind of strange, because I had tickets and could have gone to the final game, but I just don't feel anything could have compared to the incredible energy level we experienced when Kirby homered."

Robertson has been friends with Paul Molitor for several years and minces no words when speaking of the St. Paul native. "I believe Paul Molitor is the greatest athlete in St.

Paul history. I know that says a lot because there have been some great ones through the years. Paul was a three-sport star and a great natural talent; he excelled in soccer, basketball, and of course, baseball. More than that, he's a humble guy who remembers his roots. There is no doubt that Paul is exceptional in the modern age of super-stardom and media hype. He's Hall of Fame in every way."

Larry Fitzgerald, Minneapolis *Spokesman Recorder*

I was sitting with my friend Larry Fitzgerald in the press box during a game between the Twins and the Texas Rangers. Larry is an African-American journalist in the Twin Cities who is Sports Editor of the Minneapolis *Spokesman Recorder* and a radio personality with a special interest in football. Larry played college football at a high level, but he's also a baseball fan and a fellow Chicago native.

Fitz let out a sigh as he looked around the Metrodome at the empty seats. "Man, there just aren't a lot of people who seem to be interested in this team. And you could probably count on two hands the number of people of color in this building right now," Larry said.

It just so happened that there were a couple of other African-American journalists in the press box as Larry said this, and he noted the fact. "We're like some wild rice at a white rice party," Fitz said.

Wow, that's heavy. I had to admit that I hadn't really thought about the issue. Picking up my binoculars and scanning the crowd, I found that his reference to the "rice party" seemed pretty accurate.

The lack of people of color at Twins home games in the Metrodome is an important issue to the Twins. Larry thinks the Twins are doing a lot of the right things, and said "They've got a great community relations staff. They work hard and I know they're out in the community. But it's a tough sell. The team's not that good, and I think baseball has a problem from a historical perspective.

"I think you'd be surprised how distant the African-American community feels from the game of baseball due to the fact that baseball broke the color line only recently in its history. Black folks remember, or learn, that baseball only allowed Jackie Robinson to play professionally for the first time in 1947. That's not that long ago. It's something that I think baseball has to fight.

"In football, and certainly in basketball, the sports are at least perceived to be more inclusive. Baseball may be viewed in the black community as exclusionary."

I'm not black, but I think Larry has something there, and I wonder if there are ways that baseball can improve its image in the black community.

"The Twins especially are trying hard to make some changes," Fitzgerald said. "They do quite a bit of advertising in our newspapers, and like I said, they're in the community. Plus, they need to put a better ball-club on the field."

Jim Souhan, Minneapolis *StarTribune*

Jim Souhan writes a lot of baseball as a columnist for the Minneapolis StarTribune. *His take on some of the goings-on in baseball during the spring of 1999 would be hilarious if it wasn't so dead on. The following material is from a column he wrote in May of '99.*

So you've signed your big time free agent, giving him $15 million a year, chartered flights from his kitchenette to the ballpark, 18 luxury suites and the island chain of his choice.

Now what are you going to give him to make him behave? Other than Prozac?

Last week Baltimore's Albert Belle threw a fit in the Orioles clubhouse, throwing bats into his locker, breaking one, after being called out on strikes.

Then Dodgers pitcher Kevin Brown did something much more foolish. He took a bat to a toilet in the Dodgers clubhouse after someone flushed while he was taking a shower, scalding him. In short, Brown signed a contract worth $105 million, then endangered his right arm before ever throwing a pitch that counted.

"Sometimes it's better to get that out," Dodgers manager Davey Johnson said. "No one was hurt by it. You can repair a toilet."

Johnson was doing what he's paid to do: take the heat off his temperamental stars. Another one, outfielder Gary Sheffield, left the Dodgers' camp for two days to attend to "personal business" after telling the Los Angeles *Times* he was considering retirement.

Never mind that Sheffield will make $10 million this season on a deal that averages $15 million a year over the life of his contract. He's unhappy that his surgically repaired right shoulder is still sore, that the Dodgers have banned facial hair below the lip and earrings while in uniform, and that Johnson is making him move from right field to left.

Upon returning from his sabbatical (didn't baseball players have four months off this winter?), Sheffield didn't dismiss retirement talk.

"I always feel like that when I get injured," Said Sheffield, who turned 31 in November 1999. "Is it worth it, what I have to do just to get on the baseball field? People say that's a lot of money, but not everything is dollars and cents. I just have to keep an open mind both ways."

Here's the anti-Ripken on:

The switch from right field to left: "I really don't feel like I'm accomplishing anything when I'm out there. I went two games without a ball hit to me. I don't feel I've learned anything there.... Obviously, I'm not comfortable.... If I'm embarrassed, I can't do it. And I'll just say I can't do it."

His health: "I'm not going to play if I'm not 100 percent. I'm done sacrificing myself."

Retirement: "Just the grind of everything, every day, has been [wearing] on me, and you can only take so much. But you're supposed to honor the things you agree to, and that's what I'm trying to do, but it's hard."

Eric Nelson, WCCO-TV

Eric Nelson is a Twin Cities television journalist who also has a background in radio and print. He's done baseball play-by-play for the Golden Gophers and is a traveler of the highest order. A road trip with Nelson is always an adventure. If you're heading to Coors Field with Eric, don't be surprised if you end up at Bank One Ballpark in Phoenix the next day.

Nelson firmly believes the Minnesota Twins need a new ballpark. "I know that a new stadium is not a panacea. It's not a cure-all. Baseball certainly needs to recognize the problems inherent in the current morass that is Major League Baseball; baseball is in dire need of some form of revenue-sharing like the National Football League's. But you know, we're being left behind by other cities around the country.

"We need a ballpark in the Twin Cities if baseball is going to survive here. Cleveland was so dead 15 years ago that they had to tag its toe. But now, as Drew Carey would say, 'Cleveland Rocks.' Cleveland has been revitalized—not just by baseball, but

The iron man: Cal Ripken, Jr. in spring training

by the entire process that the stadium was a part of. It's museums and the Rock and Roll Hall of Fame; it's everything.

"The Minnesota Twins had a down year this year, about as low as you can go. But they were still drawing an average of 14,000 to a game. In a reasonably good year they draw 20,000-25,000, and those are people coming downtown on a regular basis. You've got 81 games a year. Why turn your back on that?

"I think ownership around the league is making a colossal mistake by letting salaries escalate as they have. Ownership makes a lot of other mistakes as well. Greed certainly plays a role for some of the large market big-money teams. But you do have to spend money, and I think Minnesota fans are turned off by the cheap approach that has been used by the Twins the past couple of years.

"You know, Camden Yards is both the best thing and the worst thing to happen to the game of baseball, and in a way to the NFL as well. Since Camden came around in the early 1990's, it's become the new standard by which sports facilities are measured. It used to be that stadiums were measured against each other and they were relatively comparable— Kaufmann Stadium, Tiger Stadium, Wrigley Field—but after Camden was built, every owner decided he needed

a cash cow. They all want a throwback park with revenue-enhancing suites. In the 90's, there's been a stadium explosion. Once Camden came on the landscape it fostered new parks everywhere. And in a way, Camden yards is a microcosm of the greed that has become a part of the game.

"People ask me why, if the Metrodome was good enough for the Minnesota Twins in 1987 and 1991, isn't it good enough now? After all, they drew 3 million fans in 1992. I believe the answer is that even then, the Metrodome was a middle-of-the-road ballpark. A little below average. At that time, the Metrodome could be compared with Veterans' Stadium in Philadelphia, Riverfront in Cincinnati, Three Rivers in Pittsburgh. But now it's compared with Coors, Camden, Jacobs and the ballpark at Arlington. Sports has undergone a metamorphosis. It's not necessarily good, but there has been a critical change. The Twin Cities has to make a decision. I think we need to get in line and get ourselves a first-rate facility that we can be proud of."

Scott Miller,
St. Paul *Pioneer Press*

When Scott Miller was the beat baseball writer for the St. Paul *Pioneer Press*, it was fun to chat with him before games and find out what he thought the vibe was as far as the ballclub. Scott, though not a cynic, was certainly not an optimist, except on the issue of the stadium referendum that St. Paul voters would be asked to consider come November. I remember talking to Scott in late September 1999 and having him tell me he thought that the issue had a shot at passing.

At the time, however, he was not too happy with the *Pioneer Press* for failing to send him on a late-season road trip with the Twins. "It's incredible," said Miller. "The doggone paper is too cheap to send me on the road with the team when they're the town newspaper that you'd think should be making every effort to inform the voters, if not to try to gain votes. This will definitely cost St. Paul votes on election day. I don't get it, and I think it's strange." He has a point. If the Minnesota Vikings were 2 and 10 late in the football season, would the *StarTribune* cease to send its top football writer with the team? With such a critical vote looming on the horizon the message sent by the *Pioneer Press* was not a positive one.

Miller talked about the challenges relating to a new stadium for the Twins. "I've traveled to a lot of towns that have built ballparks, and one thing the new stadiums have in common is that they all seem to fit into the landscape and bring something positive to those towns. In other cities, the mayors and the city councils seem to somehow work together to get things done. But now we have a wildcard with a new governor who doesn't seem to give a damn about baseball and a public that shows little or no enthusiasm for anything relating to the process."

"Before Jesse Ventura became governor, I believe the major problem in getting a ballpark built was Carl Pohlad and the inept stadium campaign that was launched in 1997. Now, with a governor who doesn't care, the difficulty goes well beyond that, well beyond the public relations fiasco of the $80 million (Pohlad loan) that was supposed to be a gift but wasn't. It looks to me now as though, even with potential buyers in place, this whole thing is contingent on the referendum. And if the referendum is voted down, what buyer would want to step into the morass? I admire Taylor and Naegle for stepping up and being willing to take a shot to save baseball for the Twin Cities. There's no question in my mind that we deserve baseball in this market, and that the fans would be supportive if a stadium project were undertaken. If we build it, they will come."

I asked Scott if he felt the Metrodome was a large part of the attendance problem, as we looked around the thinly occupied stadium a half-hour before game time.

"They did a lousy job of looking into the future when they built the Metrodome. This thing wasn't built to go a long way as far as quality goes. And it's just a flat-out lousy place to watch a ballgame from a lot of the seats. It wasn't built for baseball.

"Even if it's forty-degrees cold or ninety-degrees hot, I'd rather see the game played outside. But I think you've got to put a roof on whatever it is that's built. I believe it's important to go with the latest in technology and to go all the way."

The Media Veterans' Perspective

Charlie Walters, St. Paul *Pioneer Press*

Charlie Walters is a sports columnist for the St. Paul *Pioneer Press*. Walters looks at the game of baseball as a former player. One day, while we were standing around the batting cages before the Twins played the Detroit Tigers, Walters spoke to me about his short professional career.

In 1968 he dueled with a young Vida Blue. At the time Blue was leading his minor league team in strike-outs, and Charlie was second or third at the time with his Wisconsin Rapids squad. During their pre-game chatter, Blue would spar with Walters regarding the number of strike-outs that the two of them would record.

"'How many are you gonna punch out, Charlie?' Blue would ask me. I'd have 13 or 14 strike-outs in some games, but nobody could fan them like that guy [Blue]," recalled Walters.

"Vida won that game one to nothing as I remember," said Walters. "The next year, I went to the big leagues—straight from class A to the majors. I had just turned 21 or so when I went up. I was with the Twins in 1969."

Walters tells a story about a young minor leaguer named Rick Dempsey who went on to star with the Baltimore Orioles.

When Dempsey was 18 he was sent down to the New York Penn league and was feeling miserable about it. As Walters recalls, Dempsey was sitting teary-eyed in the corner of the dugout. Charlie went over and talked to him and told him to hang in there. "Eight years later he's the MVP of the World Series, and when he saw me he gave me his hat from the game. He remembered me for the words of consolation I'd spoken to him eight years earlier. That impressed me."

Charlie doesn't see the same level of interest in baseball by today's kids as there was when he was growing up. "There's too many other things for kids to do today. Kids have different values. I don't think it's all bad, there's just not the same kind of interest that we used to have, pick-up games and things like that."

Charlie watches the home run races of the past couple years with a bit of caution, "I'm a little skeptical about everything," he says with a mild snicker. "I don't know if the balls are livelier—you look close at some of these guys, they're bigger, stronger, more muscular, and they work out ten months a year. In the old days we'd play the game hard for six months, then play golf for six months and kind of let go of baseball for a while."

As for McGwire and any Andro or other power-enhancing stuff, Walter says, "I don't like it, but baseball allows it, so it's all right, it's within the rules." When he looks at McGwire's mammoth arms and shoulders he does have questions, he said, but Walters finally shrugs and says, "It may be hard to get that big and there could be a little something to the Andro question, but all these guys are just bigger, stronger, and they hit more balls in the off-season. They're probably better ballplayers.

"And I don't really know about the impression that the power hitting is a result of poorer pitching. I watch some of these guys throw and they are still throwing 90-plus miles per hour. There may be some deterioration, but I don't know.

"I do respect Tom Kelly, though, and he says the pitching is thinning

out, that the hitting is better than the pitching.

"I give the hitters credit more than I take away from the pitchers. I think that some of these young Twins pitchers have pretty good stuff. Maybe they're not mentally ready.

"Guys are extremely good hitters in the major leagues. That's always been the case."

Walters, as usual, exhibited great foresight at the end of the 1998 season when he said he thought a new ballpark in the Twin Cities would require tangible political change and removal of Carl Pohlad as owner of the team. Charlie thinks that Carl is not a bad guy, but that his public image has degenerated to the point where he needs to go. "I'm objective. I hope we get a new ballpark, but we need to get some new people involved."

Herb Carneal, Twins Radio

Herb Carneal is a legend in Minnesota, known as an excellent broadcaster and as a man who has been around the game for many moons and seen a lot of baseball. The 1999 season was Herb's 38th year of broadcasting Twins baseball, and he is second only to Ernie Harwell of the Detroit Tigers in active longevity.

In fact, Ernie Harwell is a fan of Herb Carneal, referring to the Twins icon as "…perhaps the most solid guy in baseball behind a microphone. He's the way you like a ballplayer to be, steady, consistent and always ready to work. One of the best ever."

Herb knows baseball from the inside. He loves the game, is a Twins fan as well as a team employee and spends many a pre-game meal telling stories and sharing insights with former Twins Public Relations director and current official scorer Tom Mee, Associated Press journalist Barry Fritz and others. These can be power baseball sessions, whether Herb wants to admit it or not.

In one such session in early 1999, Carneal sounded a familiar theme: "Today's ballplayers keep themselves in better shape than most of the old guys, and one reason is they have better training equipment to work with.

"And they travel a lot better than before; there's no comparison between trains and modern jet aircraft.

"But I really believe the great players of years gone by would be great players today, too. As far as the home runs being hit, it's very difficult to compare something that happened in 1998 to something that occurred in 1927—more than 70 years ago."

Herb respects what Mark McGwire and Sammy Sosa have done for the game of baseball, but he does see boundaries that should be observed by fans of the longball: "I don't like to see fans boo their own players because the pitcher walks a McGwire or Sosa. I

don't think that's a good thing. The most important thing about a baseball game is to win the game. Home runs are incidental to the contest.

"The home run chase should not take precedence over everything else."

Carneal had some thoughts on the supplements reportedly taken by McGwire (Androstendione and Creatine) and Sosa. Classified as a dietary supplement, Androstendione is permitted in baseball, but is banned by the Olympics, the NCAA and the NFL. Major League Baseball has commissioned a study of Andro by Harvard scientists. For now, however, Andro is legal in baseball and that fact is important to Carneal.

"Hey, I can't even pronounce them, but they are legal. Given their legality, they (Andro and Creatine) don't necessarily cheapen McGwire's record."

Carneal stops short of endorsing the supplements, noting, "I'm a cautious sort. You don't know what the side effects might be in ten to twenty years, what the reaction might be."

There is no doubt that today's players, whether they rely on supplements or not, are more concerned about physical fitness than were the great players of yesteryear. Babe Ruth was not known for his passion for fitness, or for keeping decent hours. (Carneal recalled the time a roommate of Ruth's stated, "I don't room

The author with Ernie Harwell, entering his 60th year of
broadcasting Tigers baseball, at the Metrodome late 1999.

with the Babe, I room with his suitcase.") Quite the contrary, the Babe was known for large scale consumption of beer and hot dogs. A product like Creatine? Surely you jest. Today's ballplayer is a different animal, just as the game is a different beast. Getting results is a part of the business, and maintaining and pushing the body is improving the power product. You can't compare apples and oranges.

Talking to Carneal later in the season, I asked him about the increase he's seen in the time it takes to complete a Major League Baseball game.

"I've done a lot of games in 38 years," he said. "We need to do something to speed up the pace of games.

It's not that I want to get home earlier; I'm okay with 3-hour games as long as there is something going on. But now there's too much delay, with pitchers off the mound, hitters consistently stepping out of the box.

"We've got a lot of 4-2 games that are taking 3 1/2 hours."

He's right, of course. And Frank Robinson, with whom I talked at the All Star Game, is working on behalf of the powers in baseball to increase the pace of games in both leagues.

Overly long baseball games are a particular pet peeve of Robinson's, but despite his efforts, the American League average of 2 hours and 53 minutes per game in 1996—down 3 minutes from 1995—jumped to three hours in 1999. The three hour baseball game is a reality.

It looks like we need another program, Frank.

Carneal believes baseball games that drag on too long are hurting baseball in general, but particularly with young people.

"I'm hoping for a resurgence in the game, and I think people are paying attention beyond the home-run race, but we've got a real problem here [with over-long games]. Especially with young people who want something to happen.

"I remember the 1965 World Series between the Twins and the Dodgers. The longest game lasted 2 hours and 37 minutes!

"People talk about television adding delays, well, those games were televised! They've probably added another 30 seconds for advertising between innings today, but that only explains nine minutes."

Carneal's next comment reflects some of Twins General Manager Terry Ryan's beliefs:

"The other thing, and maybe the main thing, is that the umpires have got to call strikes. The belt's not a strike anymore, which it used to be and still should be. And the knees; the knee is a strike. Some of these guys are not calling good pitches that are in the strike zone, strikes.

"With some dilution of the pitching, and I think there has been some of that, combined with some reluctant umpires, the whole thing just gets more difficult. There are more 3-ball counts, more long at-bats, and the game sometimes tends to drag along."

And as a result, Major League Baseball games today take longer to complete than ever before in the game's history.

Dick Bremer, Twins TV

I always learn something when I talk to Dick Bremer, the point man on the Minnesota Twins TV broadcasts and an astute observer of the Major League Baseball scene. Dick made comments about the 1998 season that would apply later in the 1999 campaign.

The 1998 squad played pretty well in May, June, July and August with the usual ups and downs along the way. September, though not quite as bad as 1999, was nevertheless dreadful, with very few well-played ballgames. Baseball's long season has a purpose: to separate the men from the boys. "It gets tougher later in the year," Bremer said.

"It seems like every year some teams stay competitive for 100 games or so, but the last two months tell the tale of how good a team really is. In the past you can find examples of low-budget teams like Montreal and Pittsburgh who were very tough in the early going, and then faded. It's my guess the Twins may not have enough talent to play a full season."

Bremer was proven right by the Twins' finish in 1999. In the month of September the Minnesota Twins won 7 and lost 21. Throw in an 0-2-1 record (yes, a tie on the 1999 season's final day) for October and they closed the year with more than three losses for every victory in the final 30 games. That would be unacceptable at any level of baseball.

This kind of "fade" can be looked at two ways. The lower-budget teams tend to go with younger players who are less battle-tested than veterans who have more knowledge of the long season. Most young players have simply not been through the grind of the 162-game campaign.

Teams with larger budgets can stockpile more quality players and bring them off the bench offensively, defensively and to the mound. They have more weapons. It should also be said that losing can become contagious. Brad Radke pitched well, but was unable to stop the bleeding late in the year.

Serving up youth is a tough way to go in Major League Baseball, but Bremer (along with the Twins organization) remembers when the Twins went that route in the early 1980's, with exceptional results.

"The Twins tore things up in the early 80's when they decided to go in a different direction. There were some great prospects and the team was patched together with young players and guys like Roy Smalley and Butch Wynegar. That class of Hrbek, Gaetti, Viola, Brunansky, and later, Puckett had a lot of talent. You can build a team with young players, but there has to be a lot of talent to make up for shortcomings in other areas. Those guys were awfully strong and certainly not typical.

"Do they have comparable talent at the present time? I don't know. Time is always the test. I like some of the young pitchers, but they certainly lack power. It would be nice to see [David] Ortiz develop."

Speaking at the end of the 1999 season, Bremer talked of what he views as the largest single challenge facing the game today.

"We have an ongoing situation of economic inequity in baseball. The payroll tends to rule the game today. A big payroll provides a team with a definite short-term benefit, but what about the game? What about Montreal, Oakland and Minnesota, to name a few? This is the issue that baseball has to face going forward, certainly the critical issue of today.

"I think a lot of problems in the game have been overshadowed by the home run races of the last couple of years. The home run contest between Mark McGwire and Sammy Sosa has been good for baseball; baseball needed something like that. But there are still big issues that need to be dealt with."

What about suggestions that have been floated regarding reducing the number of teams in baseball by getting rid of the revenue-challenged?

"Maybe that's what needs to be done," Bremer said. "Tighten the league up by letting teams die; boost the quality of the talent pool for the remaining teams. Just let go of the Montreals and the Minnesotas."

I couldn't tell if he was serious. That's us you're talking about, Dick, our Minnesota Twins.

"Forget about North Carolina, too," he added.

It's hard to forget about Charlotte, North Carolina when there are 10 million people within a 100 mile radius of the state's capital city. There must be a lot of them who would love to have a Major League Baseball team.

Roger Buxton, WMNN Radio

It was a slow, late July afternoon during the 1999 season when I struck up a conversation with Roger Buxton of WMNN Radio. Roger is a sports director who attends the vast majority of Twins home games (and usually makes it through to the end of the game). As we were chatting about the current state of events surrounding the Twins, the ballclub and the stadium issue, we thought about the prospects facing the team.

We both agreed that the proposal to get a third of the financing for a new stadium from the team, another third from the city of Minneapolis and the last third from the state might have flown in 1997, before the Carl Pohlad faux pas of presenting an $86 million dollar loan as a gift.

"That really soured things," said Buxton. "If we had worked the 33% solution without the blunder that was made, I think it could have worked here like it did in Detroit. It worked there because the fans supported a similar concept of shared responsibility. I don't think it's going to fly in Minnesota."

We got to talking about Eric Milton and the promise that the young left-hander shows on some occasions. "Milton is still a very young pitcher and sometimes we tend to forget that. What is he, 23 or 24 years old? (Milton turned 24 during the 1999 season.) Sometimes it seems as though Eric tends to over-think. He can get pretty slow out there and I've heard Tom Kelly say that Milton seems to slow down when he has men on base."

I agree with that last assessment. Milton sometimes delivers pitches at a pace that seems to work against him, but boy, does he have good stuff! He's a complete pitcher when he really gets it going, and it's amazing that he hasn't won more ballgames. On this July 26 date, as the Twins prepared to face Oakland, the Twins had won 22 and lost 21 in their last 43 games. During that positive stretch, Eric Milton stayed stuck on three wins. How is it possible that Milton would not get a piece of the Twins playing over .500 baseball for six weeks? Milton was 8-14 with a 5.60 ERA in 1998 and pitched better than that.

In 1998, after the all star break, I had the chance to watch the Twins play what was at the time an important four-game series with Cleveland. The Twins split the series and ended up gaining no ground on Cleveland, which was essential if they were truly going to compete with the Indians in the second half of the season. In the fourth game of the series, Milton had a perfect game going through 5 2/3 innings and, in doing so against the powerful Indian's lineup, looked a bit reminiscent of Sandy Koufax. The Twins had a 10-0 lead when Milton, perhaps letting up a little, gave up a solo home run to David Bell that broke up the perfecto. The Twins went on to win the game 11-6.

Terry Ryan was holding court with a beat writer near where Buxton and I were standing, and I asked Roger what he thought of the job Twins leadership has been doing. "You have to give Terry Ryan credit for getting to the regular season without even knowing what his payroll is going to be. Somehow he's put a pretty respectable product on the field, and they're playing pretty good baseball right now. We'll see if they can hold up. A lot of these kids have talent, but we could sure use a couple of bangers to give us a power lift."

Terry Ryan and Tom Kelly both probably deserve kudos for getting this team to a position where they can stay on the field with just about anybody. The kids are playing well; Corey Koskie, Christian Guzman and some of the young outfielders as well as pitchers look like they're going to stay in the major leagues. Sometimes T.K. can sound pretty negative on the radio when he does his sports talk show, so I think he still gets frustrated.

Nevertheless, as Buxton noted, "These kids are lucky to be in this organization and playing for Tom Kelly. There's a lot of opportunity for the young players on this club and that's not completely a bad thing."

John Sherman, Richfield *Sun-Current*

John Sherman has been a baseball writer for the *Sun-Current* newspapers for 27 years. He's covered the local baseball scene from every possible angle and knows a great deal about the nuances of youth baseball. I asked John how he felt the state of the game was among the Metro area youth as he sees it.

"I don't see kids playing the game on their own as much as we used to," Sherman said. "You certainly don't see young people just playing catch or throwing the ball around very often anymore. We used to have a lot of fun just playing toss. When I was a boy in the late 50's and early 60's our whole day centered around pick-up games. I know I'm dating myself, but I used to

THOUGHTS ON AN EMINENT MEDIA VETERAN:
SID HARTMAN

It is disheartening that while several of the teams around both leagues are loading up with overpriced talent, the Twins are trying to make do with reasonably solid has-beens, a few never-weres, and of course, the kids. While the Twins are opportunity central for the farm system, the burden for the success of the Twins farm program falls largely on Director of Minor League Operations Jim Rantz.

Rantz, who frequently attends Twins ballgames at the Metrodome, has to be proud in many ways of some of the young talent that has been pushed to the forefront by the budget constraints of Minnesota's big club.

I kind of like Rantz. But frequently, he comes under fire from one of the Twin Cities' preeminent sports figures, Sid Hartman. Sid likes to criticize Rantz's efforts, and he frequently does so in the public arena.

I kind of like Sid, too. I see him at the Metrodome more often than I see any other journalist in the Twin Cities, and that tells me that Sid is one hard-working reporter. Yes, it's his job to be at the Metrodome before home ball-games to do reports for WCCO radio, but Sid puts energy into the task of covering a sub-par major league ballclub, and I have respect for him as an extremely hard working nose-to-the grindstone reporter. Sid can be abrasive, but it's darned hard to beat him to a story.

Sid being one of the hardest-working journalists in the world, it would be nice if he didn't feel it necessary to use the media dining room as a platform from which to criticize Jim Rantz for his supposed failures. It's just a simple matter of common courtesy that one would think Mr. Hartman could observe in the twilight of his grand career.

play ball from mid-morning until dusk or until we were ordered home by adults.

"There were always kids waiting to get into our games. If the sides weren't fair we made them fair. Any ball that landed in the weeds beyond the outfield was an automatic double. It was pretty raw baseball, but I can tell you we loved the game.

"I'm not faulting the youth of today. Certainly they have a lot of demands on their time. Baseball may not be as high a priority as it was for us, and that may not be a bad thing. It's a different world today."

Sherman conitnued, "I do believe that in the 1990's and going into the next century that there aren't as many young people who'll know the joy of an informal pick-up game. If our games were really going well, we wouldn't even break for lunch. I think you learn something about leadership, fair play, and participation in the group by not having any supervision.

"There's a new ball field where we used to play our games. I rarely see a game there. We would have died to have a ball field like the one that now stands empty in the Forest Crest neighborhood of North Bloomington. Perhaps someday the kids in the neighborhood will realize just how lucky they are."

Sherman has seen a lot of great players come out of the South Metro during his quarter century of baseball writing. He first saw former Gopher star pitcher Matt Scanlon when Scanlon was 14 years old and playing some Babe Ruth ball. "He was already throwing in the high 70 or low 80 mph range at that age," Sherman said. "I saw him throw an 11 inning no-hitter in American Legion ball a few years later. When he got to the University he could concentrate on his hitting and now he hits the cover off the ball. I think he has a shot at the big leagues."

I asked Sherman if Scanlon was the best high school player he had ever seen. "No, I don't think so. Matt was an outstanding ballplayer. But I think the best I ever saw in high school was Tom Nevers of Edina. He was hitting big home runs at the high school level well before his senior year. I thought Tom Nevers was a 'can't miss,' but there's no guarantee he's going to get a shot at the major leagues."

A player like Tom Nevers speaks again to the absolute challenge of becoming a big league ballplayer. Nevers was the best player that Sherman had ever seen in 27 years on the beat. Tommy may be out of baseball this year after playing for several years in the minor leagues. He's been looking for a break over the past couple years, but so far it has not been forthcoming.

John Sherman's friend, Greg Kleven, recommended Kent Hrbek to Calvin Griffith as a prospect who would perhaps one day do some good for the Minnesota Twins. Kleven, Sherman recalls, influenced Calvin to tell his staff about the big left-handed power hitter in Bloomington. "I guess Greg was a little better judge of talent than I am," laughed Sherman. ◉

4

UNIVERSITY OF MINNESOTA

The Golden Gophers

The University of Minnesota has what is arguably the finest college baseball program in the northern states. It's certainly an arguable point because you are going to get a fight from some other schools in the land of ice and snow, most notably (in the Midwest) the University of Michigan. After all, Michigan has a slight lead in head-to-head competition with the Gophers and has won its fair share of Big 10 titles. Michigan has also had a large number of All-America players. But no northern school and few southern schools can match the Golden Gophers' three national titles in the span of nine years. (1956, 1960 and 1964.)

All of the national titles came during the 31-year reign of Dick "Chief" Siebert (1948-1978).

The Gophers have laid claim to a total of 22 All-Americans and Dick Siebert was the winningest coach in Golden Gopher history until current coach John Anderson came along.

John Anderson

John Anderson, as the coach of the Minnesota Gopher baseball team, knows that there is a significant disparity between northern and southern baseball programs.

"When you look at an Alabama or a Miami, one of the first things you notice in their schedule is the number of home games that they play. They're playing 36 or more home dates, while we're struggling in Minnesota for three decent conference weekends a year."

Anderson strongly believes that the college baseball season should be moved back in fairness to all northern teams, not just Minnesota.

"We're just asking for a level playing field. We would like to have a legitimate chance to get to Omaha (site of the College World Series). We're not getting to the college World Series and it's really a question of fairness," Anderson said.

1999 GOLDEN GOPHER ROSTER

No.	Name	Pos.	B-T	Ht.	Wt.	Yr.	Born	Hometown (Last School)
1	Mike Arlt	OF	B-R	5-9	170	Jr	4-16-77	Lakeville, Minn.
2	Scott Welch	IF	L-R	6-0	170	Fr	11-16-79	Missoula, Mont. (Loyola Sacred Heart)
3	Jeremy Negen	C	R-R	6-0	200	Jr	1-2-78	Blomkest, Minn. (Willmar)
4	Matt Scanlon	3B/C	L-R	5-11	180	Jr	6-19-78	Richfield, Minn.
6	Ben Birk	P	L-L	6-5	210	Jr	11-6-77	St. Paul, Minn. (Cretin-Derham Hall)
7	Mark Devore	IF	L-R	5-11	170	Jr	11-7-76	Bloomington, Minn. (Jefferson)
9	Robb Quinlan	IF/OF	R-R	6-1	195	Sr	3-17-77	Maplewood, Minn. (Hill-Murray)
10	Kurt Haring	P	R-R	5-11	170	So	11-27-77	Champlin, Minn. (Champlin Park)
13	Adam Horton	1B	L-L	6-2	190	Jr	6-26-76	New Ulm, Minn.
15	Rick Brosseau	IF	L-R	5-11	175	So	9-22-78	North Oaks, Minn. (Hill-Murray)
17	Paul Hartmann	C	B-R	6-1	190	Fr	11-25-78	Red Wing, Minn.
18	Bob DeWitt	P	L-L	6-0	185	Jr	11-17-76	Wausau, Wis. (West)
20	Chad Trail	P	B-R	6-0	180	Fr	2-7-79	Paducah, Ky. (Tilghman)
22	Jason Kennedy	OF	R-R	6-2	195	Fr	10-24-78	Shorewood, Minn. (Minnetonka)
23	Scott Howard	OF	B-R	5-11	180	Fr	7-21-78	Rosemount, Minn.
27	Nick McCauley	P	R-R	5-11	180	Fr	12-3-79	Richland Center, Wis.
28	Jeremy Beaulieu	C	R-R	5-11	175	So	5-31-79	Shoreview, Minn. (Mounds View)
29	Rob LaRue	1B/OF	R-R	6-4	244	So	11-5-78	Minnetonka, Minn.
30	Jack Harmahan	IF	L-R	6-2	200	Fr	3-4-80	St. Paul, Minn. (Cretin-Derham Hall)
32	Nick Mueller	IF	L-R	6-2	185	Fr	10-24-78	St. Paul Minn. (St. Bernard's)
33	Matt Brosseau	IF	R-R	6-0	190	Sr	6-3-76	North Oaks, Minn. (Mounds View)
34	Kelly Werner	P	R-L	6-3	215	Jr	2-1-77	Eau Claire, Wis. (Memorial)
35	Andy Persby	P	R-R	6-3	215	So	5-2-78	North St. Paul, Minn. (Hill-Murray)
36	Frank Wagner	P	L-L	6-2	215	Jr	9-25-77	Miles City, Mont. (Custer County)
37	Brandon Kitzerow	P	R-R	6-0	180	Jr	2-20-77	Circle Pines, Minn. (Centennial)
38	Vince Gangl	P	R-R	6-2	195	Jr	3-23-77	Nashwauk, Minn. (Nashwauk-Keewatin)
39	Nathan Bennett	P	L-L	6-6	230	Jr	7-18-76	Arroyo Grande, Calif. (Coastal Christian/Okla.)
40	Dan McGrath	P	L-L	6-1	190	Jr	4-4-77	Victoria, Australia (De La Salle College)
41	Jon Nuss	IF	R-R	6-1	190	Fr	6-8-79	Bloomington, Minn. (Jefferson)
42	Brad Pautz	P	R-R	6-3	190	Sr	1-3-77	Reedsville, Wis.
43	Chadd Clarey	P	R-R	5-11	180	Jr	10-12-76	Rochester, Minn. (Des Moines Area C.C.)
44	Aron Amundson	P/IF	L-R	6-4	215	Sr	8-1-76	Mandan, N.D. (University of Oklahoma)
45	Chris Guetzlaff	OF	R-R	6-1	195	Fr	8-26-78	Sun Prairie, Wis.
46	Josh Holthaus	C/IF	R-R	5-11	210	So	5-28-79	Monticello, Minn.
47	Jim Egan	DH/1	R-R	6-4	225	Sr	9-8-75	Brooklyn Center, Minn. (Champlin Park)
48	Jason Shupe	B P	L-R	6-4	215	So	11-13-77	Spencer, Wis.
49	Joe Schmidt	OF	R-R	6-1	195	Fr	2-9-79	North St. Paul, Minn. (Hill-Murray)
51	James Downs	C	R-R	6-0	175	Fr	4-9-79	Lino Lakes, Minn. (Centennial)
52	Mike Kobow	P	R-R	6-4	190	Fr	4-9-79	Hutchinson, Minn.
53	Eric Gangl	C	R-R	5-9	170	Jr	3-12-77	Nashwauk, Minn. (Nashwauk-Keewatin)

Head Coach: John Anderson **Assistant Head Coach:** Rob Fornasiere **Pitching Coach:** Todd Oakes
Volunteer Coach: Lee Swenson **Strength Coach:** Brad Arnett **Athletic Trainer:** Andrea Rudser

Minnesota Baseball "By the Numbers"

84 Winning Seasons
17 Big ten Titles
22 NCAA appearances
3 NCAA titles

36 consecutive winning seasons
5 College World Series appearances
only **5** losing seasons in the last **64** years
7 alumni currently on major league rosters

1999 PRO-ALUMNI ROSTER

NAME	POS.	UM YEARS	PRESENT PRO CLUB-AFFILIATION
Jim Brower	P	1992-94	Cleveland Indians-AAA
Jason Dobis	P	1995-98	Oakland Athletics-A
Kai Freeman	P	1996-98	Chicago White Sox-Rookie
Brent Gates	IF	1989-91	Minnesota Twins-Majors
Mark Groebner	OF	1995-98	Montreal Expos-A
Shane Gunderson	C/OF	1993-95	Minnesota Twins-AA
Steve Huls	IF	1994-96	Minnesota Twins-A
Ryan Lefebvre	IF	1990-93	Cleveland Indians-A (Former)
Kerry Ligtenberg	P	1992-94	Atlanta Braves-Majors
Tim McIntosh	C	1984-86	New York Yankees-AAA
Mark Merila	IF	1991-94	San Diego Padres-Majors
Paul Molitor	IF	1975-77	Minnesota Twins-Majors (Former)
Charlie Nelson	OF	1991-94	Los Angeles Dodgers-AA
Greg Olson	C	1980-82	Atlanta Braves-Majors (Former)
Justin Pederson	P	1994-97	Kansas City Royals-A
Brian Raabe	IF	1987-90	New York Yankees-AAA
Jeff Schmidt	P	1990-92	Cleveland Indians-AAA
Craig Selander	OF	1996-98	Minnesota Twins-Rookie
Terry Steinbach	C	1981-83	Minnesota Twins-Majors
Dan Wilson	C	1988-90	Seattle Mariners-Majors
George Thomas	Coach	1956-57	Boston Red Sox-Majors (Former) Minnesota Head Coach (1979-81)
Herb Isakson	Coach		Volunteer Coach (1966-97)

"There's no official starting date for college baseball, we all get 22 weeks, we all get 22 weeks total, so while the southern teams are outside practicing, Minnesota and other northern teams are in the dead of winter."

Coach Anderson has Big Ten Commissioner Jim Delaney firmly in his corner. "Commissioner Delaney is becoming active in stating our mission as a conference to compete nationally not only in baseball, but in all sports. We definitely think Minnesota should have a shot at winning the Sears Cup (awarded for best overall athletic program in combined men's and women's play). But because of the climate, our spring sports are holding us up from having any chance to win the Sears Cup."

It wasn't long after my own experience in the Big Ten that the University of Wisconsin dropped its baseball program; I was stunned when the announcement was made in the 1980's. Anderson says other Athletic Directors are considering similar actions in the face of both gender equity issues and an inability to compete with the southern schools in baseball.

This is not as far-fetched as it sounds. After qualifying for the NCAA

college world series history

1956

Minnesota captured its first national championship with a 12-1 rout of Arizona. The Golden Gophers avenged their only loss of the tournament as Jerry Thomas earned the complete game victory and tournament MVP honors. For Thomas, it was his second victory against the Wildcats. In the second game of the tournament, he allowed just one run and three hits in a 3-1 win. Team captain Bill Horning provided the fireworks in the championship game with two home runs, four hits and five RBIs. Minnesota shortstop Jerry Kindall would make history 20 years later when as head coach of the Arizona Wildcats, he led his team to three national championships. He is the only man to play on and coach a College World Series national champion.

1960

The Golden Gophers claimed the 1960 national championship with a heart-stopping 2-1 10-inning victory against USC. With the bases loaded in the bottom of the 10th, third baseman Cal Rollof drew a five-pitch walk which scored Dave Pflepsen from third and gave Minnesota the title. The Gophers and the Trojans met three times in the double-elimination tournament. In the first matchup, Minnesota rallied from an 11-2 seventh inning deficit and defeated USC 12-11 in 10 innings. After a 3-1 Gopher victory against Oklahoma State, USC captured their own extra inning victory with a 4-3 win in 11 innings which set up the one-game, winner-take-all championship game. Second baseman John Erickson was named tournament MVP after his outstanding defensive play and clutch hitting.

1964

Minnesota's 5-1 victory over the top-ranked Missouri Tigers gave the Golden Gophers their third national championship in nine years. Minnesota rebounded from a 4-1 loss to Missouri in a game which saw the Golden Gophers manage just one hit. In the championship game, Joe

Dave Winfield (above) earned College World Series MVP honors in 1973, while Joe Pollack (below) earned three victories on the mound for the Golden Gophers in 1964.

Pollack stifled the Tiger offense and allowed just four hits. Of the Gophers' four wins in the tournament, Pollack earned three of the victories.

1973

After a nine-year absence, Minnesota made its return to the College World Series a memorable one. The Golden Gopher's Dave Winfield turned in one of the tournament's most remarkable performances in its history. In the opener against Oklahoma, Winfield struck out 14 Sooners and allowed just six hits in a 1-0 masterpiece. After being shutout 3-0 by Arizona State, the Golden Gophers defeated Georgia Southern 6-2 behind a solo home run by Winfield. Facing a semifinal matchup with USC, Winfield was back on the mound and dominated for eight innings. Winfield struck out 15 as the Gophers led 7-0 heading into the ninth inning. After a Trojan batter was called safe at first on a controversial double play attempt, Head Coach Dick Siebert was ejected from the game for protesting the call. USC went on to post eight runs on eight hits with two errors and a passed ball. Winfield was relieved after allowing four hits and three runs. The Trojans claimed the wild 8-7 victory en route to eliminating Minnesota and capturing the national championship. Winfield was named tournament MVP.

1977

Minnesota dropped its first game in the College World Series to Cal State-Los Angeles and were eliminated two games later by top-ranked Arizona State. Seeded second in the tournament, the Golden Gophers bounced back from their first round loss with a 4-3, 11-inning victory over Baylor. Facing the potent Sun Devil offense, Minnesota scored twice in the first inning to take an early lead. Arizona State, who entered the game averaging over nine runs per contest, scored seven runs in the next three innings and cruised to an 8-4 victory. Tom Mee led the Gopher effort with three hits and two runs scored.

Golden Gopher World Series Records

Single-Game Records

Hitting for the Cycle: Jerry Kindall vs. Mississippi, 6/11/56

Most Double Plays - both teams: 8; Minnesota (4) vs. Oklahoma State (4), 6/18/60

Largest Margin Overcome for Victory: 9 (in the seventh inning); Minnesota vs. USC, 6/17/60 (12-11, 10 inn.)

Series Records

Lowest ERA: 0.50; 1 er in 18 innings pitched, Jerry Thomas, 1956 (tied for record)

Most Wins: 3; Joseph Pollack, 1964 (tied for record)

Most Complete Games: 3; Joseph Pollack, 1964 (tied for record)

Championship Game Records

Most Home Runs: 2; Bob Horning vs. Arizona, 6/14/56 (tied for record)

Most Total Bases: 10; Bob Horning vs. Arizona, 6/14/56

Most RBIs: 5; Bill Horning vs. Arizona, 6/14/56 (tied for record)

Most Sacrifice Bunts: 2; Archie Clark vs. Missouri, 6/18/64 (tied for record)

Most Innings Pitched: 10; Jim Rantz vs. Southern Cal, 6/20/60

Largest Winning Margin: 11, Minnesota vs. Arizona, 6/14/56 (12-1)

A TOUGH PROGRAM

I was standing outside of Rocky Miller Park in Evanston, Illinois in the spring of 1979 when the Minnesota baseball Gophers climbed off the bus to play a double-header against the Northwestern Wildcats. I must have been retrieving a ball or something to have been so close to the unloading bus and I remember the look of the guys who were exiting. They were bigger-than-average, short-haired guys who looked ready to play after a night of rest following the eight-hour drive from Minneapolis. This will be a test, I thought.

I had been in the Northwestern football locker room, which is converted to a visitors basketball locker room for Big 10 games, when Kevin McHale and Michael Thompson walked in a few months earlier. How, I wondered, would Northwestern be able to cover these guys? They couldn't. That memory came back to me as I saw George Thomas's squad enter Rocky Miller.

University of Minnesota baseball has been solid for many years. The University claims the cream of the crop in a baseball-savvy state, which emphasizes ground-up learning in its youth programs and has excellent high school teams throughout. ◯

tournament in 1999, Providence College dropped its baseball program in the face of Title IX gender equity demands.

Anderson would like to see the baseball schedule for northern teams moved back from a starting date in early April to a start in mid-May. "If I could bring Michigan, Arizona State, Illinois, and the University of Miami to Minnesota in June and July, I know that we would draw very well. That's when baseball is supposed to be played, in the summertime. Our facili-

ties are inadequate for hosting a regional tournament; our press box and grandstands are viewed as inadequate by the NCAA. Ohio State and Notre Dame have developed new baseball facilities, and they're ready to host regionals. We should be heading in that direction here."

Anderson believes he could privately raise the $5 million or so it would require to really make a new Dick Siebert field shine, but he has to offer more than a few weekends of cold-weather baseball each season to

all-americans/coaching records

Dan Wilson, 1990 All-American

*Wayne Knapp, 1960-61
All-American*

ALL-AMERICANS

Name	Pos.	Year(s)
Paul Giel	P	1952-54
Jerry Kindall	SS	1956
Jerry Thomas	P	1956
Jack McCartan	3B	1958
Ron Causton	OF	1959
Larry Bertelsen	P	1960
Wayne Knapp	P	1960-61
Jon Andresen	2B	1963
Ron Wojciak	C	1964
Noel Jenke	OF	1969
Dennis Zacho	1B	1967
Mike Walseth	1B	1969
Dave Winfield	P	1973
Paul Molitor	SS	1976-77
Dan Morgan	P	1977
Greg Olson	C	1982
Brian Raabe	2B	1990
Dan Wilson	C	1990
Brent Gates	SS	1991
Mark Merila	2B	1993-94
Shane Gunderson	C	1995

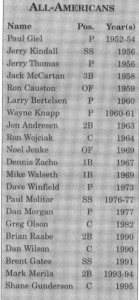

*Paul Molitor, 1976-77
All-American*

ALL-TIME COACHING RECORDS

Coach	Years	All Games	Win %	Big Ten Games	Win %
Walter Wilmot	1908-1910	36-20-3	.636	9-12	.429
Wilkie Clarke	1911	13-7-1	.643	4-4	.500
Dr. Denny Sullivan	1913-14	19-14-3	.570	7-9	.438
Frosty Thomas	1915	13-6	.684	3-6	.333
Bee Lawler, Russell Ford	1922	6-11	.333	2-6	.250
Lee R. Watrous Jr.*	1923-26	32-39-0	.450	17-21	.447
George "Potsy" Clark	1927	5-8-1	.393	3-4	.429
A.H. Bergman	1928-30	27-34-1	.444	10-22	.313
Frank G. McCormick	1931-41	138-89-1	.607	62-54	.534
David MacMillan	1942-47	67-35-1	.655	28-30	.483
Dick "Chief" Siebert	1948-78	754-360-8	.676	295-151-3	.660
George Thomas	1979-81	95-43	.688	39-13	.750
John Anderson	**1982-**	**605-384-3**	**.611**	**252-142**	**.640**

Minnesota's first full-time, paid baseball coach was Lee Watrous in 1923. Volunteer or part-time coaches led the team from 1876 through 1922.

Dick Siebert is the winningest coach in Golden Gopher history (754-360-8).

the boosters who would support such a project. Says Anderson, "I believe we could get it done. But there has to be a reason for us to go ahead with a substantial effort like this. The northern schools really need to have the college baseball season moved back."

From the Gophers to the Big Leagues

The Shooter, Charlie Walters, of the St. Paul *Pioneer Press,* made note of the fact that when Jim Brower of Minnetonka was promoted from AAA ball to the major leagues, he became the eleventh former Gopher in John Anderson's 17 years at Minnesota to reach the major leagues.

Robb Quinlan

In the spring of 1999, I spent a delightful morning sitting next to Robb Quinlan's parents at a Gopher baseball breakfast.

Robb was a dominant player in college baseball for a few years and an All-American. Robb was the Big 10's MVP in 1999. Later in the summer he was the MVP of the class A Northwest League, leading the league in RBI's with 67. Robb joined his brother Tom in professional baseball when the Anaheim Angels took him in the tenth round of the June '99 amateur baseball draft.

Things are looking very good for Robb Quinlan, but we won't jinx him by calling him a "can't-miss prospect."

5

A SMALL-COLLEGE SUCCESS STORY

Dennis Denning, St. Thomas

St. Thomas hired a new coach for its NCAA Division III baseball team in 1994. Dennis Denning took the helm of the Tommies' baseball program and led the team to Minnesota Intercollegiate Athletic Conference (MIAC) titles in 1996, 1997 and 1998. The next step after the conference championship was the NCAA regional tournament. The team to beat was Wisconsin-Oshkosh, a perennial power in Division III baseball that knocked off the Tommies in each of Denning's first three years. Finally, in 1999, the Tommies defeated Oshkosh in two one-run games in the regional tourney to advance to the World Series.

"We got a little lucky this year," said coach Denning. "We beat the number one team in division three (Oshkosh) then beat the new number one, Marietta, Ohio in a 4-1 ballgame. Then we knocked off William Paterson 10-7. Ultimately we made it to the championship game against North Carolina Wesleyan, and our luck kind of changed. We lost 1-0 in the final, but we sure could have won it. They played great defense and turned well-hit balls by our guys into double plays in both the 8th and 9th innings.

"Yep, if we'd had any luck in that final, we'd have won it. But breaks go both ways. In the first game against Marietta we hit into six double plays and still won."

(A note: the author played for Denison University in Granville, Ohio before transferring to Northwestern. Denison was in the Ohio Conference with Marietta and the author recalls some football-score sized losses to the southern Ohio baseball power.)

Dennis can now laugh at the memory of that double play by Wesleyan in the 9th inning of the championship game. "Our guy hits a rocket right back at the pitcher, who waves his glove at it because there's just no way he's gonna catch it. But he does manage to deflect the ball up in

Dennis Dennig

successful coach (at the high school and college levels) and a parent. Dennis' son Wes, a former Golden Gopher standout, recently left the Montreal Expos minor league system to pursue a career in law enforcement in Prior Lake, Minnesota. Although he was making advancements each year, Wes felt it was time to get on with his life and escape the inherent poverty of baseball in the low minors.

"Wes was making $850 a month with the Expos, about $5,000 a year to pursue his career as a ballplayer. That's just not enough money—certainly not enough to live on. He saw all his friends getting on with their lives, he's got a girl, and the job he took with Prior Lake pays him very well the first year, so there is no comparison."

Part of what makes Dennis Denning an exceptional baseball coach is his candid approach to people and events, and his great honest energy is flowing now.

"What they pay these kids in the minor leagues is ridiculous. I'll tell you it's just sick, and I think it's hurting the game. It's crazy at the other end too, with some of the money these guys are making. Baseball is not healthy. On the low end you have all these poor kids in the minors, and you're starting to see a lot more Latin players in the game at the low levels because the money, bad as it is, is better than where they

the air—straight up, and then straight back down to the pitcher, who catches it and starts a double play. We had the bases loaded with one out, and we got nothing out of it but a loss. A tough way to go, but that's baseball."

Yes, that is baseball, and when you have been around the game as long and in as many ways as Dennis Denning, you're bound to see a lot of wild and wonderful stuff.

Denning has been a high-level college player (at St. Thomas), a professional baseball player (in the minor leagues), a town-baller, an umpire, a come from. But you're losing a lot of the home-grown kids, and there is something wrong with that.

"And the game is insanely top-heavy. I know we can't go back, that this can't be done, but I wish we could somehow start over and make the maximum salary for a big leaguer $250,000 or maybe a half-million bucks a year, for the top guys. The agents have played a big role in wrecking the game by making the money nuts, demanding these crazy, outrageously huge salaries."

I reminded Dennis that agents are usually lawyers doing their best for a client. That's their job.

"Well, yeah, lawyers," Denning laughed.

"Whatever. Agents have hurt the game. And I don't understand the role of unions in baseball. Unions have always had a role in society, or at least they used to have a role, but it's no good for baseball. The money is wrecking the game, and the fans and the general public can't relate to a lot of the new stuff, the money, the jerks who can't handle the money or the pressure."

What about your job, Dennis, do you still love the game?

"Oh yeah," Denning replies. "I'm very lucky to have been surrounded by people who understand the game, understand what we're trying to do. The key is to surround yourself with good people. At St. Thomas, everybody

graduates on time, which means in four years, not in five or six. None of my kids gets any money to play baseball here. There are no athletic scholarships at the Division III level. The only financial aid goes to kids who demonstrate a real need. But we have fun here."

Denning was the baseball coach at Paul Molitor's old high school, Cretin-Derham Hall, after Molitor left. His Cretin teams had a lot of success, and he coached some terrific players, among them Chris Wienke (who gave up pro baseball to quarterback Florida State's National Champion football team), Tim Thomas, Mark Wegner and a bunch of others. Cretin's new coach and Denning's friend Jimmy O'Neill had a squad that won 66 games in a row, close to a national record, before losing to eventual 1999 champion Hastings High School in the state tournament. "That is something," Denning says. "But the St. Paul City Conference isn't what it used to be."

Denning knows Paul Molitor today and remembers the first time he saw the then pint-sized ballplayer in 5th grade at the gym. He didn't look special until he started to run around and throw. "He wasn't very big, but he had a great arm even then. And he had baseball instincts. I told another guy there, 'We're gonna see this kid in the bigs.'

"And sure enough he's proven to be one of the best ever. I bought sea-

Final 1999 ABCA Div. III Baseball National Poll/June 2

School	Record	Pts	Last Poll
1. North Carolina Wesleyan	42-9	240	5
2. St. Thomas (Minn.)	**42-7**	**232**	**17**
3. Cal Lutheran	33-14	223	17
4. William Paterson (N.J.)	31-14	217	rv
5. Marietta (Ohio)	50-8	205	4
6. Cortland (N.Y.) State	35-10	203	7
7t. Aurora (Ill.)	38-8	188	10
7t. Brandeis (Mass.)	33-10	188	8
9. Wis.-Oshkosh	34-4	168	1
10. Carthage (Wis.)	45-6-1	166	3
11. Chapman (Calif.)	39-5	155	2
12. Ohio Wesleyan	34-16	149	28
13. New Jersey	32-11	143	23
14. Virginia Wesleyan	29-15	123	rv
15. Ithaca (N.Y.)	27-16	122	15
16. Amherst (Mass.)	25-10	115	21
17. Southwestern (Texas)	42-9	102	9
18. Anderson (Ind.)	36-14-1	97	16
19. Montclair (N.J.) State	28-18	93	19
20t. Southern Maine	36-13	85	11
20t. Augustana (Ill.)	32-13	85	rv
22. St. Scholastica (Minn.)	35-12-1	74	27
23. Mount St. Mary (N.Y.)	29-10-2	57	rv
24t. Simpson (Iowa)	32-14	43	25
24t. Wis.-Stevens Point	31-10	43	13
26. Allegheny (Pa.)	36-10	41	12
27. Bridgewater (Va.)	26-19	38.5	29
28. Rowan (N.J.)	36-8	36	6
29. Wooster (Ohio)	35-14	20	22
30. Methodist (N.C.)	29-13	19.5	14

1999 Minnesota Intercollegiate Athletic Conference Baseball Final Regular Season Standings

	Conf	All
St. Thomas	*19-1	42-7
St. Olaf	14-6	26-11
Macalester	11-9	22-17
St. John's	11-9	20-16
Gustavus	10-10	18-18
St. Mary's	10-10	17-15
Conc.-M'head	10-10	19-21
Bethel	7-13	20-18-2
Augsburg	7-13	13-26
Carleton	6-14	8-30
Hamline	5-15	12-21

*clinched title, NCAA berth

son tickets for the Twins when he came here at the end of his career. I thought I'd do my share to support that. But I don't like going to the dome to watch baseball, although we play there occasionally. I like outdoor baseball. And when Molitor was finished, I dropped the tickets."

The Denning Philosophy

Tom Kelly, Jr. (the son of Minnesota Twins Manager Tom Kelly) is a pitcher for St. Thomas, a right-hander who went 4-0 last year for the Tommies. His first year he played the outfield, and in his second year he moved to second base. Now he's a pitcher who had success as a junior and "has come a long way," said Denning. "He's just a regular guy on this team who needs to show

control as a pitcher, and who might work his way into the rotation for us."

What does it take to have success in baseball at St. Thomas? "I don't have any expectations as far as wins and losses. I want the individual to have high expectations, so I like self-motivators who can get themselves going. I'm not going to stand behind 'em and kick 'em in the rear end. I don't want to have to talk to players all the time—I'm not a coach who gives pep talks.

"But if you are a kid who loves the game, you're going to have a good experience in our program. That's what I hope."

Denning's Playing Career

Dennis Denning, besides being a coach, is a former player who has lived a life filled with baseball. He gave up playing the game at the town ball level not that long ago. In 1966 he played all 29 innings for the Miami Marlins in a 4-3 victory over St. Petersburg, in what was at the time a record length for a professional baseball game.

Denning played for some outstanding coaches while he was in the Florida State League, working with such people as Sparky Anderson, Billy DeMars, Cal Ripken, Sr., Jim Frey and Joe Altobelli. Denning, who was an instructor for the young Paul Molitor, also played for George Bamberger in the minor leagues. Ironically, Molitor played for Bamberger himself as a member of Bambie's Bombers in Milwaukee. Molitor, in fact, played for Bamberger in the World Series in 1982.

Denning saw Johnny Bench in the minor leagues and didn't foresee the Hall of Fame catcher that Bench was destined to be. "Sometimes it's hard to recognize where players may be going when you see them in the minors. A guy who may go on to become an outstanding ballplayer might not show you much when you see him in a certain game," said Denning.

One of Denning's favorite stories involves the late, great Satchel Paige. While Denning was playing in the Florida State League with the Miami Marlins, Paige was signed to pitch a game for the team. It was a move by the owner of the team to gain publicity for the ballclub.

Denning tells the story:

"We were in the running for the championship of our league when we were told that the owner of the team had signed Satchel Paige, who we knew was retired and had to be in his 60's. It was bad enough that we had signed him to pitch any game, but he was going to pitch in an important game, a league game. I'm a young college guy, and I'm mad as can be because here they have signed this old man to pitch a game for us! What are the odds we're going to win?"

"Well old Satchel showed up, and he was an interesting looking man to say the least: real tall, about 6'3", thin as can be, with long arms. Here comes Satchel smoking the cigarettes and all the pitchers, all the young guys are listening to the stories he was telling and enjoying his stuff.

"When he warmed up, he didn't go down to the bullpen like a regular pitcher would; instead, he pitched out in the grass in front of our dugout with a cigarette dangling from his mouth. We asked him, 'What's the number one thing you got to have to be a successful pitcher, Satch?' And he said, 'Control, boys, control.' He gave me a cigarette and told me to put it on the plate and then he started pitching and threw the ball right over the cigarette. He had me move the cigarette around to the other side of the plate and he would keep throwing the ball right over it. It was something to see.

"He wasn't a role model but he sure was a character and a good guy, I thought. He was an old grandpa type but here's the punch line: He could still pitch!

"He probably threw 76 or 78 miles per hour, which is what a good high school pitcher throws as far as velocity, and he kept it right at the knees. There was some movement on those pitches, too.

"He started the game for us and we beat the Twins club that played in the Florida State League 4-3. He must have really been terrific thirty or forty years before.

"I'll never forget how we were, a bunch of cocky young guys, watching Satchel Paige in disbelief. He had better control than anybody on our team! I still get a thrill out of recalling that experience."

Denning's Record at St. Thomas

In 1999 the University of St. Thomas finished 42-7 overall and 19-1 in it's conference to tie a record that the school already held for most conference wins. St. Thomas became the first MIAC team to reach the Division III College World Series. Dennis Denning coached for 17 years at St. Paul's Cretin-Durham Hall High School, where his teams posted a 378-76 record. His Cretin teams captured an unprecedented 6 state titles, 11 regional titles, 12 Twin Cities titles, and 15 conference titles. Denning's successor at Cretin, Jim O'Neill, has led the team to a 128–7 record over the last five seasons. Cretin won 66 consecutive games, falling two short of tying the high school record of 68 consecutive wins.

St. Thomas in Cuba

Denning took the University of St. Thomas 'Tommies' to Cuba in January 2000 to play a couple of games against teams from the University of Havana. He is hoping for follow-up games that would be played in the Twin Cities. This trip was made possible by a $100,000 grant from the Pohlad Family Foundation to the University of St. Thomas. The grant is to be used to support continuing baseball competition between Cuban and local Twin Cities college teams.

By the way, the Tommies won both games. ◯

6

TWINS MANAGEMENT SPEAKS

Terry Ryan
General Manager

Terry Ryan is the General Manager of the Minnesota Twins. Terry spoke to our Optimist Group during the season in 1998. Though this particular speaking engagement took place over a year ago, I believe the comments that follow jibe with Terry's thinking today. Terry came to our meeting as a courtesy to me, as a representative of the Twins. He was under no obligation to speak to our small group at 7:30 a.m. during a busy time of the season. He also did not have to bring an autographed Molitor bat that the Richfield Optimists used to raise $500 for our programs. (The Optimists International is a "friend of youth.") Terry Ryan's job is not to reason why—it is to do or to fail. Terry's job is to put a quality baseball team on the field.

He began by talking about the Twins' struggles simply to remain competitive.

"There is no question that the Minnesota Twins face a tremendous battle. The New York Yankees, the Atlanta Braves and the Los Angeles Dodgers; these teams and others have enormous payrolls that make it very difficult for the Pittsburghs, the Minnesotas, the Montreals, etc. to compete day in and day out with those kind of organizations. We simply don't have the kind of funding that will allow us an equal footing with the well-financed organizations.

"I'm not here to make excuses for our ballclub. It's my job to put the best possible team on the field and they are expected to perform at the highest level possible. There are no excuses and I'm not going to make any.

"We draft about 80% pitchers. This organization has struggled with pitching and that's no secret. Some of the players have been disappointments, and you can look at a Frankie Rodriguez as one of those. We expected more of Frankie. This organization has struggled with pitching and we need to improve in that area.

"Offensively, I expected better power from this [1998] team. The corner position players (1st and 3rd base, left and right field) are supposed to hit for power. We've been lacking the production that we expected. Cordova, Lawton, Ortiz, Coomer—we expected more from them.

"We feel we found some good players; if you look at Terry Steinbach, Paul Molitor and others, I think we've done all right.

"There are a lot of things that are good about the game of baseball today. The home run race has been a healthy experience for baseball. The Chicago Cubs, with Sammy Sosa and a team that has struggled, still fill the place day in and day out. I think Ken Griffey is the best player in the game today; I think he appeals to young people and he's a good competitor. Ken Griffey is a tremendous ballplayer.

"We need to market the positive things about the game. I don't believe the Metrodome is the problem. A good club will draw fans to the seats. We didn't have any problem putting people in the ballpark in 1991 and we drew 3 million in 1992. I don't worry too much about where we play; that's an excuse and a distraction.

"There are new economics in the game of baseball. Concessions, parking, suite revenue; these are all important sources of revenue that a team needs to increase its capabilities. The business of baseball has certainly changed and will continue to change going forward. Baseball does need to look at some things.

"I like interleague play, as it gives the fan a chance to see special players and special teams from the other league. When the Chicago Cubs come to town to play the Twins, I know a lot of the crowd is there to see Sammy Sosa or Kerry Wood, and that's okay. The same thing when Mark McGwire and the St. Louis Cardinals come to town. I believe it's a good thing to be able to see the great players of the game from either league.

"I believe that offense in baseball is becoming too dominant. There's no break for a pitcher with a designated hitter, which was a fundamental change to the way the game is played. The pitchers seem to really have it rough right now. We need the umpires to call some strikes. There are some problems with the umpires as well. The strike zones are dictated by whoever is behind the plate. An umpire like Joe Brinkman, for example, has a different strike zone than Ken Kaiser.

"It used to be that the strike zone was from the belt to the lower part of the knee. Now the strike zone is from the high thigh to the top of the knee. That's a small area for the pitcher to work with. Given the strength of today's hitters, guys like McGwire or Sosa or any number of power hitters, that small area is easier for a hitter to cover. The good offensive players can keyhole your pitch.

"As I say, there are some very good things about the game of baseball and the Minnesota Twins that don't get a lot of attention. This organization is highly involved in the community, the state and the Upper Midwest as a whole. We do as much as we can for charity and we have made a special focus of youth baseball.

"Many, many players have charities and it seems to go largely unnoticed. Molitor, Coomer, Puckett and a lot more guys on the Twins contribute thousands and thousands of dollars to charities that actually get things done. They're not just fat cat athletes.

"I know the money is out of whack. We all know it. I have to pay these things, negotiate them, and the money is out of whack. I believe agents get the benefit of the excesses of dollars. Where will it end? I don't know.

"Baseball is still a wonderful game. You can get a group of kids in the ballpark for a few dollars and we really try to make the whole thing affordable. We work with the community to enable children to see baseball games. And if there's any sport that's affordable, it's ours. When you look at some-

thing like the Molitor family pack and how that works out I think we're presenting real value to the family."

An Interview with Dave St. Peter, Vice President of Communications for the Minnesota Twins

Dave St. Peter has been VP of Corporate Communications for the Twins for 10 years. An important part of his job is helping the team convey enthusiasm and a positive image to the public in general and Twins fans in particular. That isn't always easy in the context of changes in contemporary professional baseball and the way it's run. Drumming up fan support for "billionaire owners" insistent on their need for public financial support, or for "whining multi-millionaire athletes" who went on strike for whatever it was they demanded, is an increasing challenge. Consequently, I started our conversation, which took place in late 1998, by asking St. Peter whether baseball is going to be able to solve some of its image problems.

Certainly there are issues and hurdles that the game itself will have to deal with and overcome; current challenges include player relations, labor issues, revenue sharing, and income discrepancies between large markets and small markets. We don't have all the answers yet, but there's been progress made in those areas.

Unfortunately, there are also parts of the game that are dangerously unhealthy, and I think one of those is especially troublesome here in Minnesota where we've had some significant challenges in terms of how we overcome the lack of revenues in our attempt to keep this team viable for the long term.

Still, I believe that the game of baseball is in the midst of a powerful recovery. In terms of the state of the game as it relates to kids, I think we'd all like to believe that what has taken place within the last couple of years—the home run chase and some other good things, some of the real positive stories—will have a lasting impact. But more importantly, I don't think there's any question that baseball needs to continue to do what it's already doing, and more, to restore the game's status as the national pastime. It's going to be difficult. It's 1999—not 1989, not 1979, and definitely not 1955. Baseball has to adjust to today's fast-paced society. I see kids playing video games, I see kids hanging out and watching more TV than they used to watch; it's challenging. Baseball is doing some things to attract more kids to the game, though. For exam-

ple, you're going to start hearing about a two-on-two, four-on-four game called Yard Ball which is being promoted nationally and is designed specifically to eliminate the need to round up 20 guys to play baseball. Locally, the Twins are going to remain focused on trying to bridge the gap between baseball and inner city youth with their urban center.

What are some of the things you've done as far as bringing kids to the park and exposing them to the game? I know you do some good work.

There really are two ways to involve kids. There's what we're doing in neighborhoods to get kids to play, and then there's our effort to bring kids to the Major League Baseball stadium, i.e. the Metrodome, to introduce them to the game of baseball that way.

The Twins have been active in this for a number of years, and I think Kirby Puckett deserves a lot of the credit. When Kirby signed his record-breaking contract following the '92 season, it included a clause in which he basically agreed to purchase 30,000 seats each year for urban youngsters through the Twins Care program. (That kind of program wasn't really new to baseball; back in the 1970's Dave Winfield and a lot of other players had been buying tickets for kids to attend games at the Jack Murphy stadium.) Kirby and the Twins Care program helped bring such efforts up to date. Puckett isn't the only player who has been involved; Paul Molitor will probably bring 25,000 kids to the ballpark himself this year, and Brad Radke, Ron Coomer and others all contribute dollars so kids can come to the ballpark. That's important because this game has so many good things happening. Too often in some urban settings we can no longer rely on dads to bring their sons to a ballgame. That rite of passage is no longer common in urban areas because there are too many families that are not "typical" model families. There are single-parent families and families with both parents working, so we often have to try to get to these kids through their youth groups, Boys and Girls Clubs, local park and recreation programs, or the YMCA to bring the kids out here. Hopefully we're providing them an outlet as well as some exposure to a game that we hope will create the kind of childhood memories many of us have of attending our first major league game, whether it was at the old Met, or Yankee Stadium, or Tiger Stadium.

It was Wrigley Field for me.

That's a great park, and we love playing there.

This year we will probably provide upwards of 80,000 to 90,000 free tickets specifically to youth groups, a number from the urban core and some from what we call out-state Minnesota. That's a lot of tickets and it's important to the Twins that folks recognize what's going on.

Let's switch subjects before we talk about stadium debates. What are some of your observations on Paul Molitor? The thing I find so impressive is the names that he's being compared with: Honus Wagner, Tris Speaker, Willie Mays. What are your thoughts?

Well, it's tough for me to say enough about Paul on the baseball side—obviously I'm a fan and I'm just like everybody else. And its just marvelous what he does today at his age, the high level at which he can play this game. There are days when he's still the best player on the field, and at 42 years old, that's pretty darn good. But more important, I think, is where he is in terms of history. What's impressive about Paul as a person is that, in a day and an era where players are often criticized for their lack of knowledge of the game or its history, he is very cognizant of where he is in his career. More importantly, he's very respectful of the names that he's compared with, and I think he's truly touched and honored by that, and he has a tremendous sense of humility. I've had the privilege of working with some first class individuals here, whose approach to the game is not necessarily just to win, but also to convey high standards in all their activities, on and off the field. Guys like Kent Hrbek, Kirby Puckett, Dave Winfield—the list goes on. I will tell you, Paul Molitor is the most professional baseball player that I've ever dealt with. He's very cerebral; when you say something to him, Paul will actually take the time to listen and to think before he gives an answer. If I give Paul a memo about a potential interview, or a potential opportunity in the community, he'll read it. Too often in today's fast-paced society, you don't get that type of response from players, but Paul and Linda Molitor have done some tremendous things in this community. They care, they "get it," they understand that fan support is what drives this bus and that without the fans and without a recognition of a team's responsibility to give back to the community, this game has no future. I think the Molitors have been a tremendous example for young players in our clubhouse.

It has been important to have Paul Molitor here, and not necessarily to pick up the pieces, but to be here and be a presence within the Clubhouse, even if he's a bit different type of leader than Kirby was. I think that was important for us in terms of his role in the business, which in part

is to help demonstrate to those guys that there is a right way to do things and there's a wrong way to do things. And we've been very blessed, I think, to have had Kirby Puckett and Paul Molitor here.

Let's switch directions here, Dave. You know there's a stadium debate that's been going on around here, and the public has not been receptive to the idea of being taxed on anything. There's been a lot of political grandstanding, in my mind. Opponents of a ballpark have what's almost a mantra, "We won't spend dime one to help rich people," which oversimplifies things dramatically. I grew up near Wrigley Field in Chicago. I believe that an outdoor ballpark located in either downtown would just be a tremendous gift to the city and to the state. What are some of your thoughts on this?

Well, certainly there are reasons for that, probably compounded by the fact that we have struggled in the field and the Twins have fallen a bit out of favor in the sense that we just have not been competitive. And there's skepticism brought on by the issues of the ballpark debate. Unfortunately, we're dealing with a situation where ownership groups have been characterized as selfish billionaires and have been villainized whenever the issue is discussed. Every time I hear the name

Carl Pohlad, I typically hear the word billionaire attached to it. And you know folks in the state are somewhat fickle, they have a "What have you done for me lately?" attitude. There's very little memory of the Twins world championships in 1987 and 1991 and virtually no memory of the fact that Carl Pohlad stepped in and kept the Twins from moving to Tampa/St. Pete in 1984. And that, I think, is frustrating for everybody involved. Throughout the debate, the best thing that's happened is that we've seen a change of heart in three other communities whose struggles with this issue led many legislators and people here to argue, "look at San Diego, look at Cincinnati, look at Pittsburgh; they're saying no." Well, those communities have all said yes recently. They found a way to create a stadium and get the job done.

Of course, the ballclub has a responsibility and the business community has a responsibility because they stand to benefit. And you know the legislature and/or any kind of governmental body has a responsibility. Obviously, that area is open to debate. But I think it's clear that drawing 30,000-40,000 people a night into the downtown area is going to have a positive impact throughout the state of Minnesota. That's a part of the debate that we hope will be back at the table someday if, or more likely

when, the debate heats up once again.

In Denver, they use a kind of tourist tax. I used to live in Denver, and where the ballpark is now used to be the the edge of reality in downtown Denver. There's been such a revitalization of downtown Denver along with a wonderful ballpark where the fans are no better than our fans but truly have found a lot of joy. What are some of your thoughts on the new ballparks, and on what might work here?

Well, I think before Denver built Coors Field, there were like three liquor licenses in a six- to eight-block radius in that area, and now there are about 80. I mean it's some incredible number. Camden Yards in Baltimore was one of the first modern but nostalgic-type ballparks, and when you look at it and at Coors Field and at Cleveland's Jacob's Field, they're all wonderful places, they all have nuances, they all have blended into the fabric of the cities where they exist. From the Twins' standpoint, and from the Minnesota public's standpoint, I don't think there's any question that we'd already be constructing a stadium if we could've found a way to fly 2.5 million Minnesotans to Baltimore to look at Camden Yards.

There's a lot of debate here on whether we need a roofed stadium.

Certainly, from the Twins' standpoint, we recognize that you can save a lot of money by not putting a roof on, but we also recognize that we draw 30-35% of our fans from outside the metro area. And fans don't want to drive from Des Moines or Sioux Falls if they're likely to get rained out.

We're not even at the ballpark design stages, yet we're very site neutral. I think we feel as though wherever the ballpark is going to be built, if one is going to be built, the city and its leaders need to come to the forefront, and hopefully that is what will happen. The ballpark debate might have been best characterized by what happened the last night of the [1998] legislature, when 11 out of 12 Minneapolis legislators voted against a project that's going to bring an incredible amount of revenue to their city. Unfortunately, that's one example that might tell you where we are, that we had very little chance of getting anything through that night. So, some things need to happen. I think time needs to pass and maybe the biggest thing is that some of this so-called "poison" in the air needs to lift, but how does that happen? I don't know. Winning baseball games would help, but it's not quite that simple. Somehow, some of the dynamics need to change here and we'll see if any ownership dynamics change.

Do you think the Twins can rally more business leaders in the community, particularly in the Twin Cities, to pick up a fair share of the burden in keeping the team in Minnesota?

Yes, but I think it's important for it to happen in the front end of the process, versus the back end. By that I mean that the next time we go to the legislature, one of the elements that may need to be in place is to have commitments already in hand for season ticket seats, for club seats, for naming rights. In essence, we have to demonstrate to people throughout the state that there is a market for a new stadium, and that it is something that businesses support. That might be critical. That was not in place before. There certainly was a feeling there that there would be surveying done and there were some business leaders who'd stepped forward, but was there anything concrete done? No. Certainly, the next time it may be part of the strategy to bring some of that into the front end; obviously, we need to find a more effective way to communicate the incredible economic impact that a ballpark can have. Somehow we need to find a way, if Minneapolis is the site, to demonstrate to people how a ballpark can be the driving force behind riverfront development in Minneapolis, not unlike what we're seeing

Norm Coleman do so effectively in St. Paul with some of the projects that he's initiated along the city's riverfront. ◯

HISTORICAL PERSPECTIVE:
CALVIN GRIFFITH

I was checking my arriving faxes one day when I noted that I had received a Twins press release announcing that Calvin Griffith had died at the age of 87. Calvin died at his second home in Melbourne, Florida October 20, 1999 from complications of heart and kidney problems. He actually looked pretty good to me the last time I had seen him at the Metrodome, in September of '99.

Calvin Griffith owned the Washington Senators and their successor, the Minnesota Twins, for three decades. Calvin was the type of owner that doesn't exist anymore. He ran the baseball club like a family business. Baseball was changing after the Second World War, but Calvin ran his team in a style reminiscent of simpler days. The Twins won one pennant and two division titles during his tenure in the Twin Cities, but he did it his own way, refusing to pay big salaries, and running the team close to the vest with a large number of family involved. By the 1970's Calvin was one of the few remaining owners who, in a changing game, made his living solely from the game of baseball.

"People who call me cheap never had to make a payroll," he said in the early 1980's, his last years in Minnesota. "This is one club that always pays its bills."

Calvin brought the state of Minnesota its first major league sports team in 1961. Thirty-nine seasons later, the Minnesota Twins have given the state countless baseball memories by making three World Series appearances, winning in 1987 and 1991, as well as hosting two All Star Games in 1965 and 1985.

Calvin's baseball roots ran deep. Calvin Griffith, who was born in Montreal in 1911, was a nephew of Clark Griffith, the National League pitching star of the late 1800's, a founder of the American League, a manager and then-owner of the Washington Senators.

As the Senators' bat boy, Calvin Griffith watched Walter Johnson win the seventh game of the 1924 World Series against the New York Giants.

Calvin played college baseball and was active in minor league baseball as a player and as an executive. In 1941 he returned to Washington to run concession stands at Griffith Stadium.

When Clark Griffith died in October 1955, Calvin was named president of the Senators.

There are pictures of presidents throwing the opening day first ball in the Twins executive offices. There are some wonderful photos of presidents ranging from Truman to Eisenhower throwing the opening strike. It's interesting to me to think of Calvin being on the scene through those historic portraits.

The Twins won divisional titles in 1969 and 1970, but with the arrival of free agency in 1976 the Twins lost several top players. Baseball had made a fundamental change. Calvin Griffith was unwilling and, he would say, unable to meet mounting salary demands.

Calvin's big mishap occurred in September of 1978 when he told a civic group in the town of Waseca, Minnesota that he enjoyed Minnesota and that, "We came here because you've got good, hard-working white people here".

The Minneapolis *Star* called for Griffith to sell the team in a front-page editorial. Calvin has always claimed that his remarks were taken out of context.

Interestingly, Calvin had been told that there was in the audience that day a "Nick Coleman," whom Calvin thought to be a politician by that name. In fact, the Nick Coleman in attendance was a young journalist for the Minneapolis *Star*, who now writes for the *Pioneer Press*.

Hall of Famer Rod Carew went to the California Angels as a free agent in 1979 after stating that he did not want to keep playing on Calvin Griffith's "plantation."

In 1982 the Twins moved from Metropolitan Stadium in suburban Bloomington to the Metrodome in downtown Minneapolis. The payroll was only one third the major league average, and the team lost 102 games while winning only 60.

In 1984 a business task force drew up a marketing plan to win back the fans, and then asked for $125,000 from Griffith to implement it. He refused to spend the money. In August 1984 he and his sister Thelma sold their 52% interest in the Twins to Carl Pohlad for $32 million. The Twins

World Series title in 1987 can be viewed as a tribute to Calvin's personnel skills. Calvin was always known as having a sharp eye for baseball talent. He was responsible for Minnesota fans being able to watch the likes of Hall of Famers Harmon Killebrew and Rod Carew, as well as Bob Allison, Tony Oliva, Bert Blyleven, Jim Kaat, Gary Gaetti, Kent Hrbek, Frank Viola and Kirby Puckett, among others.

Calvin has a sister, Mildred Cronin, the widow of Joe Cronin, the Hall of Fame Senators shortstop and manager who became president of the American League. ◐

Salaries for 1998/1999

What the highest-paid Twins were scheduled to make in '98 and '99.

1998

DH	Paul Molitor	$4.25 million
C	Terry Steinbach (re-negotiated down)	$2.85 million
P	Rick Aguilera	$2.75 million
SS	Pat Mears	$2.50 million
OF	Marty Cordova	$2.00 million
OF	Otis Nixon	$2.00 million
P	Bob Tewksbury	$1.75 million
P	Brad Radke	$1.40 million

1999

P	Rick Aguilera	$3.25 million
OF	Marty Cordova	$3.00 million
P	Brad Radke	$2.25 million
OF	Matt Lawton	$1.7 million
P	Mike Trombley	$1.475 million
IF	Ron Coomer	$1.1 million

A TWINS PERSPECTIVE

Tom Kelly, Manager

Tom Kelly will be entering his fifteenth year as manager of the Minnesota Twins in the year 2000.

Kelly, whose nickname is T.K., was born in Minnesota in the small town of Graceville. He'll celebrate his fiftieth birthday midway throughout the 2000 season, and he has the longest tenure of any active manager or head coach in all of professional sports.

It has been an interesting ride for the Twins skipper, who replaced Ray Miller late in the 1986 season. Kelly was a long-time minor leaguer, spending twelve years as a player at the grassroots level of professional baseball. In 1975 he came up to the Minnesota Twins club long enough to officially hit close to his weight: he achieved a .181 average in 127 at-bats, including one home run, a shot off Vern Rhule in Detroit. Kelly was an excellent minor league player but was one of those guys who was destined to be just that: a reliable AAA per-

former with limited potential in the big leagues.

Many people in baseball believe Tom Kelly is one of the best managers in baseball. In Kelly's first full year as manager of the Twins, the team won the American League Western division with an 85-77 record, stunned the baseball world by defeating Detroit in the playoffs, and knocked out the St. Louis Cardinals in the World Series. Kelly wasn't much older than many of his players on that squad, and he helped the young ballclub to a monumental success.

"He was a good fit for that team," a member of the '87 team told me. "I think he had a lot of fun that first year, when we won it all. I don't think I've ever seen him as genuinely excited as he was after we beat St. Louis." The Twins would win the West again in 1991, with a record of 95-67. Again they made it to the World Series, where they defeated the Atlanta Braves four games to three. Once again Tom Kelly was named the

American League Manager of the Year.

In 1992 Kelly was also rated the American League's finest Skipper by *Baseball America*, despite the Twins failure to make the playoffs. 1992 would be the last time in the '90's the club would win more than eighty games in a season. Minnesota has played sub-.500 baseball every year since.

It's not surprising that Kelly was highly respected, considering he had won two World Series titles in his first five seasons as a full-time manager. What is interesting is that in 1998, after five consecutive finishes of fourth place or lower, Kelly was rated the American League's second-best manager by *Baseball America*. How can a man whose team does not succeed be considered one of the premier leaders in the game, you might ask?

The answer is, perhaps, both simple and complex. For the past five years the Twins have had no chance to contend for a World Series title. They haven't even had a *good chance* to finish above where they have. Tom Kelly arguably gets the most out of the limited talent pool that he is given. He succeeds in putting a team on the field that tries to win every time it's out there.

I heard Kelly say on one occasion, "You just make the moves that you think are the best. If you win that's fine, and if you lose that's fine."

That is an oversimplification of the tenacity with which Tom Kelly teams face every game.

When I heard Kelly make that comment, I thought to myself that it gives the impression that the man doesn't give a flip whether they win or loose. I don't believe that to be the case.

Kelly comes off as a gruff field general with little tolerance for the petty or the insignificant. Listening to Kelly on a weekend morning radio show, one can't help but think that he doesn't care what anybody else thinks. On occasion, the way he treats the callers, who are generally fans, is little short of rude.

I don't know if Kelly knows how he sounds or not. I know that it is not Tom Kelly at his best.

You need to watch Kelly on the field to appreciate him as a manager. The players almost universally respect him. Paul Molitor told me "You've got to play hard for T.K., or you're not going to be out there for very long. He wants his players to work hard and bring a good attitude and self-control to the way they play the game. Even when this team has been in some very down times, you rarely see any quit out of his players, and you'll never see a white flag from him."

It's fascinating to watch Kelly pitch batting practice and run the pre-game drills. He spent a lot of time in the different minor leagues learning and teaching the fundamentals of baseball. (Kelly had a number of first place finishes as a minor league manager.)

When Kelly throws batting practice, he leans into his pitches and works hard to put the ball where his players need to see it. He is a great left-handed batting practice pitcher who could get a lot of people out in my town ball league. He still has a very good arm. One time he walked by me, mumbling, "I'm over the hill." T.K. doesn't look very far over-the-hill to me.

One of the coaches, I think it was Scott Ullger, told me a story about Kelly stepping into the breach on little notice when he was managing in the minor leagues, and throwing a 1-0 shutout. I certainly believe it; T.K. was no pitcher, but I'll bet he could be crafty.

All the while he is throwing BP, he will talk to the hitters on where they are showing weakness, or make a crack to loosen up a tight ballplayer. The players listen, if they are smart, and move quickly and with purpose in and out of the cage.

One day, while Kelly was doing a radio briefing, Jacque Jones was screwing around with Matt Lawton. Kelly said something to the effect of "knock it off" and Jones slowed, but didn't stop, his banter with Lawton.

"I'm getting tired of it," Kelly suddenly barked. "I said knock it off!"

Jones, a fine young center fielder and no dummy, took the direct hint and went immediately back to work.

Some people speak of Tom Kelly's "dog house." I'm not certain that it doesn't exist. To get there, a player seems to have to do a couple of things: not play Tom Kelly baseball (defined as aggressive, selfless team play), or not live up to the talent that God has given him. Which would seem to apply to David Ortiz.

Ortiz hit .277 for Minnesota in 1998. Toward the end of that year, Kelly was making it clear that he was unhappy with Ortiz's attitude and physical condition. He was hitting the ball pretty well, but he came back from an injury out of shape, and it showed.

Ortiz was expected to play first base and give the Twins some home run power at first base during the 1999 season. When Ortiz had a lousy spring training and let it affect his attitude, Kelly made it clear that he was not going north with the ballclub.

Ortiz never made a meaningful contribution in 1999 to a team that desperately needed his power. Doug Mientkiewicz was a much better defensive first baseman than Ortiz, but he didn't deliver nearly the power that Ortiz might have. We'll never know whether the team would have done better with Ortiz. To say that David Ortiz stayed in the minor leagues because he couldn't get out of a "dog house" may not be true, but a lot of the "geniuses" in the media seemed to think that we could have used him.

Personally, I very much like the fact that Tom Kelly is old school. On the subject of his players having a sense of history, Kelly said "Most of these guys know that we won the World Series in 1991, but we've got guys on this team who don't know who Harmon Killebrew is."

"A lot of young players today have an attitude that says, 'OK, I've made it.' They have so much to learn about the game. Some of our guys do give me a little hope, though."

I think Kelly has a good heart, even though he doesn't wear it on his sleeve very often. One day I spotted him out at shortstop working with Twins coach Ron Gardenhire's son. "Gardy's" son Toby looked like a pretty good ballplayer, and Kelly was helping him with work around the second base bag. I watched them for quite a while. Kelly was really working with the kid. That's what he does best.

Kelly's view of the game was expressed clearly when he talked one day about the New York Yankees. "The Yankees are a club with a lot of guys who can get you out of trouble. Offensively and defensively, they have a number of players that can help you. I look around the league and I see a lot of teams that have guys who can get you into trouble and can't get you out."

I found an interesting statistic about Tom Kelly, the player, that I think relates to what is important to him as a coach. In 1972, Kelly lead the Pacific Coast League in fewest grounded-into double plays (4) and took part in the most double plays by an outfielder. Tom Kelly, besides being a player who obviously hustled and was solid fundamentally, was a player who tried to keep his team "out of trouble" by playing the right way. This is a practice he has carried into managing; if you want to play for Tom Kelly, you have to play the game the right way.

These days, the Twins have too many guys who can get you into trouble and not enough that can get you out. There's not a whole lot that Tom Kelly can do about that.

Denny Hocking

Denny Hocking, the Twins' 52nd-round draft choice in 1989, has displayed extraordinary versatility in the field, playing every defensive position except pitcher and catcher in 1999. Hocking could start a game at shortstop and move out to left field, only to end up at second base to close the game. He's probably not going to play pitcher or catcher, but hey, he was drafted as a catcher out of junior college.

"I figure it's just a matter of time," Hocking says with a laugh. "The catcher's gear, the 'tools of ignorance,' as they're known, have always fit me well."

When guys who have played the game of baseball look at Denny Hocking, they'd like to think they're seeing themselves wearing his number, 7. Guys who play the game like to view themselves as players who hustle and do the little things well. Hocking pays these qualities more than just lip service. After handling over 500 chances at seven different positions in 1999, he finally made his first error on August 15 against the Yankees in New York. He hit some balls hard in 1999 as well, with his batting average up 70 points from the low 200's of 1998. Hocking had a five-hit game and a grand slam among his offensive accomplishments in '99.

It's the way you play the game that keeps you a Tom Kelly favorite, right Denny?

"I think T.K. likes me because I understand the game at this level, in this dimension," says professor Hocking, sounding overly profound for a moment.

"What I mean is that I put myself in situations before they happen. I knew last year ('98) that I would often come in to play defense in the late innings. All it would take was for T.K. to look down the bench toward

Denny Hocking

me; if we're winning in the 8th inning, I'm going in. I would have myself prepared on the bench so that just a nod would be signal enough, no 'Hey Denny' needed," said Hocking.

"This year my role has expanded because there are so many young guys to educate about our system. They need to learn how to adjust, and I've got no problem with that. It's part of my job."

You seldom see Hocking walking around without a smile. He's having fun doing something he loves, longshot that he was, and he knows well the inherent joy of the game. I didn't hear a word of complaint when he was bumped from the starting short-stop position by prize rookie Cristian Guzman (I was listening), and for that I admire him.

Okay, so were you disappointed not to start?

"Of course I was," says Hocking "Who wouldn't be? Everybody who plays the game, even the last guy on the bench, wants to start. Maybe I'll get another shot next year, or maybe it will be somewhere else. I don't know.

"But I'll tell you what. I think I make this team better by being a part of it, and I'm going to continue to battle every day, to do the extra things every day. Don't be a cancer, be a good person, a team player; that's what you've got to do."

The everyman ballplayer inside of me is jumping up and down, shouting, "That's right, that's right!"

Hocking continues, "Man, I'm a karma person. I think good things happen to good people. Things are going to work out the way they're supposed to."

I was going to ask him about the stadium question, but thought better of it. Bad karma. I asked him instead about a bench-clearing mini-brawl in which the Twins had recently partici-pated. Hocking was already laughing.

"You watch baseball fights, they're almost always ridiculous. And you know what? It's always the guys in the bullpens that want to fight! They're always the first guys out there, ready to battle.

"The position players, they don't want to get hurt. This isn't like football or hockey where everybody's got hel-mets or gloves. If a real punch gets landed in a baseball fight, it hurts! Who wants a serious injury from one of these things? But the bullpen, they're always ready to lead the charge. It must get awfully boring out there in the bullpen!"

Matt Lawton

Matt Lawton is a great guy. At least he's always shown me a lot of cour-tesy, and he gave me some insights into what it was like to be a teammate of Paul Molitor as Paul approached retirement.

That's why when Lawton became involved in a spitting brouhaha in Toronto on August 31 1999, I was sur-prised, to say the least. Aiming a quid is not Lawton's style.

It seems that in the seventh inning, while Lawton was playing right field, he ran into the corner, chasing a long foul ball. A fan there was heckling Lawton and even flashed an obscene gesture toward Matty. The obnoxious fan, who was white, then directed a racial epithet towards Lawton, who is black. At that point, Lawton spat at the young man.

Matt Lawton

"I knew I was in trouble the minute I did it", Lawton said. "There was no good that was going to come of this; I had made a mistake."

The young fan claimed he was hit in the face by the Lawton spitball and was heard to threaten a lawsuit. Fortunately for Lawton, the scene was caught on videotape and the fan was seen gesturing toward Lawton, and Lawton was seen spitting toward, but not on the fan. "Man, I'm glad the tape showed that I didn't do what he said I did," Lawton said.

After the game of September 2, the last game in the Toronto series, Lawton apologized to the fan and in turn, the young fan apologized for his behavior. Lawton gave the fan an autographed baseball, and hoped to put the entire incident in the rear view mirror. "I can't say he was that bad a kid," Lawton said. "He actually seemed like a pretty decent guy."

The Toronto Police Department had actually begun an investigation of the incident but decided to back off when an agreement was reached by the two parties. Sometimes weird things happen to good people, and this must have been one of those times. I'm glad for Matty that this one blew over. These little nickel-and-dime things can escalate when you're in the public eye.

Brent Gates

Slumps are the bane of an offensive player's existence. When a ballplayer isn't hitting, life couldn't get much worse. In the beginning of the 1998 season, Twins infielder and former Gopher All-American Brent Gates had a prolonged slump that was gnawing at him.

When Gates took an 0-for-19 at the plate late in April of the '98 season, his batting average had dropped to .051. Gates had never hit .051 in his life.

"When you go on for days and days and you're not hitting, it starts to eat away at you. I mean, physically. I haven't been feeling that well lately," the 6' 1" 190-pound Gates said, with a hint of a smile.

Slumps become both mental and physical: physical because the hitter is not, for whatever reason, dropping the ball in there for hits, and mental because baseball is a thinking man's game and the oh-fors start to work their way inside your head.

Gates went from April 14th to May 2nd without a base hit, and although his role has been primarily as a utility infielder, Gates has always been regarded as a solid offensive player. For awhile there, Gates had the "hex."

A slump is a very personal experience for a ballplayer. Some guys will take extra batting practice to see if that will help them sting the ball a lit-tle bit harder. Or maybe the extra BP will help a ground ball grow some "eyes."

Other guys would rather avoid batting practice when they're slumping. Just get away from the whole thing for a little while and see if maybe that will open things up. A ballplayer will try anything that can bring a change in the situation to break the dreaded slump.

When Gates finally got a couple of hits in a victory over the Baltimore Orioles, he raised his average to .093. He wasn't the only guy on the team who was struggling early in the season. When Denny Hocking and Gates were in the lineup against the Yankees early in the '98 season, Hocking was hitting .094 and Gates was at .093.

"Not being able to play every day makes it tougher," Gates said. "Sometimes I go to the plate after sitting on the bench for a couple days and it can be tough. But I've never struggled like I have recently. I feel like I'm going to get on a good roll, but it takes time."

Gates would get it going during the 1998 season; he hit over .300 from June to the end of the season, finishing with a respectable batting average of .249.

Ron Coomer

Ron Coomer was waiting his turn to get into the batting cage before the night's game against Kansas City while I was talking with Scott Miller, the St. Paul *Pioneer Press* baseball writer.

We were conversing about the relative lack of recognition that was accompanying the probable departure of Paul Molitor from the game of baseball. There would be no going away party for Molitor, because he wouldn't want one. But there wasn't much being said anywhere about the future first ballot Hall of Famer's imminent transition into post-player status.

Coomer overheard us talking and asked the question, "Where's the recognition for Paul Molitor that is extended to Wayne Gretzky and John Elway? Paul's an elite, Hall of Fame type player, and it seems that he never receives the recognition that he should."

I mentioned to Coomer that Paul was a low profile type of guy, who played in small markets most of his career. Heck, when he was MVP of the World Series with Toronto, he wasn't even in the United States. "Neither was Gretzky," Coomer said. "Yeah, but that's hockey, the national game up there. Gretzky's the greatest hockey player to ever play the game," I replied.

"There should be more recognition," Coomer repeated.

It was nice to hear the Twins' future All Star speak as a fan of his friend. I told Coomer that when he has a going away party in ten years or so, I'll be there. "Doggone right you're going to be there," he says to Miller and myself, "If I'm still playing in ten years, there's going to be a heck of a party at my retirement. You're all going to be invited."

You have to love Coomer. He plays the game with passion and it comes through every time you see him, even when things are going as tough as they have been for the Twins (and for Coomer in the second half of 1999). He keeps a smile on his face and a good word on his lips. Ron Coomer plays the game with passion. It's fun to be around Ron Coomer in a baseball environment.

Terry Steinbach

I've always liked what catcher Terry Steinbach has to say about pitchers, and he has worked with dozens of hurlers in his time. Terry knows that pitching is never an easy task, even for the great ones, and for the less-than-great there is a tremendous amount of mental challenge. Steinbach provides a level of comfort for young pitchers given his experience as an All-Star-caliber backstop.

A three-time American League All Star, Steinbach was the MVP of the 1988 All Star Game while playing for the Oakland Athletics. He had the unique experience of homering in his first All Star at-bat, and drove in the game-winning run with a base hit later in the game.

Given the youthful nature of the Twins pitching staff, Steinbach faced a daily challenge during the '98 and '99 seasons. Terry spoke of that challenge early during the 1999 campaign.

"It's been tough being a starter around here for a number of different reasons. If an offensive player has a bad at-bat, it's just a matter of innings, maybe a day, and he can get back in the batter's box and correct it. He might homer the next time up," Steinbach said.

"But a starter pitches only once every four or five days, so it tends to get magnified if he doesn't perform well, or if he doesn't perform as well as he's capable of performing. It would be nice to simply say 'Hey, he didn't have a quality start', and just leave it at that."

But that is hard to do given the failings, inconsistencies and youthful mistakes that have plagued the Minnesota Twins pitching staff.

"We do have some days around here where the guys are not really 'on,' probably too many of them," Terry said near the midpoint of the 1999 season. "Sometimes the velocity is down, or there just isn't the movement you expect. Sometimes the defense is not what it should be. We've got some young guys, and their inexperience is going to show up on occasion."

Not only have the Twins' young starters been erratic, but Brad Radke, the ace of the Twins staff and an All Star in 1998, got off to a relatively poor start in 1999. Radke spent all of the '99 season battling to get to .500, while LaTroy Hawkins had what for him is a fair year at 5 games below 500 and a near 7.00 ERA. Hawkins is capable of much more, and the Twins organization wants LaTroy to fulfill his potential.

Eric Milton looked simply brilliant at times, like when he threw a no-hitter against the Anaheim Angels; he's certainly the best 7-11 pitcher in baseball.

Milton did earn a somewhat respectable 4.60 ERA over the course of 1999. Joe Mays looked alternately awesome and awkward, and he has an exceptional major league curve ball. Jason Ryan looked fairly tough some of the time, but will need the big league maturity that only comes with experience.

"They're young guys," Steinbach says a couple more times with a grin. "They're all going to get better."

Steinbach remembers when Twins pitchers held their own against the best offenses in baseball.

"From 1987 to 1992 it seemed like it was either Oakland or Minnesota coming out of the American League West year after year," Steinbach said. "When I was playing for Oakland during its World Series year of 1989, we played a lot of key games in the Metrodome. This has

◀ Eric Milton readies to throw the final pitch of his Sept. 11, 1999 no-hitter vs. the Anaheim Angels.

He fires… ▶

◀ …and he's got it! Jeff Davanon of the Angels strikes out.

Teammates rush ▶ to congratulate the young Twins lefty.

◄ Paul Molitor's
final at bat.
A line drive base hit
off Doug Jones of
Cleveland.
Hit number 3319.

Trademark ►
head-first
dive into
3rd base.

◄ Run scored
number 1782,
the final
time across
home plate,
good for
15th on the
all-time list.

◀ ESPN's Chris
Berman with
New York Yankees
Manager Joe Torre
at Detroit's Tiger
Stadium.

Astute baseball ▶
writer Peter
Gammons talks
shop with
Tom Kelly at
Fenway Park.

◀ Berman and Gammons
at the 1999 All Star
Game at Fenway Park.

Future Hall of Fame pitcher Dennis Eckersley with
young Detroit Tiger All Star catcher Brad Ausmus.

The author in his element at Fenway Park, Boston.

Another injury during a physically tough final year for Paul Molitor. This one is a sprained ankle on August 15, 1998 vs. Boston.

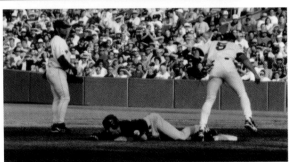

"A-Rod": Alex Rodriguez of the Seattle Mariners.

He perfect-gamed the Twins as a Yankee on May 17, 1998.
David Wells visits the Metrodome with Toronto in 1999.

Photographer Sandy Thompson captures Molitor the little boy
in the future Hall-of-Famer during the 1998 season.

How big
is your
bubble?

The Molitor
"Ball Trick"

A moment of reflection during his final game in Minnesota, September 27, 1998.

A great combination of talents at shortstop: Boston's Nomar Garciaparra.

On the way to 70: Mark McGwire launches number 36 at the Metrodome on June 27, 1998.

One of the all-time greats prepares to take his final at bat. September 27, 1998.

◀ The Twins' young pitching staff
provides hope for the future.
Will Jason Ryan succeed in the
big leagues?

▼ Ron Coomer in his hometown
of Chicago, at Wrigley Field.
The building in the background
provided roof-top viewing
for the author.

T.K. at work.

A joyful day: Paul Molitor's number 4 jersey is retired
by the Milwaukee Brewers. June 11, 1999.

Bob Uecker and Bud Selig lead the cheers.

Molitor and family enjoy a laugh with Hall-of-Fame Brewer Robin Yount.

Molitor and Yount add some life to the Brewer dugout on a warm, drizzly June evening.

▲ Tony Oliva volunteered his
time to help make Richfield,
Minnesota's "Quicksteps Fest"
a success. He ripped a few
line drives, as well.

◄ One of the state of
Minnesota's top senior
baseball players, Jim Wheeler.

The Minnesota Saints at Terry Park in Ft. Myers, Florida, during the Roy Hobbs World Series 30 and over. The Author is 3rd from the left, top row.

Photo: Greg Wegner

The author loosens up before a Roy Hobbs World Series game.

"You can't beat fun at the old ballpark." City of Palms Park, spring training home of the Boston Red Sox, is one of five Lee County, Florida sites of the Rob Hobbs World Series.

A Norman Rockwell-esque Twins dugout scene, late season 1998.

The author with Paul Molitor and University of Minnesota baseball coach John Anderson
at the annual pro-alumni game at the Metrodome, February 7, 1999.

Terry Steinbach with Wade Boggs

always been regarded as a very tough place for visiting teams to play. There have been some great Twins clubs that have played in this park."

"I remember some big, turning point type games against the Twins over the years. I remember a 1991 game against the Twins out in Oakland in which we jumped out fast, took a big lead early, must have been 6 or 7 runs up. Those guys [the Twins] just kept picking away at our lead, narrowing it down, until Brian Harper hit one out to win it."

Steinbach looked out at the big baggie in right field. "That was a 'turning point' for the Twins in '91, perhaps."

I can tell Terry's not too comfortable with the expression "turning point"; he's probably seen too many of them, a lot of imaginary momentum swings. But he continues:

"They (the Twins) ended up taking the series from us, and it was a big series. That team had a lot of talent. And I remember right here in 1992—I think it was in August—Eric Fox hit a homer off Rick Aguilera. That was at the opposite end of the spectrum;

another 'turning point.' I do know the Twins' season took a turn for the worse after that series."

Well, that *was* a turning point. Kind of like too many Mexicans at the Alamo. The 1992 season went south after the sweep at the Metrodome at the hands of the Athletics. Like the Titanic, the rest of the decade sank after the sweep by Oakland in that summer of '92.

In mid-November 1999, the Minnesota Twins received the news that they were expecting: Terry Steinbach would retire.

The press conference to announce the retirement was scheduled for November 16th in the Twins media dining room. Steinbach probably won't have his picture on the walls like Puckett, Hrbek and Carew. (I noticed Harmon Killebrew was missing from the dining room.) But Terry Steinbach was a valuable addition to the Twins during his time in Minnesota.

Twins General Manager Terry Ryan spoke first. "The Minnesota Twins recognize that this is a joyous day for the Steinbach family, which gains a full-time father. But it is a sad day for the Twins organization, as we lose a full-time catcher. I guess you could say his wife Mary won out, and she'll bring Terry home to Corcoran, Minnesota."

Terry Ryan proceeded to go over the highlights of Terry Steinbach's long and distinguished Minnesota baseball career. Steinbach was drafted by the Cleveland Indians after graduation from New Ulm High School in 1980. However, rather than play professional baseball right away, he headed for the University of Minnesota, where he played first base for John Anderson's squad until he was drafted by Oakland as an eligible junior in 1983. Steinbach was signed by former big league pitcher and Minnesotan Jim Perry.

After stops in places like Medford, Oregon, Madison, Wisconsin and Huntsville, Alabama, Terry made it to Oakland as a catcher in 1986. During the course of his major league career Steinbach caught hall-of-famers, played in the World Series and was an All Star at the major league level in the game he loved.

Steinbach looked bewildered by the large turnout of Twin Cities media people who responded to his announcement. "I didn't expect this," he said, "but it's nice of you all to be here." Most of us, and I suspect there were a couple dozen of us, attended out of affection for a baseball player who deserved respect. I know that's why I was there.

Continuing, Steinbach said, "I feel that now is the right time to get out of the game. I've spent 17 years in organized baseball, and I've been thinking about this decision all year. I've missed a lot of Memorial Days, Labor Days, Fourth of Julys. I think it's time to catch up with my family."

Steinbach mentioned some of the former players he had talked with about his decision. "I talked to Mollie, Bob Tewksbury and Jamie Quirk about my decision. It was good to council with those guys.

"I give thanks to Mr. Pohlad and to Terry Ryan for bringing me home—I always dreamed of finishing my career in Minnesota. I know my kids are ready for me to come home; a lot of times they may have wanted me to play with them but they understood that I needed rest and they would respect that. Some things have opened my eyes to my desire to spend time with them."

Steinbach is aware of the blessings his career has given him. "I won a World Series. I wish every player

WHERE HAS ALL THE POWER GONE?

No Minnesota Twin has hit thirty home runs during the regular season since three Twins hit that many in 1987. This is the most looming, glaring offensive weakness of the ballclub. Terry Ryan continues to say that finding power at the plate is a priority.

If that's true, it's hard to understand why David Ortiz was kept in AAA Salt Lake City for nearly all of the 1999 season. It appeared that Ortiz had fallen out of favor with Tom Kelly at the end of the 1998 season, and that there was some carryover into 1999. If Ortiz is in the dog house, it seems that he should be given a chance to escape. Ortiz has home run power and plays a position (first base) where the Twins have little offensive sting, except when Ron Coomer brings his 15-20 home runs over from third base. With Corey Koskie emerging at third base, it is likely that Coomer will see significant action at first. Coomer is a Tom Kelly ballplayer, but there should still be room in the Twins lineup for a David Ortiz, perhaps as a designated hitter.

We know that the Twins can manufacture runs; they're pretty darn good at scraping for victories. But you rarely find the Twins winning games with big home runs, although it does happen once in awhile. Not only do the fans like to see an occasional power display, but as Earl Weaver said, "Base hits don't kill ya. Three-run homers, those kill ya."

could have a chance to do that. You can't know what it's like until you've been there. At the All Star game it's just incredible to be around all the superstars—I had to remind myself that I was one of them! Eric Milton's no-hitter against Anaheim has to be the highlight of the last three years. The nervousness and the excitement were very real. That's what the game was about for me.

"I'm walking away from the game, I'm not running. I've enjoyed my time. I hope I'm remembered for two things: for being a consistent ballplayer and for giving 100% all of the time."

Somewhere during his statement Steinbach had made reference to possibly playing for the Hamel Hawk town team, where some former Gopher teammates play the game.

Though said in jest (I think), Hamel could no doubt use Terry's considerable skills. Hamel failed to make the state town team baseball tournament in 1999, an exception for that quality ballclub.

As the meeting ended, Twins owner Carl Pohlad stated that there would always be a place in the Minnesota Twins organization for Terry Steinbach. "He's a thoroughbred," said Pohlad. "We were fortunate to have him here for a while."

With that, it was over. Steinbach's major league career was history. Terry Steinbach turned to Terry Ryan as they arose and said, "I'm really comfortable with this, Terry. I think I'm doing the right thing."

And part of me wondered if he'd really play for Hamel.

8

PAUL MOLITOR: MORE THAN JUST A PLAYER

Why a special focus on Paul Molitor?
Because he may be the one Minnesota-born player who, more than any other, represents what is right about the game of baseball. Since his days as a high-schooler in St. Paul through college ball at the University of Minnesota and beyond, his light has shone bright upon his home state.

The People's Ballplayer

When you talk to Paul Molitor you quickly become aware that he is much more than just an outstanding professional baseball man. At the end of his career he comes across not only as a player who still has true fire in his game, but also as a human being with a lot of gratitude. He is a good man.

By the end of the 1998 baseball season, Molitor had written himself all over the record books with incredible numbers—huge, gargantuan numbers. Undeniable statistical greatness was his. Watching Paul in the cage at that time, he still appeared to be the most solid hitter on the ballclub. Crunch. Crunch. Crunch. Molitor still pounded the line drives with regularity and intensity. It was perfectly clear that he was still doing what he wanted to do.

But crushing the ball wasn't all he could do. Early in that '98 season Molitor's versatility was underscored when he dropped a perfect bunt—doing one of the little things that defined the Molitor style—to help the Twins beat the Yankees.

Ryan Lefebvre and I watched Paul from behind the cage one afternoon during the '98 season. "I'm still amazed by how quick that bat is. When you're behind the cage you flinch because you think the ball is going to get past him and hit the back of the netting you're looking through. Then he pulls the trigger and the ball is headed the other direction. What

"The numbers don't lie": Molitor behind Wagner at number eight

amazes me the most, though, is how he runs the bases. He runs like he's 25. The bat speed has always impressed me, but it's the way Paul runs, his quickness, that impresses me the most. The way he can still play physically, with both speed and base-running savvy, I think he could play like that until he's fifty years old."

Molitor played extremely well through May and into June of his final year. He had several doubles and scored a bunch of runs, slashing and sliding like the Molitor that the Twin Cities has known and loved for so many years. Then came an injury to his shoulder in early June, the first of a number of injuries that hindered his final season. The shoulder injury turned out to be a small labrum tear

of the left shoulder. Later in June, a broken rib put him on the disabled list. A sprained ankle (acquired during a play involving Nomar Garciaparra of the Red Sox) sidelined him for a week in August. Paul had taken a pounding his entire career, but the beating he was taking as he approached his 42nd birthday gave many of us cause to wonder whether he would care to do this again in '99.

Molitor kept a sense of humor about it all: "If I hadn't been injured for 500 games, my career might have ended three years ago."

I asked Paul to reflect on the home run race as he was closing out his career as a player. "I think that all the 50-home-run seasons of late pointed to the possibility of home run records being broken. A lot of the early homers by McGwire certainly help, and Sosa and McGwire are definitely pushing each other. They're bigger and stronger and I think the parks are a little bit more hitter-friendly. And I think the home run record is more approachable than some other records."

Paul the prognosticator said in June that he thought Roger Maris' home run record was in serious jeopardy in 1998, and of course he was proven correct.

Molitor spoke about his 39-game hitting streak in 1987, which ended with Molitor on deck in the bottom of the tenth inning as the winning run was scored. "It's funny," he said, "the way the home crowd went silent. Rick Manning singled home the winning run while I was waiting my turn to hit, and it was kind of strange. We won a terrific game in September, yet there was even a little booing from the Milwaukee fans who were disappointed that I didn't get to the plate."

I vividly remember learning that Molitor's 39-game streak had been put to rest as I sat in a little restaurant on the North side of Chicago, drinking coffee and reading a story about it in the sports pages of the *Chicago Tribune*.

"I was never really thinking of DiMaggio's record hitting streak of 56 games." Molitor told me "I was think-ing more of Pete Rose's 44-game streak. I was looking at second place, perhaps. I only needed five more to catch Rose, and I've only had a half-dozen hitting streaks of 17 games or more in my career. That puts DiMaggio's record in perspective. I've had a lot of five game hitting streaks. Maybe I could have caught Rose, but we'll never know."

As noted earlier, Molitor is more than just a great player; he's also a good citizen. Players on opposing teams are aware of that fact.

For example, the Major League Baseball Players Trust for Children made a $25,000 donation to Camp Heartland in honor of Molitor in August 1999. This is truly an award of his peers, as he was the winner of the 1998 Players Choice Award for Man of the Year. In accepting the donation. Neil Willanson, Camp Heartland's president and founder said, "Paul Molitor not only left an incredible legacy on the baseball field, he has left a remarkable legacy in the lives of thousands of children affected by AIDS."

Paul's creation, Camp Heartland, is now a national non-profit organization that enhances the lives of children infected with and affected by HIV/AIDS through year-round support, advocacy, recreational programs and community AIDS awareness efforts.

In addition, Molitor helps sponsor a "Fields For Kids" program (see the press release from the Pohlad Family Foundation on page 98), which makes funds available to help create new ball fields and upgrade old ones. It's more than just sprucing up old ball fields, although it is that, too. It's creating hope and spirit in neighborhoods that frequently need all the TLC that they can get.

Molitor is concerned about the health of the game of baseball among young people. "It's not where it was when I was younger. I think baseball has periods of highs and lows and there have been more lows the last few years, especially due to the work stoppages, the strikes. I know kids have a lot of choices, and the growth of soccer is a phenomenon, but I want to give the kids who want to play baseball good places to play. We're in the age of the computer and the development of the Internet and baseball is just another choice for a lot of kids, and not necessarily a first choice. But I think the past couple of years were years of inspiration for young people, with the home run races and other spectacular individual and team performances."

I asked Paul during the '98 season why he decided to come back to a team with expectations as low as any in the American League.

Molitor said, "I decided to come back because I still take pleasure in the competition. I'm at a skill level where I feel I can still contribute."

Nevertheless, he added, "This season has been difficult mentally, just trying to withstand the grind. With all the physical rehabilitation it's definitely getting tougher."

Then I watched him stand in the batting cage and rip line drive after line drive.

One of my conversations with Molitor came during the final home series of 1998; the Twins were playing Cleveland.

I had an increasingly strong feeling that Paul was going to retire, and the feeling was not diminished by the downcast atmosphere at the Metrodome and the almost palpable sense that the Twins couldn't wait to play the games, clean out their lockers and leave town.

With so few media people covering the team, it was easy to talk one-on-one with some of the players, including Molitor. "Hey Paul you're hitting too well to retire," I said.

"Yeah, in batting practice I'm hitting them pretty good," he replied.

The somber emptiness of the dome was magnified by the sight of Molitor in center field, alone, during the pre-game warm-ups.

He was reflecting, I suppose, on a lot of things and perhaps stirring a memory or two.

His teammates were leaving him alone to the point of avoiding him.

I caught Matt Lawton behind the cage and Matt said, "Paul told me it's just starting to hit him now. I think it's a shame if Paul doesn't keep playing, because he's got more baseball in him, and he's just now getting healthy. He's thinking out there."

As if by magic, during my conversation with Lawton the Metrodome speaker system filled the stadium with the poignancy of the Rolling Stones "Ain't No Use in Crying." It was no doubt a coincidence, but it was an intense moment nonetheless. I knew the game would miss him.

On September 27th 1998, Molitor was taking what would turn out to be his final batting practice as a major leaguer before the game with Cleveland.

The usual suspects were around the cage: the beat writers and others who surmised that they may be witnessing the final hitting exhibition of a hall-of-famer while he still wore a major league uniform.

Amazingly, Molitor thanked me for my efforts during the course of the year. I wondered why—I had done nothing out of the ordinary for him.

But I've come to understand that is just the way he is, a true gentleman, a man of courtesy and class, full-time.

"Even when you're going good, you make a lot of outs."
–Paul Molitor (shown here with Dan Wilson)

POHLAD FAMILY CHARITIES
MINNESOTA TWINS COMMUNITY FUND
CARL & ELOISE POHLAD FAMILY FOUNDATION
TUESDAY, APRIL 6, 1999

Minneapolis, Minnesota—The Minnesota Twins Community Fund, in partnership with Northwest Airlines and the Pepsi Cola Company, today announced plans to award $250,000 in grants in 1999 and 2000 designed to improve baseball and/or softball facilities for children throughout the upper midwest.

Created and supported by the Twins Community Fund, Northwest Airlines and Pepsi, and named in honor of St. Paul native and future Hall of Famer Paul Molitor, the Molitor Fields for Kids program will make grants ranging from $500-$5,000 to small nonprofit organizations and local governments that operate youth baseball and/or softball programs.

"The Twins Community Fund is committed to providing expanded baseball and softball programs for children living throughout the region," said Twins Community Fund president Bob Pohlad.

"Moreover, we're thrilled to have this opportunity to ensure Paul Molitor's legacy with children throughout the region via the introduction of the Molitor Fields program."

Molitor Field grants of up to $5,000 will be available for major renovation projects including new grass, infields, fencing and dugouts. Grants of up to $2,000 will be available for other items needed to enhance local baseball and/or softball facilities such as bleachers and scoreboards.

Established in 1991, the Twins Community Fund is a Pohlad Family Charity focused on providing expanded recreation and education opportunities for youngsters. Over the past eight years the Community Fund has contributed nearly $1 Million to Upper Midwest organizations. The healthy development of children is the primary interest of the Fund, with a large percentage of the funds used to support programs created and/or operated by the Minnesota Twins, Major League Baseball and local community partners.

Paul Molitor and Ricky Henderson

Before Molitor left the field to go up to the locker room for final preparations for the evening's game, I asked him how he felt the team had been handled during a difficult 1998 season.

Paul did not hesitate for an instant before stating that the team still felt togetherness. "Being a bottom-division team hasn't kept this club from being a close team. Tom Kelly has been outstanding on a daily basis; he works at staying positive even during blowouts—and there have been a few of those this year."

There is no question in my mind that Molitor is destined to manage at the big league level, and I think of all the areas in which he could guide his players: from baserunning strategies and techniques, to developing an approach to pitchers, to helping players express frustration without going nuts. He will be a fine coach.

Molitor, throughout his career, has been able to persevere.

In baseball, as in life, that's the greatest gift of all.

Tom Mee on Molitor

Tom Mee, the Twins' public address announcer, has known Paul Molitor for a long time. His son, also named Tom, was a teammate of Molitor at the University of Minnesota and a very good baseball player in his own right. Tom Mee Sr. has known Paul Molitor's mom for many years as well. During a conversation in 1998, Mee talked a little bit about Molitor.

Molitor, number 3255. This hit off of Allen Watson tied
Mollie for tenth on the all time list with Eddie Murray.

"Paul has been a great player for the game of baseball for a long time. The guy is a cinch hall-of-famer, and a lot of his contributions were related to the fact that he was such a great team player. It's been wonderful having a chance to watch him play here, even in the twilight of his career.

"He still has that real good quickness. He's been a natural leader on any team he's played with, from Little League to the University of Minnesota to the major leagues. That's a distinguishing feature about Molitor, a quality you don't create in a ballplayer. It's gotta be there inside the individual.

"Every team needs leadership that isn't forced. Paul Molitor is a catalyst, and Tom Kelly loved having him in the lineup every day. With some of his injuries staying is that lineup has been tough. But he's still the ignitor," which is a good nickname for Paul.

"We needed some guys with a little power to drive Paul in more often."

Tom Mee is in the group that believes the Twins absolutely have to find some power hitting to improve. He was hoping the Twins would add some power to the lineup during the 1998-99 off-season, and he was still hoping the Twins would add some strength during the 1999-2000 off-season.

"The way we have to manufacture runs, we might need three base hits to score one run," Mee said. "There was a situation recently where we had three singles and a walk in the first inning [of a game in 1999] and we only scored one run. We need to have something different happen, like getting four men on base and having all of them eventually score. The Twins don't score runs in clusters anymore, and it's very hard to score runs in bunches when you don't have the power hitting."

When Molitor Talks, People Listen

During the middle of the '99 senior baseball season I found myself in a bit of a hitting slump. When a slump occurs, I try to fight my way out of it as any ballplayer does, by taking some extra hitting and also by doing some reading on the subject of hitting. Purely by accident, in a National Geographic of all places, I came across a comment by Rod Cross, an Australian physicist, who claims that a baseball bat's "sweet spot" is really a "sweet zone" 5.9" to 7" from the end of the bat.

At that point of the summer I sure as heck wasn't hitting it on that location very often, which gave even more power to a statement Paul Molitor made at the Metrodome's batting cage: "Even when you're going good, you make a lot of outs." Paul tends to say a lot of things that make you think; when Molitor talks about hitting, it's a little bit like Merrill Lynch talking about investments. I can't get that statement out of my mind, and it gives me some comfort to think that no matter what, in baseball you're going to make a lot of outs.

Of course, that didn't help me with the hitting problem I was having right then. At that point in the town ball season I tended to have a couple of good games, followed by a couple of no-hit games. When Molitor made his statement about "even when you're going good," I mentioned to him about the "sweet spot" scientific revelation. I couldn't tell if he heard me as he was readying himself to enter the cage, and when he did it was POW, POW, POW.

As usual.

Yeah, he may make a lot of outs, but some ballplayers make fewer outs than others.

Molitor Honored in Milwaukee

Photographer Sandy Thompson attended Paul Molitor's "Jersey Retirement Day" in Milwaukee Wisconsin on June 11, 1999. The Brewers were host to the Twins on a drizzly Friday evening. Here is Sandy's description of that event.

"It was a very hot day, and we knew the rainstorms were coming. We had gone onto the field prior to the cere-mony when the rain and lightening came. The wind blew the chairs off of the stage that was set up on the pitcher's mound.

"During the rain we waited in a stadium tunnel. Players passed us by, smiling and looking out expectantly. They must have known we were wait-ing for the Molitor ceremony. When the rain finally stopped, we proceeded back to the field and it seemed like things got going quite quickly.

"I saw a commotion over by the Brewers dugout, and Paul started to stride across the field. He looked over-whelmed as he saw his friends, a large group including former players, Bob Uecker and Bud Selig among others, gathered at the stage.

"Paul was obviously humbled, and he appeared teary-eyed. But he never stopped smiling or lost the look of extreme joy that shone from his features.

"He immediately shook hands with Robin Yount and then Jim Gantner. He was surrounded by pho-tographers and TV cameras. He made his way on to the stage and sat down.

"Paul was very attentive to his family members, especially for the first 10 to 15 minutes of the cere-mony. He glanced over at family, sub-tly waving and smiling while occasionally pointing and acknowl-edging his guests.

"Bob Uecker took the stage first and made humorous, but respectful, references to Paul's style of play. There were pictures on the scoreboard throughout the ceremony showing Paul's history as a Brewer, a few mar-riage photos, and pictures of Paul as a young boy. The crowd frequently applauded and cheered.

"At one point, Paul seemed con-cerned that Uecker's seat was going to be too wet for him to sit back down on, since it had started to sprin-kle again. Paul was trying to ask for a towel, but no one responded. The guest of honor was being ignored.

"Paul laughed the most when a young child from his charity, Camp Heartland, spoke. He seemed tickled by what the child said, and was gen-uinely pleased by the child's courage.

"Robin Yount spoke admiringly of Paul's integrity and passion for the game, his work ethic and his grace as a teammate.

"Interestingly, Sal Bando sat very still and, while attentive, did not speak at the ceremony.

"Jim Gantner spoke at length about his relationship with Paul. His sincerity was very flattering towards his former teammate, and Paul looked up at him with a quiet respect. He seemed very proud that Gantner spoke of him with such high regard. (Note: Gantner, Yount and Molitor played together for over 15 years.)

"Paul grew teary-eyed when he spoke to the crowd. He actually held his emotions in check quite well, until he said he'd go in the Hall of Fame as a Milwaukee Brewer. That seemed to get him.

"The crowd cheered for a long time in recognition of his 'Hall' statement. Paul wiped a tear and applauded when his name was added to the other Brewers whose numbers have been retired: Rollie Fingers, Hank Aaron and Robin Yount. Paul is just the fourth Brewer, or Brave, to have his number retired.

"Paul hugged everyone on stage. Terry Steinbach and Ron Coomer gave a gift to Paul from the Twins. Their exchange was a joyous one.

"After the ceremony the stage cleared and the tarps remained on the field. Although the rain was picking up, Paul stood on the field while a number of people approached him to shake his hand.

"He went to the Brewers dugout and stood with Ron Jackson and Robin Yount, laughing and tossing a ball in the air with one hand. He was waiting for the O.K. to go onto the field to throw out the opening pitch. His brother threw out the first pitch and Paul the second, to Robin Yount, after which

The Molitor "Salute" at Fenway: Lawton, Meares, Molitor, and Walker

Paul Molitor prior to his last game at home.
September 27, 1998

they hugged and shared a quiet moment.

"It was over. I took a few pictures of the crowd. A lot of people were hoping to get an autograph from Paul, but the Brewers ushered him away, basically telling Paul that it was his day, and not a day for signing.

"There were a number of nice signs printed in honor of his day. A lot of people were wearing the number 4, as well.

"It began raining immediately after the ceremony, and the game with the Twins was delayed. It really poured down rain the better part of the night. When we left at 1:30 a.m., they were still playing, trying to get the game in.

"By the end of the game, only the die-hards remained. It wasn't a perfect night weather-wise, but it was appropriate, given the outdoor baseball environment. Despite the rain, it was a beautiful evening.

"Looking back, what stands out over time is the grace with which Paul conducted himself during the evening. He was very reflective and contemplative, yet shared his joy with all of those around him. He even had time to give me a smile.

"Typical of the Molitor style was his concern regarding Uecker's chair. When no one heard his plea for a towel, he just let it go. There are people who might have made a big deal out of it, but not Paul. That's not his style.

"I should note that the Twins dugout was very quiet and respectful during the ceremony. They were watching a good friend being honored, and were sharing in the moment.

"I believe it was a capacity crowd at County Stadium, though I am not certain. It looked full. No one who was there will soon forget the night.

"Paul spent no time staying around to talk about his achievements. When it was over, he was on his way to tend to family and friends.

"Milwaukee loves Paul Molitor, and that was the message of the evening."

Molitor to Stay with Twins— As Coach

The Twins received both good news and bad news regarding team personnel within a few weeks of the failure of the ballpark referendum.

First the good news: Paul Molitor signed on with the Twins to be a coach on Tom Kelly's staff. Note the date—November 23rd, 1999. It may mark the beginning of a long-time coaching career.

Molitor will be a "bench coach" in name only. He will actively work with players in all areas, with a special focus on improving the skills of young players. Paul says he still has an intensity and passion for baseball that will allow him to remain committed to the game and to his former teammates.

"I guess I'm in no hurry to leave," he said. "I respect this organization."

But why stay in Minnesota, when the offer from new Seattle General Manager Pat Gillarek was so strong? Seattle has a beautiful new facility, good crowds, and arguably a better ballclub. So why?

I saw Paul at a Twins function after he had made his decision to stay. When I asked him about Seattle, he said with an enigmatic Mollie smile, "Tempting, don't you think? But I'm staying here." Then he turned and walked away. No real answer there.

I figure he may be in the Twin Cities to work out an apprenticeship with Tom Kelly. Maybe he'll be a candidate to succeed Kelly as manager of the Twins if Kelly moves on. In any case, he'll add experience that will embellish an already impressive resume that includes studying the game from both the field and the advantageous perch of the TV booth.

But perhaps more than any of this, I think Paul is staying home for family. He'll have plenty of time for moving as the years go by; that day will come.

For now, he can relax and enjoy this time on the Twins bench. He's a born student of the game of baseball. Managing, when it comes, may take him anywhere, and he'll be ready. Even if you're Paul Molitor, you've got to be ready if you're going to lead a major league ballclub. ◎

Molitor's Rankings
Among the All-Time Leaders

HITS - Over 2800

1.	Pete Rose	4256
2.	Ty Cobb	4191
3.	Hank Aaron	3771
4.	Stan Musial	3630
5.	Tris Speaker	3514
6.	Carl Yastrzemski	3419
7.	Honus Wagner	3415
8.	**PAUL MOLITOR**	**3319**
9.	Eddie Collins	3315
10.	Willie Mays	3283
11.	Eddie Murray	3255
12.	Nap Lajoie	3242
13.	George Brett	3154
14.	Paul Waner	3152
15.	Robin Yount	3142
16.	Dave Winfield	3110
17.	Rod Carew	3053
18.	Lou Brock	3023
19.	Al Kaline	3007
20.	Roberto Clemente	3000
21.	Cap Anson	2995
22.	Sam Rice	2987
23.	Sam Crawford	2961
24.	Frank Robinson	2943
25.	Willie Keeler	2932
26.	Jake Beckley	2930
	Rogers Hornsby	2930
28.	Tony Gwynn	2928
29.	Al Simmons	2927
30.	Wade Boggs	2922

DOUBLES - Over 500

1.	Tris Speaker	792
2.	Pete Rose	746
3.	Stan Musial	725
4.	Ty Cobb	724
5.	George Brett	665
6.	Nap Lajoie	657
7.	Carl Yastrzemski	646
8.	Honus Wagner	640
9.	Hank Aaron	624
10.	Paul Waner	605
	PAUL MOLITOR	**605**
12.	Robin Yount	583
13.	Charlie Gehringer	574
14.	Wade Boggs	564
15.	Eddie Murray	560
16.	Cal Ripken	544
17.	Harry Heilmann	542
18.	Rogers Hornsby	541
19.	Joe Medwick	540
	Dave Winfield	540
21.	Al Simmons	539
22.	Lou Gehrig	534
23.	Al Oliver	529
24.	Cap Anson	528
	Frank Robinson	528
26.	Dave Parker	526
27.	Ted Williams	525
28.	Willie Mays	523
29.	Ed Delahanty	522
30.	Joe Cronin	515

25 Years of World Series MVPs

1974 – Rollie Fingers, Oakland (AL)
1975 – Pete Rose, Cincinnati (NL)
1976 – Johnny Bench, Cincinnati (NL)
1977 – Reggie Jackson, New York (AL)
1978 – Bucky Dent, New York (AL)
1979 – Willie Stargell, Pittsburgh (NL)
1980 – Mike Schmidt, Philadelphia (NL)
1981 – Ron Cey, Pedro Guerrero and
　　　　Steve Yeager, Los Angeles (NL)
1982 – Darrell Porter, St. Louis (NL)
1983 – Rick Dempsey, Baltimore (AL)
1984 – Alan Trammell, Detroit (AL)
1985 – Bret Saberhagen, Kansas City (AL)
1986 – Ray Knight, New York, (NL)
1987 – Frank Viola, Minnesota (AL)
1988 – Orel Hershiser, Los Angeles (NL)
1989 – Dave Stewart, Oakland (Al)
1990 – Jose Rijo, Cincinnati (NL)
1991 – Jack Morris, Minnesota (AL)
1992 – Pat Borders, Toronto (AL)
1993 – PAUL MOLITOR, Toronto (AL)
1994 – No Series (STRIKE)
1995 – Tom Glavine, Atlanta (NL)
1996 – John Wetteland, New York (AL)
1997 – Livan Hernandez, Florida (NL)
1998 – Scott Brosius, New York (AL)
1999 – Mariano Rivera, New York (AL)

NOTES FROM THE MIDSUMMER CLASSIC

Denver, Coors Stadium, 1998

All-Stars and Beanie Babies®

As I was preparing to enter Coors Field for the 1998 All Star game, I was walking along the stadium wall near the press gate area. There was a little corridor that I was moving through and it suddenly occurred to me that I was being offered money by a number of women and a few men. I could see one hundred-dollar bills in their hands and, for the life of me, I couldn't figure out what was going on. Did they want to buy a ticket? The game was a sell-out, that must be it. Did they want to buy my media pass? That wasn't going to happen, of course. Maybe they wanted the new sport coat that I had just purchased that afternoon. Part of me was thinking that it was very interesting that these women were determined to gain entrance into the All Star game.

After entering through the press turnstile, I was handed what appeared to be a little stuffed animal. As I got onto the elevator to be transported to the press box a fellow next to me lamented that he only had one "Beanie Baby" though he had two children. "It's going to be tough to decide who gets this one," he said.

I looked at him and looked at my little stuffed bear that was decorated with stars both blue and red. It was an easy decision to give my stuffed animal to this gentleman from the media. I never asked his name and was happy to do the right thing.

Only later when the talk of the press box was the fervor for the Beanie Babies did it occur to me that I had given away what people were now selling for a few hundred dollars. One of the media guys went down to where people were lined up outside the stadium during the game—hundreds of them, he said—sold his beanie for $200 and was back at work before the next inning started.

Ah, greed, the other national pas-time. It really makes this country go around.

Mark McGwire

It was a privilege to spend a few minutes with Mark McGwire at the 1998 All Star Game. I mentioned to McGwire that Roger Maris had once said that home runs were the result of hard work and prepara-tion, not luck. He agreed with Maris, up to a point.

"I am always working on my game as a hitter, just like I work on defense. During batting practice I try to discipline myself and to get things working together. Sometimes I'll focus on a certain area where my swing could use work."

"It's all about timing and hitting a ball that is moving with power. So you need to get extension with the arms and follow-through with your swing. Roger Maris had an exceptional swing with a lot of follow through. I work on weight transfer a lot even when I'm just swinging the bat to get loose. I definitely push myself to be the best hitter I can be."

McGwire paused for a moment and added: "I can't tell you how much I respect Roger Maris and what he accomplished. I'm grateful to be drawing these comparisons."

Boston, Fenway Park, 1999

All Star Game, So-So Seats

The media area that had been desig-nated for the peons at Coors Field a year earlier was in the right field bleach-ers. They were great seats, far removed from home plate but with a good visual line. It was nice to be able to watch the game from that vantage point.

In Boston the location for those "low on the totem pole" members of the media was the "Cronin Room," named after Hall of Fame shortstop and manager Joe Cronin (and brother-in-law of Calvin Griffith), hidden behind the left field grandstands of Fenway Park. Those of us in the press who feel fortunate to have had our credential applications OK'd generally choose not to argue with seating assignments.

Yes, you're clearly in the lower echelon of the media contingent, and your seat assignment lets you know that you are second tier, but at least you're in the ballpark.

The seat assignment on this occa-sion was at a table in front of a TV set in The Cronin Room. Don't get me wrong, I'm not complaining in the least. I liked Cronin. When I explored the little rooms connected to the aux-iliary media area, I learned that Pedro Martinez was going on camera in a small studio in a few minutes.

I waited and watched the surprisingly diminutive Red Sox pitching ace answer the usual questions. "How are you going to get out the great hitters of the National League," etc.... Pedro's answer to that particular question was "It will take a little bit of skill and a little bit of luck. I know they are good hitters but I'm a good pitcher, too. I look forward to the challenge," he said. He was sweating under the lights, and his face was glowing radiantly. He looked like a Dominican angel.

The Cronin Room itself was decorated with numerous interesting old pictures of former Red Sox players, with a special emphasis on Ted Williams, who was a special guest of honor at the 70th All Star game. Ted was to throw out the first pitch and would be particularly honored before the game by the century's finest living ballplayers as well as the current All Stars. In the Cronin Room, the pictures of Ted reflected his growth as a player and his image at different stages of his career was revealing. He always looked confident in the photos.

One of the best pictures on the wall of the Cronin Room is Williams standing with his friend Johnny Pesky at Fenway. Pesky, an excellent shortstop who managed the Red Sox in 1964, looked so small next to the powerfully built Williams. Earlier that day, I had seen Pesky leaning against the wall on Yawkey Way, the street that runs next to Fenway's third base line. He was signing autographs for a group of fans. I noticed how simply he was dressed. He was simply pleasing some of the faithful, and his humility was striking.

The Cronin Room had a TV set that the media would watch the game from. As game time approached I slipped out of The Cronin Room (we were not locked in there) and walked throughout the interior of Fenway as the late arrivals moved quickly to their seats. I picked up a sausage with extra onions and stuck my head out the gangway and watched the flying Thunderbirds noisily zoom over in perfect formation. As I looked to the field, there was Ted being surrounded by some of the greatest names in the game. It was a wonderful sight.

When a policeman told me to move from my position at the top of the stairs, I moved to the next aisle over and stuck my head out again. Some of the fans were standing as Pedro Martinez took the mound and began his warm-ups. I was able to maintain my spot as I watched Pedro strike out the side in incredible fashion. First, he struck out Barry Larkin, then he struck out Larry Walker, and then he struck out Sammy Sosa in an intense battle of the great Dominicans. What a sight. Holy smokes!

The excitement of Pedro's big entrance had the raucous crowd in Fenway on its feet applauding maniacally, and I was undisturbed in my prime location for several minutes. I knew I was watching pitching mastery. This had to be one of the finest displays of the craft that had ever been witnessed at any All Star Game. I knew that I was privileged.

When the crowd settled, I slid back into the bowels of Fenway and started working my way back to The Cronin Room. I stopped for another sausage with onions, relish and peppers. Man, are they good.

Mark McGwire: The Home Run King

When Mark McGwire stepped into the cage for the semi-final round of the 1999 All Star game home run contest he looked eager to perform. He waved his bat in a manner that suggested he was ready for the challenge, unlike the previous year when a tired-looking McGwire didn't get good pitches to hit and retired early from the contest.

On this evening of the "home run derby," McGwire was ready. He hit a number of long fly balls over the fence to open the competition, in what is really a glorified batting practice. Nonetheless, the crowd was enthralled by the majesty of his arching shots.

After 13 of McGwire's rocket launches had zoomed into the night sky and beyond the walls of Fenway,

Mark McGwire: Longest home run in the Medtrodome, hit when he was with Oakland

the crowd rewarded him with applause and shouts of approval in a yawning, expanding exclamation of gratitude for having witnessed such a display.

Some of McGwire's blasts were launched above the Green Monster and into the light standard, with its oversized Coke bottle midway up the pole. The standards literally came under attack from McGwire as his blasts went careening into the dozens of light bulb fixtures. Like a vision from the movie "The Natural," in which Robert Redford's character, Roy Hobbs, explodes the night sky with his dramatic home run, it was spectacular.

McGwire is a good man, though he is larger than life. To the many thousands who witnessed his display that night, it was a moment that won't soon be forgotten. For the first time in my experience watching Mark McGwire, I knew that I was watching the greatest home run hitter of all time.

Ozzie Smith: One of the Best Shortstops Ever

Everyone knows Ozzie Smith as one of the greatest shortstops ever to have played the game. While he was with the St. Louis Cardinals, from which he retired in 1997, his regular appearances at Wrigley Field were a must-see event for serious infielders. As I was looking for an interview at the 1999 All Star Game, I found Smith sitting quietly on the National League bench. He would later be honored as one of this century's 100 finest baseball players.

I decided to ask him if he was interested in coaching, as I didn't want to simply fawn over him. (Not fawning was a challenge, since whenever I looked at him, my mind would recall Ozzie deep in the hole at short, framed against the Wrigley ivy, unleashing his off balance throw to get a Cub base runner just in time.) Smith replied, "I'm a dad now. I'm really enjoying being with my kids. They are 17, 12 and 9 years old, and I don't want to coach right now. Maybe I'll coach my kids a little later in life."

Ozzie does media work for CNN, *Sports Illustrated* and *This Week in Baseball*. Does he enjoy watching the game from the vantage point of the press box? What does he think of the shortstops patrolling his former position? "I think some of the guys playing short need to work on the fundamentals. You've got to get into the proper position to field the baseball. It's interesting that some of these players have so much talent, but I sometimes find them lacking in the fundamentals."

As I listen to the Hall of Fame shortstop it occurs to me that Ozzie Smith would be a great coach, especially for a certain style of player. For me!! I wonder what it would take to get him to come out to Minnetonka and work with an old guy who could desperately use his guidance.

As if he was reading my thoughts, Ozzie's gazes at me from the bench with his soft, knowing eyes. "I loved the great rivalry between the Cubs and the Cardinals. Those were boisterous, happy crowds that showed up at both ballparks. I always felt appreciated in Chicago. We had a lot of fun back then, but I don't want to be back in the game right now."

So Ozzie, of the great shortstops in the game today, who would you take as your shortstop for a money game. "You can't go wrong with any of the three A.L. All-Stars (Jeter, Garciaparra, or Vizquel). But I think for one game with all things being equal I would take the Mets' Rey Ordoñez. I think he has the best instincts of any shortstop in the game. He's very fundamentally sound."

Smith would be proven right on that last point. Ordoñez would become the first shortstop in major league history to play 100 errorless games in a row. He accomplished this feat at the end of the 1999 season.

Ivan Rodriguez

As I boarded the media shuttle from the homerun derby to the hotel I found myself in the midst of the entourage of Ivan Rodriguez. I had a conversation with Rodriguez's strength and conditioning coach and noted that there appeared to be six or seven people connected to the fine Texas catcher on the bus.

We may have been the only people on the bus and it was a good chance to talk to people who knew the little catcher known as "Pudge." We chatted for a while, and I came to like the small army that works with Rodriguez. He doesn't travel light; more like a rock star.

Pudge himself was not on the bus. Ivan Rodriguez, it should be noted, is not pudgy. He's built more like a little tank with a cannon arm he uses to throw out base runners at the highest percentage in baseball. I have seen him at the Metrodome launching enormous homeruns into the bleachers, a stunning picture given his relative lack of size.

The strength and conditioning man told me that Rodriguez eats right, works out consistently and has a natural body for baseball. All the typical clichés you would expect from one of his posse.

I eat right (well, not that bad), work out consistently (at least a couple times a week), and have a decent baseball body (could use a little muscle, you say?). What's the difference?

Like night and day.

Ivan Rodriguez won the Most Valuable Player Award in the American League in 1999 after having a tremendous season. He was a spark plug on a Texas Ranger team that had an excellent regular season (beating the Twins all 12 times they played in

'99) and won the Western Division title.

Early in 1999 Rodriguez set a Texas Rangers record by driving in nine runs in a game against Seattle. Amazingly, he set the record in only the first three innings of the ballgame. Rodriguez hit a three-run homer in the first inning, a two-run single in the second inning and his first career grand slam in the third inning in what may be a Major League Baseball record.

Ron Coomer:
A Long Road to Stardom

Ron Coomer was a small celebrity at the 1999 All Star game in Boston. During the major media press confer-

ence, which allowed journalists good access to the players, Coomer expressed his gratitude for being a part of the festivities. He was truly humbled.

"It's a wonderful thing for me to be here. I never expected that I would be selected, because we had a few other guys who I thought were more worthy. Brad Radke, for one, is an All Star pitcher who was in the game last year and probably should be here today.

"I spent eight full years and part of a ninth in the minor leagues before I got a shot with Minnesota. To make it to the All Star Game is just unbelievable, absolutely a dream come true.

An appreciative Ron Coomer at the All Star Game. Fenway, 1999.

"I had some awfully good years in AAA baseball (Coomer hit .338 for Albuquerque in 1994 and .322 for part of 1995 before being called up). I really wasn't sure if I was ever going to get a shot at the big time. In my heart I thought I could play there, but this is just amazing."

Ron Coomer was released by Huntsville during the 1990 season. He was flat out of baseball.

Ron Coomer standing alongside Mark McGwire at first base, at the 1999 baseball classic, is one of the many stories that make baseball great.

Jeff Zimmerman: Miracles Can Happen

I ran into Scott Taylor of the Winnipeg *Free Press*, who related a marvelous comeback story about one of the players in the '99 All Star Game:

"How about the story of Jeff Zimmerman. What a terrific tale. A Canadian, Jeff was a member of the Canadian National Team when it failed to make the Olympic games and his career appeared to be over. Jeff went to France to play baseball!

"When he returned from France he drove to Winnipeg from Carseland. Alberta, where his mother owns a hotel, to try out for the Winnipeg team in the Northern League (the same league as the St. Paul Saints). Zimmerman paid $25 for the privilege of trying out for Winnipeg.

"After he threw two pitches,

Scott Taylor with former Northern Leaguer Jeff Zimmerman

coach Hal Lanier gave him his money back.

"It was Reid Nichols of the Texas Rangers who finally gave Zimmerman his chance. He went from A ball to AAA ball in three months, didn't look like he would make the Rangers in 1999, got called up, and was in the 1999 All Star game."

Do you believe in miracles? Zimmerman's story is even more miraculous than Ron Coomer's.

Matt Damon

Before the All Star game got underway at Fenway, I got a chance to talk to film star Matt Damon.

Damon had been hanging out with Kevin Costner and had participated in the Home Run Derby, although not too successfully. "I didn't hit real well, did I?" he said. "It was a great experience, but I guess I'm still good-field no-hit."

I asked Matt if he had played much baseball in his life. He said that he had played a lot as a young boy in Little League, but he hadn't played much in high school. "I would have liked to, but it didn't work out."

Matt Damon spent a lot of his time looking with awe at his heroes, both present and past. I caught him checking out Sammy Sosa from a few feet away and, while I'm not sure Sammy would know Matt Damon, Matt Damon sure as heck knows Sammy. I'm aware also that many

women would have liked to be standing where I was, next to the cinema superstar. But I have to believe that Damon enjoyed being on the field at Fenway more than making any movie.

"Did you ever play any pick-up baseball when you were growing up?" I asked.

"Yeah, all the time. We'd find a way to play ball any way we could when I was a kid."

So Matt Damon was a ballplayer. He didn't look too bad in the cage during his chance at batting practice. I liked him more for the fact he loves baseball, and I thought I'd catch a Matt Damon flick when I got back home.

John Wetteland

Texas Ranger All-Star John Wetteland, who was an outstanding relief pitcher with the Yankees and the Expos before landing in Texas, was hunkered down next to the right field bullpen with a bunch of kids who had finished their Home Run Derby responsibilities in the outfield, shagging balls for some of baseball's best hitters. Wetteland was in a crouch and thrilling the kids with a conversation about what it takes to succeed in baseball. I caught him talking about "focus" and "determination." It was some pretty heavy stuff for young kids, but vital if they could understand what he was trying to say.

Two hours before game time,

Wetteland was giving of himself to these kids. It was an extraordinary sign of his willingness to mentor children and teach them about the game of baseball.

Orlando Cepeda

Orlando Cepeda was a tremendous ballplayer for the San Francisco Giants from 1959-1973. Cepeda participated in eleven All Star games and three World Series. He has fond memories of the All Star game and is the honorary captain for the 1999 National League All Star team. He hit four home runs during his All Star appearances. Orlando Cepeda entered the Hall-of-Fame in 1999.

For Cepeda, however, the greatest thrill of his career was participating in his first big league baseball game. "I knew that my dream had come true. I knew I was playing in the major leagues. That is still my greatest thrill in baseball."

Anthony the Street Vendor

Just outside of Fenway park there was a food vendor named Anthony, whose cart I frequently patronized when I ventured outside the ballpark. The big friendly Italian would shout, "It's not a game without sausage, guys!" in his thick Boston accent, and his pitch would echo, "Extra long, sweet and hot, Italian sausage, sautéed sweet peppers and onions, Cajun chicken, sirloin steak tips." By the end of the All Star break I had sampled them all and can affirm Anthony's mantra of "absolutely delicious."

Anthony's friendly face was one that I would look for each time I was on Yawkey way. There's something about food at the ballpark that tastes better than food almost anywhere else. When the food itself is truly delicious and you can enjoy it in the shadow of Fenway park, well, it just doesn't get any better than that.

Carlton Fisk

Carlton Fisk commented on the fact that a new Fenway park is in the works. "The new park won't erase the memories of the old Fenway. But to remain competitive we're going to have to have a new park here."

Joe Torre

"I remember what Tim McCarver used to say about Bob Gibson, and it reminds me of Pedro Martinez. He used to say about Gibson, 'He's very lucky. Whenever he pitches, the other team doesn't score any runs.' Pedro can stop any hitter when he is on."

Facts and Statistics

Willie Mayes, Hank Aaron and Stan Musial each played in 24 All Star games. Harmon Killebrew participated in 11 All Star contests for the Minnesota Twins and Tony Oliva participated in 6. Rod Carew participated in 15 All Star games.

In 1946 at Fenway, Ted Williams participated in the most one-sided All Star contest ever played. Ted Williams went four for four with two home runs, five RBI's, and four runs scored. Holy smokes! The American League routed the Nationals 12–0.

Jose Cardenal: "It's not like yesterday."

It seems like only yesterday that current Yankees first base/outfield coach Jose Cardenal was thrashing around in the ivy at Wrigley Field looking for a lost ball, shrieking in Spanish just below my seat in the left field bleachers. It seems like yesterday to both of us. "I loved my time in Wrigley," said Jose "Those are good memories for me. I loved the fans at that ballpark.

"But the game isn't like it was yesterday. The players don't listen to me too much; they only listen to the money. They're the world champions; they know everything or think they know everything."

His comments make me dislike the Yankees more than ever. I really don't mind the fact that they are a great baseball club with a great tradition, but I don't like the fact that they think they know everything. What fun is invulnerability anyway?

Greg Maddux

Greg Maddux still reminds me of a schoolboy, with his baby face and youthful expressions. When Maddux is asked about the power in the game today, he replies that he believes it's the hitters more than the pitchers.

"I think the hitters have gotten better. I feel the pitching has maybe thinned out a hair by expansion. It's a reflection on how good the power hitters are. They've gotten better, they're staying healthy and they're not missing their pitches."

Maddux doesn't feel the dilution of weaker pitching has played a significant role in baseball today.

"I just don't think there's that much difference between now and a couple of years ago. Sammy Sosa works so hard and he shows that hard work pays off. He loves the game so much. The people in the game and the fans of the game return that love to Sammy. He's an amazing ballplayer. Mark McGwire is just a scary strong hitter. If he gets it, it's going to go a long way. You've got to try and make McGwire miss the ball. He's such a good low-ball hitter that when you pitch him down and throw a good pitch, sometimes he still makes you pay for it."

10

BREAKS OF THE GAME: THEY CAN MAKE ALL THE DIFFERENCE

John Castino:
A Career Cut Short

My Minnesota baseball ties run deep for a non-native. For example, my high school varsity baseball coach, a fine gentleman by the name of Ken McGonagle, lettered for the Gophers in 1951 and 1952. When McGonagle led the Evanston High School Wildkats against archrival New Trier H.S. in 1974, the Trevians, led by Ron Klein, featured an exceptional third baseman named John Castino, a future Twins player who at the time was headed for all-state honors in both basketball and baseball (á la Paul Molitor).

I didn't play much for Evanston during my junior year, but as I rode the bench and made my way around the Chicago area, I saw some good players who were a year ahead of me. Scott Sanderson (who pitched well for the Expos, Cubs and others), Charlie Liebrandt (a World Series winner with Kansas City and, pitching for

Atlanta, the victim of a Kirby Puckett home run in game six of the '91 Series), and other fine players, including Castino, who was a great high school athlete.

After high school I went to Denison University in Ohio and then to Northwestern University. Castino went on to play baseball at Rollins College in Florida, where he signed with the Twins. He was still playing third base with flair, making $21,000 as a rookie in 1979, when I watched him rip a double against the White Sox at Comiskey Park in Chicago. Castino became the American League Rookie of the Year in 1979 (the same year I was playing shortstop at Northwestern), hitting .285 with 55 RBI's and some pretty solid glove work. Life was a lot of fun for the young man from Chicago's North Shore.

"I really enjoyed that first year in the big leagues," says Castino. "It was a tremendous experience to walk into Yankee Stadium and hear the fans calling your name, the same thing with Fenway Park in Boston. Those fans would greet you the way real fans did back then; the fans appreciated good play by all players and let you know it."

The year after Castino was named top rookie in the league, Cal Griffith gave him a big raise—to $50,000 a year (Kerry Woods' raise for being the top National League rookie in 1998 was over a half-million dollars). Though the raise was small by today's standards, Castino doesn't have any second thoughts about it. "Cal was tough but pretty fair, and in 1964 Tony Oliva earned $7,000, won Rookie of the Year honors, and was raised to $10,000." When Castino was MVP of the Twins ballclub in the early 1980's, he earned his top salary of $160,000.

It all ended too soon for John Castino. In 1983, when manager Billy Gardner told him he would be the club's selection for the All Star game, a degenerative back condition that would ultimately claim his career began to make itself known. Castino missed significant time prior to the '83 break, and the decision was made to send Gary Ward to the classic instead.

Castino remembers this wistfully in our conversation, knowing that the missed All Star game would have been his last honor as a ballplayer. He'd like to have gone, though Gary Ward was worthy. The complicated spinal fusion

that was to come within a year was preceded by troublesome back pain. He didn't know what was coming then; it was to mean the end of his career as a professional ballplayer. Finished, finito. In the prime of his baseball life.

"My son has the same condition and may be giving up the game himself very soon," Castino says. "I was able to coach him a little and see his love for the game." (His son played at Edina High School in Minnesota and is currently at Rollins). "I think the love is there among today's kids for the game of baseball, but they're smarter than we were. My son and his friends are more ambitious, they work harder, and they find out what's out there college-wise for a good player. I respect that."

Now it looks like his son's baseball days may be numbered, and I asked John if he remembers the first year he couldn't play the game. At first he skirted the question, saying he remembers, but he doesn't miss it so much today: "It looks like they're having less fun than we did."

Later in the conversation John answered my question more openly.

"I was blessed with a gift from God and I worked my butt off. I love the game. And for a long time baseball was who I was, that became my identity. I'm OK now, but at the time, being forced to leave the game was the hardest thing that ever happened to me. The only thing tougher in my life was the loss of my father, when he died. Leaving the game and the people behind was very hard. I could only visualize myself as a member of that 1987 Championship team."

"I guess it just wasn't meant to be."

Roger Maris and Mark McGwire: Different Kinds of Heroes

When Roger Maris challenged for the single-season home run record in Major League Baseball, he was taking on the most honored record in sports. Maris was taking on the Herculean Babe Ruth, a figure so much larger than life that no mere shrine is befitting the Sultan of Swat. Yankee Stadium itself is the House that Ruth built.

Maris' assault on the home run record was not a popular one in its time. It was not popular in New York, nor was particularly popular around the country. New Yorkers felt that if anyone must break Ruth's record of 60 home runs in a single season, Mickey Mantle should do it. Mantle was popular with the New York media and was considered a true Yankee. Mantle suffered an infection late in the season or he may have done more to challenge the record himself.

Mickey Mantle later said about Maris' effort: "What Roger Maris accomplished in breaking Babe Ruth's record, under such tremendous pressure, is the greatest feat in the history of sports."

It is strangely ironic that when Roger Maris accomplished the heroic deed of breaking the magnificent Ruth's record, he did not become a hero. One can only speculate as to why. The times they were a-changing. Popularity, which has always been influenced to some extent by the media, was becoming overwhelmingly determined by media coverage of people and events. Roger Maris was a simple man in a sophisticated city, who would not play by the rules of Gotham.

There is a story that when Maris was told to buy new shoes that didn't look as "square" as the ones he was wearing, Maris went out and bought another two pair of the very same shoes.

Roger Maris was perceived as an unworthy heir to the throne that Ruth held. Perhaps if Maris had hit 59 home runs, rather than 61, he would have been more beloved by the media and the citizenry of New York City. For whatever reason, Maris faced a variety of abuse in the town for whose team he had exercised his home run talents.

Former Yankee player and broadcaster Tony Kubek wrote a book called 61. In it, Kubek says, "I don't know if there's ever been an athlete under more intense pressure than

Roger Maris. I remember Roger talking for hour after hour with the press. And this was a guy who had to be pushed out of the dugout to tip his hat after his 61st home run. It wasn't something that he enjoyed or that came naturally."

When Mark McGwire came to the Metrodome in 1998, he gave one press conference during the entire series. The St. Louis Cardinal media staff were capable of helping McGwire to withstand a late 1990's-style assault by the press. It is my belief that it's right for public relations people to assist any record-setting athlete in dealing with the media throng. In New York in 1961 Roger Maris had no such luxury. He was prey to the hoard.

Mark McGwire is a hero today to many baseball fans, and most importantly to many children. He is certainly a hero to his son, Casey and for that alone he is to be admired. But McGwire is not Ruthian, for baseball is different today. There can be no doubt that Mark McGwire is a significant sports figure. He did not merely break the record held by Roger Maris, he shattered it by hitting 70 home runs in 1998 and followed that by hitting 66 in 1999 to prove that it hadn't been a fluke. Truly an amazing accomplishment.

As a boy, I saw Roger Maris while he was playing with the St. Louis Cardinals in a game against the Chicago Cubs. The year must have been 1967 and the Cardinals had a fine team. Maris was a complete baseball player, who could hit, run, throw and think. He was not averse to hitting behind the runner or dropping a bunt. He was much more than a home run hitter; he was a team player. Overlooked about Roger Maris is the fact that he was a complete baseball player.

It was hard for me, though, to recognize the ordinary-looking major league ballplayer in the outfield as the holder of the all-time home run record. Could this mortal man walking in the Wrigley outfield truly be the one who had broken the almighty Ruth's record? Maris had a good game against the Cubs that day, and I can recall him hitting a long, long, foul ball that sailed over our seats in the right field grandstand. I remember Maris stepping out of the box and watching the flight of the ball as it sailed completely out of the ballpark onto Sheffield Avenue.

Watching him stand at home plate, I thought, "This is the man who broke Babe Ruth's record."

Interestingly, on the day Mark McGwire hit his record-breaking home run, he was in the physical presence of the bat with which Roger Maris had hit his 61st homer to break Ruth's record. On September 8, 1998, before the game with the Chicago Cubs that would change home run history, McGwire caressed Maris' bat and, as he would say later, "Held it close to my heart. I was certain it (breaking the record) would happen that night."

So the Cardinal McGwire tied the one-time Cardinal, one-time Yankee Roger Maris on September 7, 1998 with a home run off former Twin Mike Morgan and passed him the next night with historic number 62, pounded off Steve Trachsel in the presence of Roger Maris' family.

As number 62 settled into the Busch Stadium seats, Sammy Sosa ran in from right field to personally salute his friend. The two sluggers swapped the usual jibes of fake punches and playful banter.

McGwire was keenly aware of the historic nature of his accomplish-ment. In short order he found his son, and then he jumped into the stands to embrace the six Maris children who were seated along the first base line near the Cubs dugout.

Later, Maris' son Randy would say, "There is sadness. Mark McGwire is a fine man, but there's still a feeling of sadness. My father held the record for 37 years and we never thought we would see this day come."

Mark McGwire had accomplished the feat nearly four decades after Roger Maris had established the mark. His enormous accomplishment had come well before the end of the regular season. It was on a Sunday, October 1, 1961 that Roger Maris broke Babe Ruth's record (at 2:42 p.m., against the Boston Red Sox). McGwire had broken Maris' record

CHARLIE NELSON

I saw former Gopher and Dodger minor leaguer Charlie Nelson at the pro-alumni game in 1999. He said he was finished with the Dodgers. He had been injury-prone the previous couple of years, but felt he would give it one more shot playing center field for the St. Paul Saints.

Don Wardlow told me that Charlie looked good the first couple games of the year. "He was starting to hit the ball pretty well. There was every rea-son to believe he would be outstanding." said Wardlow.

Charlie tore up his shoulder in the fourth game of the year against Schaumburg, Illinois. It probably was the final blow and the end of his pro-fessional baseball life. ◐

with more than three weeks left in the season. He would use that time to good advantage and hit 8 more home runs to push the major league home run record to an extraordinary and daunting place.

70 home runs in one season!

Jim Morris

Out of Texas comes the story of Jim Morris, a 35-year-old high school baseball coach whose team, tired of their coach throwing fastball bullets in batting practice, told him he should still be playing. The coach, a lefty who had "pretty good stuff a while ago," was the number one pick of the Milwaukee Brewers in 1983. His career ended when he underwent surgery on his rotator cuff.

Taking up the challenge of his Reagen City Texas High School Owls team, the coach had a tryout and was clocked throwing 98 mph at the audition. Perhaps not quite believing what they had seen, the scouts requested that he come back the following day. There, in a light rain, he topped out at about 96 mph and was signed by the Tampa Bay Devil Rays. In July he was recording saves at the AA level and on July 23, 1999 he recorded his first save in AAA baseball.

On September 18, 1999, James Samuel Morris, who had been a high school baseball coach in the spring, pitched for the first time in the major leagues, as a Devil Ray.

I think it's fabulous that the kids put him up to the challenge and that Morris, a normal everyday high school coach with a big fastball, would be able to pursue his dream once again.

So there is still a little hope for all of us, that perhaps we will be rediscovered on the sandlot or at the local town ballpark by a bird-dog major league scout. Of course, it wouldn't hurt if you could throw a fastball 90+ mph at your high school baseball team to draw a little attention. ◎

11

THE AMAZING NORTHERN LEAGUE

St. Paul Saints vs. Duluth Dukes

One lovely afternoon in early June I found myself finishing up an extended weekend on the north shore of Lake Superior. My drive back towards the Twin Cities took me through the north woods and some spectacular views of Lake Superior in all its beauty at the mouth of the Cascade River. My route was going to take me through Duluth, so I decided to stop and watch the St. Paul Saints play the Duluth Dukes in a ballgame at Wade Stadium.

Wade Stadium is an enjoyable little ballpark that is the home of the Duluth-Superior Dukes. Duluth is a beautiful small town in transition from its industrial and shipping past to a future that will be more reliant on tourism and technology.

In the ballgame that was played that evening, the Saints pounded out 20 hits—18 singles and 2 doubles—and they won the ballgame 14-3 in front of the season's smallest crowd,

listed at around 1500 fans. The Dukes are averaging 1800 fans per ballgame, but the word around the league is that they must do better and draw more people to their ballpark. Since the Northern League's revival in 1993, more than a half-million fans have passed through the turnstile at Wade Stadium; in fact, fan number 500,000 was at the game that I attended that Monday night.

The Saints were playing small ball against the Dukes; 18 singles was an unusual performance for them. Catcher Carlos Mota went six for six at the plate and is a nice player who looks like he has some potential. The kids can play and I agree with Scott Taylor of the Winnipeg *Free Press* that the Northern League has players of higher quality than is generally recognized. Part of the reason for that lack of recognition is the fact that people go to Northern League games for the fun and not so much to study the quality of the players in action.

Ila Borders came in to pitch late in the game; Ila is the first woman to pitch at this level in some time. She gave up six runs on six hits with two errors behind her, and it wasn't all her fault. She looks like a steady left-hander who would be tough in the 35-and-over league. I think the boys get psyched up to face Ila and they are especially determined not to make an out against the young woman.

St. Paul's ballpark, Midway Stadium, is a quaint park situated in the Midway area between downtown Minneapolis and downtown St. Paul. When I attended a weekday game on June 16th of 1999, all of the tailgating spots had been taken by 11:00 a.m. A policeman working the game told me that if I wanted to secure a tailgating spot I should plan to arrive by 10:00 a.m.

That was the only weekday day game of the year and it was a beautiful morning for it. The Saints have picnic areas and family areas that are available for the fans looking for a particular ballpark experience. The organization is well-run from top to bottom as minor league ballclubs go.

Mike Veeck was a caring and capable marketing man as an owner. General Manager Bill Fanning works hard, and his duties include taking tickets at the gate in addition to the more traditional management responsibilities. Marty Scott, the manager, has had success in St. Paul as well as in

other locations where he managed teams before coming to the Saints.

Don Wardlow, Saints Color Commentator

Don Wardlow is the color commentator for St. Paul Saints baseball on a radio station in the Twin Cities. It happens to be a radio station that I am well acquainted with, having done some work there myself. When I was visiting the Duluth Dukes in their battle against the Saints, I wanted to visit Wardlow and his play-by-play man Jim Lucas in the press box at Wade Stadium.

Wardlow and Lucas have been calling St. Paul Saints games for a number of years. Don Wardlow is blind, but that doesn't stop him from creating one of the most interesting baseball broadcasts out there. Lucas and Wardlow make it a point of entertaining the listener with all kinds of information, no matter what the game situation may be.

You can get a few four-hour contests in the Northern League. That's a lot of time to kill on the radio. Lucas and Wardlow create an atmosphere for the listener that, similar to Saints games, is not reliant on the quality of the game itself.

Not that Wardlow is disrespectful of his team.

"The St. Paul Saints get the best out of all their people; people in management, people in marketing and the team on the field. Everyone is expected to perform at the highest level possible.

"The guys play top-notch baseball, but there are some games where, for whatever reason, things might get a little out of hand. So we try to keep the listeners entertained with trivia, player stories, a variety of baseball-related stuff."

Wardlow is appreciative of the opportunity extended to him by the Saints. He is a one-of-a-kind color man in the game today.

"It's exciting being around the game full time. I believe I'm the only blind color man in all of organized baseball. There used to be a fellow out in California who was doing this, but I believe he's gone now. I just try to do my job the best that I know how. I don't want people to think that I'm working with a disadvantage."

On the night when I was in Duluth watching the Dukes take on the Saints, Wardlow's braille writer broke. That's the braille writer that Wardlow counts on for technical assistance.

"Yeah, I remember that night real well. It's a good thing you weren't too close to me that night, because there were a few ugly words being tossed around. Not a good thing to lose the brailler." Wardlow said.

Wardlow is an optimist, as are most people in the Saints organization. Although 1999 was not a good year for the ballclub on the field, Wardlow feels it was another growth year for the team as a whole. "We're pretty established now in St. Paul. I think we've become established throughout the Twin Cities.

"The major league game makes people think of baseball, and because our season starts later we benefit from big league publicity. While there has been dissatisfaction with the Twins as a whole, that doesn't necessarily hurt us. The idea of the Twins leaving town; that would be different. The Twins should stay in the Twin Cities. I would hate to see them leave."

Wardlow is impressed by the players with whom he rubs shoulders every day during the season.

"I know it sounds like a cliché, but the guys on this team are good people. I've been around other professional ballplayers at the AA and A levels and the men there were not nearly the gentleman that we have here. None of our guys are prima donnas. Team manager Marty Scott wouldn't have it. I kid you not, he wouldn't put up with a real bad attitude."

"So the players are nice guys. Everybody stays positive, even when the season gets a little tough. I think the players make the fans feel good by welcoming them to the park. The St. Paul Saints realize that people are busy in this day and age, and the Saints don't take them for granted.

Nobody is obligated to come to Midway Stadium (the Saints' home ballpark). You need to make the fans feel welcome and do what you can to secure their enjoyment. In the Northern League, the fans are the game."

I told Wardlow that I thought Marty Scott was disappointed by Darryl Strawberry's relapse in his battle with crack addiction. I told him that I was surprised when I heard Marty come down a little bit on Straw for having his continuing battle.

"I could understand Marty feeling that. Here you have Darryl Strawberry, who Marty has helped back to the major leagues, and here Darryl is jeopardizing himself, his family and every-one who believed in him. Here's a guy (Strawberry) who battled cancer and won that fight. That should be enough. Straw should have learned his lesson and moved on. I know Marty was very disappointed in his relapse."

Wardlow is a fan of Matt Nokes, who has played for the Saints for the past couple of years. Matt Nokes has had a ten-year major league career with some tremendous success, but he wore the Saints uniform while looking for another opportunity to make the big show, much like Darryl Strawberry.

Nokes asked for a tryout with the club before the 1998 season, person-ally calling Marty Scott to ask for an

Darryl Strawberry with the St. Paul Saints, 1996.

opportunity. Nokes is a left-batting catcher who can rip a baseball when he is going good.

Nokes had stops in San Francisco, Detroit, New York with the Yankees, Baltimore and Colorado during his major league career. In 1987 he hit 32 home runs with 87 RBI while hitting .289 for the Detroit Tigers. In 1991, while playing for the Yankees, he hit .268 with 24 homers and 77 ribbies. His major league career started to tail off after that year, ending with a batting average in the low .100s in 1995.

Nokes will tell you he wasn't feeling up to par due to injuries in '95. He's still looking for an opportunity to be a major league catcher again, and it's not impossible to picture Nokes as a left-handed DH or pinch-hitter coming off the bench with some pop.

To that end, Nokes has signed a contract with the Cleveland Indians and is reporting to their camp in Homestead, Florida for the 2000 training camp with the Indians. Wardlow, for one, thinks he has a chance. "You've got Sandy Alomar, Jr. behind the plate, and although he's an All Star, his knees are in pretty lousy shape. With Matt Nokes you've got a guy who can catch once in a while and maybe give you some good at-bats. He's a great hitter and I wouldn't bet against him."

In fact, Nokes did well in the Dominican Republic league during the winter, earning his shot with Cleveland. Wardlow wishes Nokes only the best, saying, "He's really a good guy and he's a fine baseball player."

"I've got a little story about Matt that's kind of interesting. One day we were driving from the hotel to the stadium for a ballgame. As we were pulling out of the hotel, Jim Lucas saw Nokes standing around, and Nokes signaled him to pull over. Here's a guy who's a ten-year veteran of the big leagues, who could have called a limo or a cab, but instead he jumped in our car and started regaling us with stories about the Yankees. What it was like to be on the Yankees for five years and play for Steinbrenner, stuff like that. It was great.

"And that's just the way he is. He's a good guy in any league, the kind of guy you hope gets another chance. I wish him the very best."

Matt Nokes' Major League Career

Year	Team	Games	Avg.	HR	RBI
1985	San Francisco	19	.208	2	5
1986	Detroit	7	.333	1	2
1987	Detroit	135	.289	32	87
1988	Detroit	122	.251	16	53
1989	Detroit	87	.250	9	39
1990	Detroit	44	.270	3	8
	NY Yankees	92	.237	3	8
1991	NY Yankees	135	.268	24	77
1992	NY Yankees	121	.224	22	59
1993	NY Yankees	6	.249	10	35
1994	NY Yankees	28	.291	7	19
1995	Baltimore	26	.122	2	6
	Colorado	10	.182	0	0
Totals		**902**	**.254**	**136**	**422**

12

The 1969 Cubs

The greatest team of all time never to win a World Series played in Chicago. The greatest team of all time never to win a World Series didn't win the pennant, either.

The 1969 Chicago Cubs were beaten down the stretch by the "Miracle Mets" who went on to win it all for delirious New Yorkers. As happy as the New York baseball fans were, that was how devastated Chicagoans felt by the Cubs' late season collapse. The Cubs had it all that year with Don Kessinger at shortstop, Glenn Beckert at second, Ron Santo at third, and the wonderful Ernie Banks at first base. Hall of Famer Billy Williams was in left, and while there was a hole in center field, the cubs had a fabulous team and a fiery skipper in Leo Durocher.

Leo may have been a little too fiery. As the team ran into trouble in August, the wheels seemed to come off, and trouble turned into a thorough nose dive in September. The Cubs Manager put a lot of pressure on his players, and some of them did not handle it well. Players and manager, the Cubs folded. It was enough to drive a man to drink!

The Mets were very lucky that they were able to catch the Cubs from ten games back in early August. They were lucky that whenever Tom Seaver pitched, the other team didn't score many runs. The same with Jerry Koosman and Nolan Ryan. They were lucky, I tell you!

As a very young boy I participated in a contest put on by a local newspaper, the late Chicago *Daily News*.

The contest involved picking the date that the Cubs would clinch the pennant, right down to the minute that the historic event would occur. I flooded the mails with postcards (which I can still remember were 3 cents apiece) and made entries calculated to cover the times when Cub games would end, from early September through the end of the season.

I was concerned that the Cubs would clinch the pennant too early, and thus make my methodology obsolete. Those darn Cubs might clinch the pennant in August, they're playing so doggoned well!

Or so I thought in July.

As the season drew to a close, I came to realize that my postcard pursuit was an exercise in futility. The Chicago Cubs had broken down again, and the Amazin' Mets went on to win the World Series. The despondency that afflicted the mythical fans of Mudville fell on Chicago.

The late Steve Goodman, who was an extraordinary folk singer and songwriter (one of the all-time great train songs, "City of New Orleans," is his), and an avid Cubs fan, captured the city's mood when he wrote the following song:

Do they still sing the blues
In Chicago
When baseball season rolls
around?
Do the Cubbies still play
When the snow melts away
In their ivory-covered burial
ground?
When I was a boy they were my
pride and joy
But now they only bring fatigue
To the home of the brave
The land of the free
And the doormats of the
National League.

Despite giving in to the occasional twinge of despondency however, Cub fans, like Boston Red Sox fans, are a pretty tough bunch. We can live for the future. For us it seems no matter how good the prospects may have seemed at the beginning of a season, by September (or earlier) we're convinced that it's next year—always next year!—when our dreams of baseball glory will come true.

Hope springs eternal in the Cubs fan's breast!

How blessed and how fortunate Minnesota was to have two World Series winners within five years. I hope people in the state were grateful for the gift of those championships. It is a part of this state's marvelous sports history.

Heck, the Twins were like the Yankees there for a while!

It *would* be nice to keep them.

CASEY AT THE BAT

The outlook wasn't brilliant for the Mudville nine that day.
The score stood four to two with but one inning more to play.
And then when Cooney died at first, and Barrows did the same
A sickly silence fell upon the patrons of the game.

A straggling few got up to go in deep despair. The rest
Clung to that hope which springs eternal in the human breast;
They thought if only Casey could but get a whack at that—
We'd put up even money now with Casey at the bat.

But Flynn preceded Casey, as did also Jimmy Blake,
And the former was a lulu and the latter was a cake;
So upon that stricken multitude grim melancholy sat,
For there seemed but little chance of Casey's getting to the bat.

But Flynn let drive a single, to the wonderment of all,
And Blake the much despised, tore the cover off the ball;
And when the dust had lifted, and men saw what had occurred
There was Jimmy safe at second and Flynn a-hugging third.

Then from 5,000 throats and more there rose a lusty yell;
It rumbled through the valley, it rattled in the dell;
It knocked upon the mountain and recoiled upon the flat,
For Casey, mighty Casey, was advancing to the bat.

There was ease in Casey's manner as he stepped into his place;
There was pride in Casey's bearing and a smile on Casey's face.
And when, responding to the cheers, he lightly doffed his hat,
No stranger in the crowd could doubt it was Casey at the bat.

Ten thousand eyes were on him as he rubbed his hands with dirt;
Five thousand tongues applauded when he wiped them on his shirt.

Then, while the writhing pitcher ground the ball into his hip,
Defiance gleamed in Casey's eye, a sneer curled Casey's lip.

And now the leather-covered sphere came hurtling through the air,
And Casey stood a-watching it in haughty grandeur there.
Close by the sturdy batsman the ball unheeded sped—
"That ain't my style," said Casey. "Strike one," the umpire said.

From the benches, black with people, there went up a muffled roar,
Like the beating of the storm-waves on a stern and distant shore.
"Kill him! Kill the umpire!" shouted someone in the stand;
and it's likely they'd have killed him had not Casey raised his hand.

With a smile of Christian Charity great Casey's visage shone;
He stilled the rising tumult; he bade the game go on;
He signaled to the pitcher, and once more the spheroid flew;
But Casey still ignored it, and the umpire said, "Strike two."

"Fraud!" cried the maddened thousands, and echo answered fraud;
But one scornful look from Casey and the audience was awed.
They saw his face grow stern and cold, they saw his muscles strain,
And they knew that Casey wouldn't let that ball go by again.

The sneer is gone from Casey's lip, his teeth are clenched in hate;
He pounds with cruel violence his bat upon the plate.
And now the pitcher holds the ball, and now he lets it go,
And now the air is shattered by the force of Casey's blow.

Oh somewhere in this favored land the sun is shining bright;
The band is playing somewhere, and somewhere hearts are light,
And somewhere men are laughing, and somewhere children shout;
But there is no joy in Mudville—mighty Casey has struck out.

"Casey at the Bat," by Earnest L. Thayer
As it appeared in the San Francisco *Examiner*, June 3, 1888. ◎

Ozzie Rosinski:
A Great Ballplayer and
the Hand of Fate

I had the privilege of playing high school baseball with the finest high school athlete I have ever seen. Brian "Ozzie" Rosinski was first team All State in football and, though I can't remember if there was an All State team in baseball, he would have been first team in that sport as well. Ozzie was probably 6'1", about 190 pounds and gifted beyond his years. I think some kids mature faster that others, and Ozzie was a man among boys by his senior year of high school.

Oz was a Phenom. In the fall he led the Evanston High School football team to a top state ranking; in the spring he also led our baseball team to high achievement. I didn't become a starter on the Evanston Varsity until my senior year, while Ozzie had not only started but been a key player for Evanston as a sophomore and was All Conference as a junior. Heck, he may have been All Conference as a sophomore. I can't remember.

This was the old Chicago Suburban League. The Suburban League at that time, and for many years before that, was an outstanding sports conference that produced many fine athletes (John Castino of the Minnesota Twins among them). Evanston Township High School probably had a graduating class of over 1,200 students in 1975. Evanston High School was bigger than a lot of colleges, with a lot of the diversity that Minnesota strives for. Evanston should have had a strong athletic program. There were a lot of talented kids walking through those halls.

None was as talented as Ozzie, though. In our high school lineup, Ozzie was usually third in the batting order; in my senior year I frequently led off or hit second in the order. I was a fair high school player, and I did get on base for Ozzie to drive me around on a number of occasions. I recall once leading off of first base when Ozzie (who was a left-handed hitter) ripped a shot down the first-base line that to this day may be the hardest-hit ball that has ever whizzed by my head. And that wasn't the only one. I learned that on steal attempts I should always look to see what Ozzie might be doing with the ball. It was a matter of safety.

A lot of the time the ball was being deposited into the parking lot *beyond* the right field fence. On a few occasions the ball was being deposited in the street beyond the parking lot beyond the right field fence. He had that kind of power and he had that kind of stroke. Some players, the better players, seem frequently to hit the ball hard, while average players don't hit the ball with full force nearly as often. Ozzie always hit the ball hard.

But he wasn't just a hitter; he had the catlike quickness of a running back and the speed to match. He was an intelligent player who worked on his game every day. I remember watching Ozzie stretch during a practice one day and thinking to myself, I'm lucky to be playing with Oz.

And I was. In addition to being our best athlete, he was one of the nicest people in the whole school. Though he had been a starter for two years on the Evanston team, he never acted as though he was any different, any better, than the rest of us. He was a team player of the highest order.

We fell short of a state title that year (something about a shortstop who missed a tag at second base. I happen to know that tag was made), but we had a good year and won the Suburban League. There was word that Ozzie would be drafted by a major league ballclub and, though I was still just a boy, I knew that this was a big deal and that it would be a wonderful thing. Brian Rosinski was the first draft pick of the Chicago Cubs in the 1975 amateur baseball draft, and the fourth pick overall. Ski was considered the fourth-best unsigned amateur prospect in the United States of America. When the announcement was made over the school intercom I can recall that my homeroom erupted in cheers. Alhough we were kids, we knew that

something wonderful had happened and that it couldn't have happened to a nicer guy.

Ozzie was a lock. Even though statistics tell us that only 5 of the top 100 amateur baseball draftees ever see the major leagues, and only 1 in 100 newly signed professionals will have a successful major league career, Ozzie was a lock. While I was playing college baseball at Northwestern, I occasionally saw him working out in preparation for spring training at the N.U. facilities. He was getting bigger and stronger and he was hanging out with guys like Scott Sanderson and Jack Perconte (a fellow who hit .294 for Seattle in 1984 and who I would run sprints with at N.U.) and other big leaguers who used the facilities during the winter. I remember that Ozzie tore up the Texas league (playing out of Midland, Texas) in what must have been the late 1970s before he moved on to AAA Iowa and the Iowa Cubs.

I'm not clear on all that took place during Ozzie's minor league career. I know that he fought some nagging injuries and was kept on the farm due to promotions or trades that were not in his favor. I know that he performed well at every stage of his minor league journey. I seem to remember that former Cub Ty Waller was promoted ahead of Ozzie, and that perhaps a trade for an over-the-hill Bobby Murcer was not a good thing. I'm not certain of the details. I do know that Ozzie was given his release by the Cubs in the early 1980s and I remember a story that was done for a Chicago weekly in which the author quoted former Cubs General Manager Bob Kennedy as saying something to the effect that "Rosinski was a great prospect. He could play the game of baseball. I remember going to Iowa and seeing him hit a tremendous home run off a pitcher that was among the longest balls I had ever seen hit there. I know that I remember it, and the pitcher, he probably remembers it, and I'm sure that Ozzie remembers it. But we may be the only people that remember it.

"Call it life, or call it the facts of a baseball career."

Why would the fact that Ozzie never made it bother me as much as it does? Part of it was Kennedy's comment. It struck me as unfeeling at the time and it still does. But was it really? In town ball, there are lots of guys who might have made it. Who would have or could have or should have made it. In some ways, I'm one of them. We didn't make it, we never came as close as Brian Rosinski, and you have to move on with your life. The last time I saw Ozzie he was raising a nice family. (He told me that he'd be a grandfather before I had kids. So far he's right.)

He's a first-class guy, the best high school ballplayer I have ever seen, and he didn't quite make it. And that is life.

Mike Pearson, Gophers Shortstop

Mike Pearson was a shortstop for the University of Minnesota during the mid-1980s. Growing up in St. Peter, Minnesota, he was a rival of the Steinbach bothers (Tom, Tim and Terry, who later became a catcher for the Twins) before they ended up at the University of Minnesota together. Mike is cognizant of the great traditions at the University of Minnesota.

"I enjoy being a part of the tradition that is University of Minnesota baseball, a tradition that includes Paul Molitor, Dave Winfield, Terry Steinbach, and a long list of exceptional players and people," Pearson said. "It was a wonderful experience to be part of two Big 10 championships during my time at the University. I know that U of M baseball is a special program."

But, in Pearson's opinion, it's not a perfect program. "I believe that, at least in my era, there was a lack of personal interest in the ballplayers. I may be speaking only for myself, but the program didn't provide any opportunity for me to go to the next level. At that time the program let down some players who wanted to continue playing the game professionally. There was no discussion of how to continue my baseball career. There was no discussion of why I wasn't drafted and what might be available to me if I desired to continue playing.

"I wanted to keep playing baseball. I think I had the talent to at least get a shot at the minor league level. In some ways I feel the program let me down in that regard.

"What I am trying to say is, players don't spend any time with baseball scouts. My job, as a player, was simply to go 100 percent all the time and let the chips fall where they may.

"Coaches are the contact for the people involved in an athletic program. It's the function of the school to promote the organization. Mankato State outperformed the University of Minnesota in this department when I was a player. We were the Big 10 champions and not much happened for the players.

"Dean Boyer, the coach down in Mankato, rewarded his players for dedication and commitment to the team. I'm left to believe that more could have been done to market the players who wanted to stay in the game."

It's probably worth noting that when Pearson played for the Gophers, John Anderson was a "green" young coach barely older than his players. Could Anderson have done more as far as marketing his players to scouts for the big leagues? Maybe. But, personally, I remind myself that, when I was playing baseball at Northwestern, I thought I might have

what it takes to make it to the majors. Now, as I reflect on what I've learned from several years of covering baseball as a journalist and playing the game as an amateur, I realize I was simply not quite there as a player.

...and a Couple That Came to Pass

Mark Loretta, Milwaukee Brewers

Mark Loretta is a Northwestern University graduate who was an All-American shortstop while at Northwestern, as well as the Big Ten Player of the Year in 1994. He's been hitting around .300 for the Milwaukee Brewers, largely in a utility role.

"I hope I'm not being labeled," said Loretta.

I don't think he has a label as a utility player yet. The Brewers don't seem to have a regular place for him to play, so Loretta ends up playing first base one game of a series against the Twins, shortstop the next and maybe some second base before they leave town. He's a quality ballplayer whose long and graceful throws from deep short remind me of a young Molitor in Milwaukee.

Mark is a tough-looking ballplayer on the field but a soft-spoken gentleman off the field. During a conversation with him behind the batting cage, he reminded me very much of the kid I saw at Northwestern's Rocky Miller Field in Evanston, Illinois.

I hear some of the other Milwaukee Brewers refer to Loretta as "Lo." One of them is Milwaukee shortstop Jose Valentin, whose brother Javier Valentin is a catcher for the Twins. Hopefully, Javier can develop the power his brother has displayed for the Brewers. Mark Loretta is backing up a veteran shortstop who is high quality and possesses a strong bat.

"Lo is a good man," says Jose Valentin. "He's helping us, he's learning everyday," Jose says with a smile as he heads into the batting cage. On this night, June 25, 1998, Loretta is leading off and playing second base for the Brew Crew. He hits a rocket back up the middle that Twins starting pitcher Brad Radke can't quite handle. It is Radke's first career error after 142 chances in the big leagues.

"Radke is a great fielding pitcher," Loretta says later, "I feel kind of bad about that (ending his errorless streak)."

A Milwaukee writer asks me how I know Loretta. I toot my own horn and tell him that we were both shortstops at Northwestern University.

"He went a little farther in baseball than you did," the writer guessed.

I didn't answer; he can draw his own conclusions.

The Milwaukee writer watched Loretta handle a chance in the field and said, "He's the one guy everybody in the league would like to have on their team. Right now (late 1998), he's inexpensive and he plays good baseball. The Brewers are going to do everything they can to keep him."

Joe Girardi, Yankees

Baseball is not a game that can be played well if you are tight. You need to be relaxed to play baseball, at any level of the game. To that effect, the New York Yankees play a bizarre game of pepper that gets everyone involved, laughing and loose.

Every time I see the Yankees they strike me as being the most easy-going of any major league team. I always see a lot of laughter and fun shared by Yankee players before Twins games, which is kind of surprising.

We so frequently hear of troubles in the Yankee organization. These guys make a ton of money, and perhaps Steinbrenner has bought his way to team happiness. There is no question that the little boy inside every New York Yankee player is alive and well. The Yankees have the appearance of a healthy team.

Yankee catcher Joe Girardi looked like Roger Maris on the day I spoke with him. He had the crew cut of Maris, but I hesitated to ask if he was going for a Maris-like look. He might not have been, so I decided to shut up.

The Yankees are real sticklers for utilizing their exercise bungee straps;

"We swear by them," Girardi said, "you've got to be loose to play the game."

Joe played his college ball at Northwestern University, and came up to the major leagues with the Chicago Cubs. I had a chance to see him play a few times in college and I saw his first game in the big leagues with Chicago. I remember when Joe tried to help the home-plate umpire clean off home plate. Dirt must have remained on the plate, because the umpire pushed Girardi out of the way and swept it again.

Joe Girardi was the first player from Northwestern to make the majors in some time. I don't know who the last player was before Joe, and I remember a great feeling of pride when he caught his first pitch in the Bigs. For the year 2000, he returns to catch for the Cubs.

On August 23, 1999, Girardi knocked in seven runs for the New York Yankees in a single game. That gave him 20 total RBI's for the year through late August. Prior to his big game, Joe had gone 0 for 17 and was 13 for 158 for the year. His four hits in six at-bats boosted his average to .223. Joe really needed to have a big game, obviously. I know that sharing time with Jorge Posada was bothering Joe, his playing time was being further reduced in the playoffs, and the move to Chicago should be a good one for him.

13

THE GAME TODAY

People

Tony Clark

Detroit Tigers first-baseman Tony Clark is a batting practice sultan. The big left-handed hitter is a dynamo in BP and is improving as a prime time player.

One day around the cage, a ball escaped from Clark's glove and rolled over to where I was standing. At once, I picked up the ball and flipped it to the 6'6" Clark. "Thank you, sir," said the massive Detroit slugger.

I was almost shocked. No one says thank you around the batting cage, except Paul Molitor and a couple of other Twins. I have never heard a compliment from the Twins opposition for any reason. There was something so incongruous about his genuine thanks for my simple gesture.

Tony Clark has picked up a fan for life. I liked him anyway, so I hope that he doesn't end up making too much money or doing something that will cause his personality to make a transition into "overpaid big shot" mode.

Brady Anderson

When Brady Anderson was with the Baltimore Orioles in 1996 he hit fifty home runs, more than tripling his previous home run high in the major leagues. I'm sure he was "seeing the ball better," and that his "wrist got quicker," but there is a feeling around the game that he must have done something more than merely improve his stroke.

Some people in baseball believe that Brady Anderson did something to improve his physical makeup. If he was taking Creatine, and that nutritional supplement made that kind of a difference, then perhaps I could use it. I don't, and never have, had any power. Maybe I could grow some muscles, some real muscles, and start experiencing the thrill of hitting the ball out of the park consistently in senior ball.

But, what if the wrong parts of my body start growing, or hair starts sprouting on the bottom of my feet?

There are no scientific studies that can predict what these supplements will do to the human body years down the road. I guess I don't want to chance it.

Some guys just have it naturally. I'm not one of them, but I guess that's OK. I've got my health and I'm not willing to jeopardize it for amateur baseball. Now, would I think differently if I were a pro?

Phil Tasch: A Common but Very Personal Problem

My senior ballplaying friend Phil Tasch was talking about the spitting and groin-grabbing that goes on at all levels of baseball. "I go to Little League games and the kids are grabbing at their crotches. I've played for a long time, and I've noticed that when I set myself at the plate, I just can't stop myself. I just have to hitch up my jock strap a little bit. I think it's a primal male thing. And when I'm out in the field, I find myself spitting—even after I told myself not to spit because my wife is watching the game and lately she is telling me that I spit too much. Next thing you know, she's going to be telling me to stop hitching up. I'm going to have to really focus on quitting the spitting and the groin-grabbing."

Just Like Old Times

The Quicksteps play costumed exhi-bition games using 1860s rules throughout Minnesota. All of the Quicksteps members are members of The Society of American Baseball Research (SABR) and most members are historians to some extent. Bob Tholkas and Jim Wyman speak as members of the Quicksteps. The author is a member of SABR and plays with the Quicksteps.

Bob Tholkes

Bob Tholkes is the founding father of the Quicksteps old-time baseball team, and a fair left-handed hitter in his own right. His wife is the official custumer of the Quicksteps and is responsible for the historically accurate, yet unbelievably pink uniforms that we wear.

The baseball historians, of whom Tholkas is one, care about the game today, and in many cases are fans of big-league teams.

"A new stadium won't work without other fundamental economic changes. There's a dire lack of consistent revenue streams. Baseball needs to right itself and the Twins could then develop side revenues they have lacked in the past. I'm talking about stadium naming rights and the like.

"If baseball wants to maintain the current number of franchises (thirty), there will have to be revenue sharing; and it seems to me that a shake-out is still likely. I'm okay with 24 teams, or even 20 teams (he laughs), because the

The Quicksteps assemble for battle.

dilution of talent that I believe we are seeing today would be less apparent.

"I don't see people like George Steinbrenner wanting to share any of his local money, unless revenue sharing is the lesser of some other evils proposed by the owners or Bud Selig in his expanded commissioners role.

"Why would Steinbrenner want to change? He has leverage, he's winning World Series championships, things are pretty good in New York.

"The Players Union is a typical union in that it tries to do the best it can for its members. They can't mandate these huge free agent contracts, it's the owners who pay them. How can you fault the players for taking what they are given?

"The game of baseball is a lot more than what is going on in the major leagues at any particular time. It would be wonderful if the players would realize that and make some concessions. I don't know if that's going to happen, or if it will happen in time. Baseball may be returning to its grass roots state sooner than we think."

Jim Wyman

Jim Wyman is a member of SABR as well as a Quickstep. The 48-year-old first baseman from New Hampshire says "I'll play baseball anywhere, any time there is a game that needs me.

"I used to listen to the Boston Red Sox on the radio all the time when I was a kid. They used to have a pre-game memories show, and I loved that program. I'm a Red Sox fan, and that's not much different than being a Cubs fan. There haven't been a whole lot of titles.

"I just love to play ball. You can ask the other Quicksteps about my shagging balls in the summer heat in Phoenix, Arizona when the temperature was 100 something degrees. And I loved it! Just show me a field and let's play ball. Playing for the Quicksteps is enjoyable both for the baseball and the interaction with the public. SABR encourages the teaching of the history of the game, so we are all a part of that. Baseball has a long, deep history.

"Right now it looks like the Yankees are going to win the next twenty World Series, if you know what I mean. I could name five teams and be certain that one of them is going to win the World Series this year. The best owner for a ballclub the way the game is now, unfortunately, is a wealthy individual who can treat the game as a hobby and who isn't dependent on outside capital.

"The political climate at the moment is hands-off business. Congress won't look at it right now. If some franchises fold, or if the Yankees win a couple more in a row, then the Congress may stir. As far as a new ballpark in the Twin Cities, I would like to

Tony Oliva still has it! August 1999

see it done right. The Twins' fan support seems to be contingent on winning. If they're not a good ballclub, there's a lot of apathy. It's not like with the Red Sox or the Cubs. That's not good for getting a new facility, and fair-weather fans might not support a lousy team in a new ballpark."

A Neighborhood Ballpark

There is a wonderful ball field within a few yards of the front door of my home in Richfield, Minnesota, an inner-ring suburb of Minneapolis.

The backstop is adjacent to the historic Bartholomew house, which has been on its present foundation since 1852—ancient, by Minnesota standards. The site on which the ball field sits was farmland for more than 100 years, until around 1960, when it was acquired by the Richfield school system, which turned it into a baseball diamond. It's a full-size field of dimensions suitable for high school ball, for which it is still used. I think the Richfield High freshmen play there now. Perhaps because of its agricultural history it is nice and flat, with a minimum of rocks. "Lyndale Field" (named for the street that runs parallel to the first-base line) is a solid little ball-yard that I first noticed when I was visiting the home that I later purchased; Lyndale field was a selling point in the eventual procurement of my present digs.

In some ways it feels like my own personal practice field. This is largely due to the fact that for long stretches of the summer, I'm the only person using it, as I continue to prepare for my senior town ball league. In two full summers of playing in the park, I have yet to see a pick-up game break out.

There's just never anybody around to play with. Yes, some organized teams use the field for league games and a lot of soccer is played on the grounds (both organized and pick-up games), but I have never seen the kind of spontaneous, pick-up baseball game that I remember from my youth. I'm talking about the "you pick first, no-holds-barred, just for fun" kind of ballgame that can be played by perhaps eight or ten kids. With maybe two outfielders and the backstop is the catcher. First base is an extra glove, second and third bases a hat or glove as well.

When I go over to the park on a summer day, after the high school season is over and the weather in the Land of 10,000 Lakes has grown warm and humid and slightly buggy. I like to stretch out and drive balls off the batting tee to imaginary safe outfield landings.

The tee provides pitching with a velocity I can almost always handle, and the vast outfield expanse (it's well over 400 feet to a neighbor's barbecue pit just beyond the left field boundary, a rather short 360 to the street in right) affords a similar accommodation to my stroke as I picture myself spraying the balls from my ball-bag to all fields. Most everything drops in for a hit, usually for extra bases. Nobody ever throws me out, which is to be expected when the only defense is ankle-high blades of grass. Occasionally, I enjoy the company of a young fellow from the neighborhood who likes to shag baseballs for me.

I sometimes lift fly balls to this young guy, whose age I guess to be about twelve. He must live near the park because he always arrives after I've gotten started on my exercises. He circles dizzily under any fly ball too high for him, but he is a game little guy who doesn't back off from the hardball in play. He throws better then he catches, doesn't hit too badly off the tee for his age and size, but needs work in all areas so he can progress.

He used to play in a league, he says, but not any more. The idea of a pick-up game is foreign to him. "You have to have a team" he said.

"No you don't," I said. "You need to get a few of your friends to come around."

He points at me and says "You're around a lot."

Yeah, I think to myself, I guess I am. Now we need five or six more.

Umpires Make a Bad Call

Umpires feel unappreciated in today's baseball environment. Or at least they did when they decided to go on strike in July 1999. Twenty-two Major League Baseball umpires lost their jobs the following September when baseball called their bluff and gave them their pink slips. Almost as quickly as the umpires threatened to resign, it became obvious that their strike was a very bad idea. What the umpires seem to have forgotten is that they could be replaced, and that they generally were not viewed as sympathetic figures, either by the fans or by most players.

Part of this is due to the fact that the older umpires seemed tired and lazy at times. It's sad that the umpires have been let go, because there are families and livelihoods involved, but the newer umps—particularly the younger ones—seem to be better umpires, showing more hustle and energy than old veterans like the Twins' nemesis Greg Kosc or big Ken Kaiser. Perhaps the corps of new umpires will at least develop a consistent strike zone and view themselves less as the stars of the show.

Saint Thomas coach Dennis Denning remembers watching a baseball game on television during the 1998 season in which Kaiser was working a game that pitted the Chicago White Sox against the Los

Angeles Dodgers in an interleague contest. Denning remembers relaxing in his rec room, watching the first inning as the White Sox pitcher took the mound. "It might have been the pitcher's first pitch of the game. It was a fastball and it must have been deceptive, you know how they sometimes look like they're rising, and it went off the tip of the catcher's glove. I'll be doggoned if it didn't hit Ken Kaiser right in the mask. Boy, he just flipped out. Oh man was he mad. He was walking around huffing and puffing—being a baby in my opinion—

when the catcher finally got his attention and asked him for a new baseball. You could almost see the hostility in Kaiser's eyes as he just flipped the ball about 15 feet in front of home plate. Well, the pitcher and the catcher are just standing there in disbelief, you could see it. So the pitcher finally goes in and gets the baseball and walks back out to the mound.

"So he winds up and fires another fastball. It hits the catcher right in the glove, a perfect pitch, just right down the middle. Kaiser doesn't move and finally sticks out two fin-

UMPIRES WHO LOST THEIR JOBS

American League (9): Drew Coble, Jim Evans, Dale Ford, Rich Garcia, Ed Hickox, Mark Johnson, Ken Kaiser, Greg Kosc, Larry McCoy.

National League (13): Gary Darling, Bob Davidson, Bruce Dreckman, Eric Gregg, Tom Hallion, Bill Hohn, Sam Holbrook, Paul Nauert, Larry Poncino, Frank Pulli, Terry Tata, Larry Vanover, Joe West.

UMPIRES WHO ARE NEW HIRES

American League (12): Ted Barrett, Eric Cooper, Feldin Culbreth, Laz Diaz, Mike DiMuro, Doug Eddings, Mike Everitt, Marty Foster, Bill Miller, Brian OíNora, Jim Reynolds, Bill Welke.

National League (13): C.B. Bucknor, Mark Carlson, Phil Cuzzi, Paul Emmel, Andrew Fletcher, Greg Gibson, Marvin Hudson, Ron Kulpa, Alfonzo Marquez, Tony Randazzo, Brian Runge, Mark Wegner, Hunter Wendelstedt.

gers for ball two. His face is revealing total defiance.

"So here comes another pitch and it's the same thing. Right down the middle. Of course, he calls it ball three and I'm thinking to myself 'my goodness!' Well, at this point (manager) Terry Bevington comes out of the White Sox dugout and before he gets within twenty feet of Kaiser, Ken makes the big gesture saying *you're out of the game!'* It was complete histrionics," Denning said.

Denning further explained what he thought he had seen. "It must have been that Kaiser thought that they had let the first one hit him on purpose. I think there is no way that's the case; not the first pitch of the game. You don't want to turn the umpire against you right from the get-go. I'm not saying it has never happened or never could, but if it does, it's going to happen later in the game when the outcome has already been determined. You don't draw the line in the sand before the game begins."

I asked Denning if he thought the umpiring might improve as the new guys get settled in.

"Absolutely," Denning said "without a doubt. It's got to improve. I don't think they do as good a job as they could, and I know they don't do as good a job as they think they do. They need to stop thinking that they're the show. They're not. It's a great job being a major league umpire, a lot of these guys are making well into six figures. And when they've put ten years in as an umpire, they get a tremendous pension. As part of their contract they also receive something like a week of paid vacation for every year that they have worked."

"A lot of those guys, they're not going to be missed."

Spoken like a true coach.

The umpires made a very bad call when they resigned en masse in an attempt to improve their bargaining position with Major League Baseball. Baseball accepted the resignations that were submitted by 56 of the 66 umpires and said goodbye. Nine American League umpires and 13 National League umpires lost their jobs effective September 1, 1999.

Richie Phillips, the president of the Major League Umpires Association, argued that when baseball accepted the resignations, its actions were "reprehensible and oppressive," and said that, "Executing surrendered prisoners is indicative of the mindset of baseball today that has led us (the umpires) to the position we're in."

Umpires are a necessary part of the game, but they are not the reason the fans attend baseball games at the major league level. It's a very sad situation for the umpires and for their families, but members of the Association made the decision to follow as Richie Phillips led them into an abyss. "The Association isn't run by the members of the union, it's run by Richie Phillips."

The umpires' strategy never had a chance, and it ended up costing several of them their livelihoods.

The umpires became competitors with the fans for attention. They ran their own little show and became a large part of the strike zone problem that has lengthened games so dramatically. Every umpire has his own strike zone that he believes to be the proper strike zone.

THE YANKEES: DOES ANYONE ELSE HAVE A CHANCE?

Was there money to be made by betting on Kansas City to have a better record than Minnesota in 1999? A donkey would have been less of a long-shot against Secretariat in his prime than the Twins beating out the Yankees for the World Series. These Las Vegas numbers should be alarming to Major League Baseball as well as to the average fan. How much joy is there in watching a team that has absolutely no chance to compete for the grand prize? Note the accurate predictability of the top two. Why even bother to play the regular season?

Team	Odds	Team	Odds
N.Y. Yankees	2:1	Boston	500:1
Atlanta	4:1	San Francisco	500:1
Cleveland	7:1	Toronto	500:1
Los Angeles	12:1	Detroit	15,000:1
Baltimore	15:1	San Diego	30,000:1
Texas	15:1	Philadelphia	50,000:1
Anaheim	20:1	Oakland	100,000:1
Houston	20:1	Milwaukee	200,000:1
Arizona	25:1	Montreal	500,000:1
N.Y. Mets	10:1	Pittsburgh	1 million:1
Chicago Cubs	30:1	Chicago White Sox	5 million:1
Colorado	30:1	Minnesota	10 million:1
Seattle	35:1	Tampa Bay	25 million:1
Cincinnati	40:1	Kansas City	50 million:1
St. Louis	50:1	Florida	100 million:1

14

STADIUM ISSUES: IF WE BUILD IT, WILL THEY COME?

Will Cannon: A Fan's View of a Missed Opportunity

A friend of mine, Will Cannon, whose opinions on Twin Cities issues are informed by years of living and working on both sides of the river separating the towns, observed that St. Paul missed the boat in the way it directed its pro-referendum campaign. Will was sad that the referendum failed, and viewed the defeat as an opportunity missed by the capital city. His feeling was that the referendum supporters' approach had been all wrong, that the media campaign was shortsighted.

"All you heard from the Twins and (Mayor) Norm Coleman was how wonderful having the Twins in St. Paul would be for business and for the core city. If you want people to give you money for a stadium, don't talk to them about a few new restaurants or bars or a new business or two," Will said.

"They've heard all that talk; it just doesn't move them to action. To get

at their wallets, you've got to give them something with a deeper meaning. They (St. Paul officials) should have sold the package as a pro-St. Paul vote, in that St. Paul has the opportunity to take the Twins right out of Minneapolis.

"We'll take that club right out from under 'em, and we'll have one-half the Twin Cities' major-league sports action right here, with a brand new hockey team and a brand new baseball facility with the Twins playing in it."

In a way it makes some sense. Given the rivalry between the two river towns, why not sell a ballpark plan as an exclusive opportunity to seriously tweak the do-nothings on the other side of the bridge? St. Paul could be known for the next few decades as the home of the Stanley Cup-contending Minnesota Wild, and the two-time World Champion Minnesota Twins in their new digs. A gem of a ballpark squired away from the snobs in Minneapolis. With the failure of the St. Paul ballpark referendum, the opportunity to pull a fast one on "Big Minny" appears to be gone.

There is, of course, a certain irony in these comments. The fact is, a new ballpark would benefit both Minneapolis and St. Paul, as well as baseball fans in the entire region, no matter where it is located. When Major League Baseball leaves the state, all baseball fans will suffer a loss.

The Twin Cities' approach to the issue seems to be a case of cutting off your nose to spite your face.

Peter Gammons: "Something's got to give."

Peter Gammons is a guru among baseball media people. He has acquired that designation deservedly, in my opinion, because of his diligent work around the game and because he

METRODOME ODDITIES

May 4, 1999 was a historic day at the Metrodome. It was the fifteenth anniversary of the day Dave Kingman hit a ball into the one of the Metrodome roof drainage holes during a 4th inning at-bat. The ball never came down and Kingman was awarded a ground rule double by the umpires.

Ah, the Metrodome. On April 14, 1983 the roof deflated due to a tear caused by heavy Minnesota snows and a scheduled game with the California Angels was postponed. It stands as the only postponement in Metrodome baseball history.

On April 26, 1986 the roof suffered a slight tear due to high winds, causing a nine-minute delay in the bottom of the seventh inning, again verses the Angels.

On May 30, 1992 Detroit's Rob Deer popped out to shortstop Greg Gagne in consecutive at-bats, with both balls ricocheting off the ceiling.

On July 5, 1992 Minnesota's Chili Davis hit a towering fly ball to deep right field vs. Baltimore's Rick Sutcliffe. The ball bounced off a speaker in play and caromed to second-baseman Mark McLemore, who made the catch in shallow right field for an out, robbing Mr. Davis of what would have been a sure home run.

Ouch!!

shows up everywhere Major League Baseball is going on. And minor league ball, too, as I discovered when he impressed me with his knowledge of Twins prospect Michael Cuddyer at the 1999 All Star game. He's ubiquitous, and he knows his stuff.

Gammons expressed concern about the Major League Baseball situation in the Twin Cities.

"The area needs a team ownership in there that wants the ballclub. Yes, Minneapolis-St. Paul is a small big city, but it's not a tiny market, and it is a baseball town. You've got a lot of *Fortune 500* money around there that should get involved. You need a ballpark and you need an ownership that truly wants to win," Gammons said.

O.K. Peter, that makes sense, but what about a public that frankly doesn't seem to care much about the success of the Twins? Public money for a ballpark, in any form, is looking like a longshot.

"I've sensed that, and I've sensed that everybody's been so beaten down that the frustration levels are high. But I still think there's a future for baseball there—who can forget '87 or '91— and the Twins have got some good young players, some terrific guys in the minor leagues.

"Something has got to give for baseball to continue to flourish in that market. I certainly hope baseball remains in the Twin Cities."

Socrates Babacas

Socrates Babacas (which rhymes with abacus, which is appropriate because he probably uses an abacus to figure out his financing) is a Greek tycoon, at least in his own mind. He claims that he has bought an option on farmland near Lino Lakes, Minnesota, where he plans to build a combination football and baseball facility. But when he called a press conference in early January 2000, attendance was sparse, and no one from either the Minnesota Twins or the Minnesota Vikings showed up. In response to a question as to why neither organization had bothered to send anyone to a conference involving the construction of a facility for their teams, Babacas said "I don't know. I think the Vikings are busy, they are in the playoffs."

And what about the Twins, Socrates?

"I don't know."

Babacas, who sees himself as a can-do type of individual, has a reputation for trying to buy professional sports teams. He has had failures in other locations, and it strikes me that it is not a good sign that the media depend on, or even pay attention to, individuals with so little credibility. When asked about possible financing for his new facility, Socrates showed that he should be respected for his honesty.

His response was "none of your business."

Well, Socrates, financing is a big question around here, and while "none of your business" is honest, it's none too satisfying.

Perhaps Socrates should accompany John Rocker, whose comments about minorities and gays led to a decision by Major League Baseball to insist upon counseling, en route to whoever it is that is examining heads. And maybe I should go too, because I attended this press conference thinking that there may be something to it. That tells me that my hopes have gotten pretty far ahead of reality.

Perhaps we should charter a large bus so that we can take the owners of professional sports franchises with us on our visit to the shrink. Owners who pay exorbitant salaries to ballplayers who frequently don't live up to expectations should have their heads examined as well. Shawn Green is a great ballplayer, as good an all-around player as any in the game. But why would the Dodgers pay Shawn Green such an exorbitant salary after their experience of 1999, when an $80 million payroll didn't even get them close to making the playoffs? In '99 the Dodgers signed left-hander Carlos Perez to a $15.5 million three-year contract, and then optioned him to the minor leagues during the season *with a 2-10 record.*

We may not find Carl Pohlad on the bus to the shrink, by the way. The Twins don't pay $5 million for anybody (except perhaps Brad Radke in a long-term deal). I'm inclined to say "good". They may not be winners, but perhaps they are just trying to stay sane in an increasingly insane game.

Herb Carneal: We Need a Roof

"You need a retractable roof," Herb Carneal said. "People tell me, 'Herb, I really miss the old Met Stadium and the wonderful times I had at that ballpark'. But I wonder, do they miss the night games in April when it was thirty-five degrees at game time and increasingly colder as the night wore on?

"I have a feeling that people today might be a little too spoiled to put up with that on a regular basis early in the year. If we get a new ballpark in the Twin Cities, and if it isn't cost-prohibitive, I've got to think that a retractable roof would be a very good idea," Carneal said.

"Hey, don't get me wrong. I love outdoor baseball, but let's face it, you don't get the best bang for your buck if it's freezing cold or the wind is blowing forty miles per hour in springtime, which happens around here."

I don't know, Herb. I grew up going to ballgames at Wrigley Field, and that wind does come a-howling off of Lake Michigan in the spring. Some of those cold days in April are among my favorite memories at my favorite ballpark. And I remember some beautiful days as well.

I'm concerned that some men who are close to the action, such as Herb Carneal, feel a retractable roof is necessary.

Tom Tuttle: No, We Don't

I, for one, do not believe that the Twins must have a retractable roof in a new ballpark. I am in essence a fan of the elements, of all that is part and parcel of outdoor baseball. Don't get me wrong, I don't like to suffer through an athletic event in miserable weather any more than the next person. I'm just not one who insists on the need for a roof when the temperature dips or when the weather becomes otherwise inclement, as it frequently does throughout the North.

I have been to a number of Chicago Cubs ballgames in Wrigley Field when the elements did not favor humans. I remember some very brisk opening days, and a number of chilly days later in April. And I remember some of those dates and those ballgames with great affection.

A look back at Minnesota Twins home openers at the old and beloved Metropolitan Stadium, all played in April from 1962 to 1981, reveals a number of interesting facts about the weather on those occasions. Of the

TEN THINGS TO LOVE ABOUT THE DOME

The top ten favorite things about the Hubert H. Humphrey Metrodome:

1. Only chance of a rainout is if the sprinkler system fails.
2. Parking never a problem: nobody is there.
3. Great music during batting practice. Excellent acoustics.
4. Easy-going grounds people who talk to you.
5. Peg's kielbasa in the pressbox.
6. Absolutely no fear of sunburn.
7. Good chance of catching batting practice home run— not much competition.
8. Tom Kelly throwing batting practice.
9. Twins beating expensive clubs with kids.
10. Memories of 1987 and 1991. ◍

20 openers held at the Met, only one was played in 30-degree temperatures, while the temperature was in the 40s five times, the 50s eight times, the 60s three times, the 70s twice and even in the 80s on one occasion. In fact, on April 22nd, 1980 the game-time temperature was 89 with west winds gusting up to 35 mph. Over 36,000 sweltering fans saw the Twins defeat the Angels 8-1.

By contrast, the coldest opener at the Met was on April 14th, 1962, when the mercury hovered at 35 degrees, with strong winds out of the north making it feel even colder. Fewer than 10,000 people watched the California Angels defeat the Twins 12-5. Of the 20 openers, only one had a temperature below 44 degrees; 19 of the 20 openers were warmer.

My point is that this is doable for a baseball fan. True, there are many fans who would not want to attend an outdoor ballgame if the temperature were below 60 degrees. Fine. Those fans are not essential to a franchise's success. Those fans can and should attend when the comfort level is more to their liking. All major league teams really butter their bread between Memorial Day and Labor Day.

The retractable roof is a sticking point for some who believe that baseball has got away from the essentials. A retractable roof is an amenity, not a necessity. The retractable roof increases the cost of a ballpark by a minimum of $100 million. I, for one, can live without that particular accouterment.

Tom Mee: A Twins Guy Who Likes the Dome

Twins public address announcer Tom Mee is a former public relations director with the team. Tom has watched the Twins play for a long time and knows the ballclub, and the individuals who have made up the organization, as well as anyone.

Mee is a true baseball man with a quiet strength about him; he's easy to talk to and was courteous enough to share his media dining room table with me on several occasions in 1998 and 1999. One gets the feeling when talking to him that he knows more than he lets on.

The comforting voice of Tom Mee is a familiar one in the press box. It's Tom who reports at game time that, "Outside, it's forty-two degrees. Inside the Metrodome, it's seventy degrees." Sometimes, of course, he has to say something like, "The outside temperature is seventy-seven degrees; inside the Metrodome it's seventy degrees." Those are the days when the weather outside is beautiful and it is difficult to come into the dome to watch a baseball game. Minnesota has a great number of those days in the summertime.

Nevertheless, Mee is okay with the HHH Metrodome. "I suppose it's a little selfish, but I like it," he said. "The working conditions in the Metrodome are always the same. There is a consistency to the experience of working in the Metrodome, both for media people and for the ballplayers."

Yes, there is no question that the Metrodome creates an ideal working environment for the media and for people, such as the P.A announcer, who have game-related jobs to perform.

Tom appreciates the likelihood that a new ballpark will be needed for the team to continue in the Twin Cities. He is a firm believer in the necessity of a retractable roof.

"It would be foolhardy not to have a retractable roof on any ballpark that may be constructed," Mee said. "Given the weather that we have in this area, you need to put a covering on any structure to keep out the elements at the beginning and end of the year," he added. Without a roof, "we won't be able to sell advanced tickets for September, not in this market."

I mentioned to Tom that the weather wasn't guaranteed when the Twins were new to Minnesota, but the fans did show up in droves then to watch games outside in the fresh air. Mee agreed: "We led the American League in attendance from 1961 to 1970. I think those ten years were honeymoon years, and when people traveled a great distance to come to the old Metropolitan Stadium, they were taking a chance.

"But those days may be over," Mee said. "The fans are more sophisticated now. We need to assure the fans who travel, sometimes large distances, that the products they're buying will be on the shelf when they get here. The Minnesota Twins rely on the five-state market (Iowa, Wisconsin, North and South Dakota), and don't forget about Canada.

"I believe the everyday, regular fans of the Twins appreciate the Metrodome," Mee said, expanding on his rationale for the importance of an indoor venue. "There is a consistency to the experience for the fans as well. We had some tremendous times in 1987 and 1991; remember, we drew three million fans in 1992.

"There are those for whom baseball is a 'holiday' event. They come to the park when there is a perfect day once or twice a year and that will be about it. The team can't make a living off those fans."

Mee continued, "You know Phoenix built the Bank One ballpark with a half-cent sales tax that will be paid up by the year 2000. That's reasonable. They've got a retractable roof."

I don't agree with Tom about the Metrodome or about covered stadiums, but I respect and understand his sentiments.

A Stadium in Downtown St. Paul? It Makes Sense

I find the rivalry between Minneapolis and St. Paul to be foolish, bordering on immature. I have never understood the sometimes heated disagreements between the towns on opposite sides of the Mississippi River.

I suppose this is due to the fact that I am not from the Twin Cities, and in fact not from Minnesota. I understand that the rivalry, justified or not, is a tangible consideration for teams locating their professional sports franchises. I would like to see a lovely gem of a ballpark near the river in one of the Twin Towns; either city would do, but it seems to me that St. Paul would benefit greatly from a Major League Baseball team.

When I moved to Minnesota I often measured the distance between St. Paul and Minneapolis on my automobile odometer. Usually it would come out to 12 miles, sometimes 11, but the distance between the two towns cannot be measured in mere miles. It must be measured in degrees of separation.

As I said, I don't get it. Driving down Kellogg Boulevard in St. Paul, I see the brand spanking new hockey arena, with the glass gleaming against the wintry sky. It looks wonderful and will be a great addition to the vitality of St. Paul's downtown core and to the night life that frequently appears to be barely in existence in the capital city.

St. Paul needs people downtown. One Saturday evening this past winter I was in central St. Paul and needed to call a taxicab from one of the major hotels, the Radisson. On a Saturday night it took 15 minutes for a taxicab to arrive to transport us to our destination. That's not good. I asked the cabby why it took so long to get a cab at the big hotel. "There's never too many people looking for a cab in downtown St. Paul," he replied. "Most of the guys feel they will do better at the airport."

I can understand why all of the cab drivers are down at Minneapolis/ St. Paul International. *There isn't anybody in downtown St. Paul.* That's not to say that there aren't some wonderful things about the downtown area; there are. The Ordway Theater, the Science Museum, the Landmark Center and fine dining with immediate seating are all there. But for whatever reason, it's difficult for Minnesotans to envision St. Paul's downtown as a destination.

Walking the skyway that evening, we never saw another human being. This was not in the middle of the night. This was at 8:00 p.m. on a Saturday. We never saw another human being in the half-mile or so that we walked in the skyway between hotels. You could have shot a cannon down the skyway and been at no risk of injuring another human being. Even if the imaginary cannon ball broke though a glass window of the skyway and fell onto a street, it likely would strike nothing but the pavement.

Much has been made about the unusual design features of the capitol. The streets, for example, were laid out, as our Governor has observed, in a rather irregular way by our Irish and German ancestors. Some say that the city could never accommodate the influx of traffic that would bombard St. Paul if it hosted an 81-game schedule of baseball games. (The other side of that coin is that baseball's 81 home dates a year would bring not only traffic, but vitality—and economic benefits—to the city. Nothing else comes close, including theater, opera, museums, etc.) To them I say, bring me the challenge of too many people in downtown St. Paul, of people flowing in and out of the river city. We can work with that challenge.

A policeman from the K-9 unit was empathizing with me as I waited for the cab that lonely night. He felt bad that we were waiting in the cold, and I thought perhaps he was going to offer us a ride with his very protective-looking German Shepherd Dog.

"Yes, we could use a ballpark here," he said. "There's no question that it would be great. The public doesn't want to finance it with tax dollars, that's clear. But I voted in favor of the referendum because I feel the city needs more vitality. My beat takes me by the new hockey arena, and I've been watching that structure being created since they first broke ground. I think it's going to work for the whole city.

"We could use baseball in St. Paul, there's no question. Who are we kidding? Who are we kidding when we talk about downtown St. Paul having life. This is supposed to be a big city but there's no hustle or bustle. You can't even get a cab on a Saturday night! I feel like that's the reality."

Philip Bess: Architect of Stadiums on a Human Scale

Architect Philip Bess is 47 years old, and a self-described Chicago Cubs fan. Bess teaches at Andrews University in Berrion Springs, Michigan. He has worked in town planning and came to see the study of ballparks as a good fit.

Bess had something of an "ah-ha!" experience in architectural school, when he recognized that Fenway Park and Wrigley Field offered something much different from what he had seen and experienced as a youth at Los Angeles' Dodger Stadium.

Living in Boston from 1973 to 1978, just prior to entering graduate school, Bess became well acquainted with Fenway's intimate environs and its unique standing in the neighborhood.

NEW FENWAY PARK: PRESS BRIEFING
WITH RED SOX CEO JOHN HARRINGTON

"We have a special reason for meeting today: We want to present to you our plans and the model for our new Fenway Park. As most of you know, we've had an extensive outreach program for the past two months, really since mid-May, where we've been visiting with many constituents around New England and briefing them on our plans for the new ballpark. I know Fenway is loved all around the country, and it's particularly loved here in Boston, and we were very carefully deliberate in designing a new Fenway Park with the kind of amenities that we thought our fans deserved but preserving all the good parts about Fenway. So I'm hoping over the course of the next half-hour we can get you excited about telling your fans about our plans for a new Fenway Park.

"Camden Yards inspired many other teams to move forward on new classic ballparks, such as the Jake [Jacobs Field in Cleveland] and Coors Field [in Denver], and they've done a remarkably good job there.

"Most of those new ballparks have experienced situations where millions of additional fans have come into their ballparks. Now, we're embracing what they're doing in many ways, and we all realize that we needed an additional million fans in our ballpark to remain competitive. But actually in Fenway, which is the smallest and oldest ballpark in use, we have the demand for seats here in June, July and August, and so we can't satisfy the demand that our customers present to us in the summer months, here. So we have to expand and move on.

"I've learned from the experience of other teams, but I am finding it very difficult to let go of Fenway Park and Bud Selig knows what we mean by that. And all of us in the baseball environment are very historically oriented. We know tradition means a great deal to us, and we do not let go of what we have in our hand. I have worked here at Fenway most of my adult life, and it is not easy moving forward into a new ballpark.

"We studied renovation for many, many years and we actually spent $80 million on this ballpark from 1981 through early 1990. We know what renovations can do for this ballpark, and we are really maxed out on the renovations that you can do on this ballpark. We have had great architects studying the possibility of renovating the park. Hellmuth, Obata, Kassabaum the premier architects and renowned restoration specialists and Walsh Brothers looked at it, and we simply determined based on their recommendations that you cannot rebuild Fenway Park in place, it is just totally impractical and unreasonable from an economic point of view, and our footprint is way too small to build a modern ballpark with the amenities the fans need.

"We are facing the future with our hearts in our hand, here.

"I have got to move on, myself; I cannot get involved in the emotion of what we are doing at Fenway Park.

"But after a great deal of work with our architects and engineers, we have designed a new ballpark for space that is right next door. We are going to move home plate 206 yards down the street. We believe that we have captured the essence of Fenway Park, and that when you view the model and the renderings that we have here, if you can put yourself in a seat as you view these renderings, I think you actually will be able to say to yourselves, 'We envision ourselves sitting right in Fenway Park.'

"So we are presenting it to you, and I hope you will embrace it. We have the ultimate All Star here in Boston with us for the All Star Game, and that is our Ted Williams. He is going to be throwing out the first ball tomorrow night. And Ted said in Dan Shaughnessy's book, which was published this spring, that he cannot wait to see a new ballpark for Boston. Our childhood hero and great All-Star, Ted, understands what we have here, because he played so many years here, but he too, is ready to move on to a new ballpark. He speaks for our fans in many ways. We have had our plans up on our Web site for these two months, and we have received about 20,000 e-mails in response to our plans. And 90 percent of those people have asked us to build a ballpark as soon as possible. And we did a poll a few weeks ago, and 80 percent of the fans were in agreement with the idea of building a new ballpark. We are encouraged by what was presented, and we are hopeful we can move forward expeditiously on it."

"I came to realize that ballparks could be much more interesting, and provide a very different and full experience, than what is currently the direction of Major League Baseball."

Bess is the author of *City Baseball Magic,* which is available in reprint, through Knothole Press, St. Paul, Minnesota.

Your ideas are gaining a platform for discussion in the Twin Cities.

The more the idea of a small urban ballpark gets out there, the better I think it's going to be for the Twin Cities. The traditional urban ballpark fits a smaller area and maximizes the space available; it lends itself better to fitting in with existing streets and blocks.

Most of today's parks are enormous revenue machines intended for corporate interests. They are Goliaths, with a lot of overkill in their design. They are not marketed to the average baseball fan, but rather to corporations and upscale individuals.

What we would be talking about for St. Paul is a more cleverly designed urban ballpark. Today's ballpark can be designed much tighter, both horizontally and vertically.

Is baseball ready for such a transformation?

We tried pursuing ballpark work in the early '90's but Major League Baseball was not interested in what we were doing. Times are changing, both in stadium design and in the game itself.

Baseball can't sustain itself on its present course. There is reason to believe the economics of baseball could cause the game to collapse upon itself.

The game is headed for $150 Million contracts in the year 2000. No stadium can generate enough revenue to keep up with continually escalating costs. Baseball cannot, realistically, expect to pass such enormous salaries on to the fan.

We voted down a stadium referendum in St. Paul, 58% to 42%. What do you think the public's message is?

St. Paul, and Minnesota as a whole, are saying we're not going to be subsidizing tremendous player salaries or assisting ownership in paying them.

I believe the no vote on the referendum in St. Paul sent a great message. It was not a bad thing. The people took a stand for the reform of the game. I think they recognize baseball as a community asset, but if baseball doesn't get its salary structure in order, the greatest ballpark ideas are not going to matter.

You have had a lot of exposure in the Twin Cities. Have the Twins talked to you?

No (he laughs).

Would you talk to them?

It couldn't hurt for us to have a conversation. I'm not sure the Twins see the big picture yet. There is a lot of pressure from Major League Baseball to conform to the current state of affairs, and that is to build overscaled stadiums.

The tradition now is that teams don't pay for ballparks. New and bigger is better, and nobody looks beyond that.

I'm told you are okay with Baltimore's Camden Yards design. What did the architects Hellmuth, Obata, Kassabaum do right at Camden? And, playing devil's advocate, what's wrong with the mega-structures?

Camden Yards is not too bad from my architectural viewpoint. It's the warehouse that makes it work. There are a few things right about the design.

But Camden's program could be accommodated on an even smaller footprint than it currently utilizes. Hellmuth, Obata, Kassabaum, the same company that built the disastrous Comiskey Park, was held in tight reign by the Orioles. Camden still has some spatial inefficiencies in its design.

Traditional urban ballparks are about the game of baseball, and not all the side shows. Traditional ballparks are less expensive to build, and also put the fans closer to the game. They work better in a mixed-use environment, and add to the neighborhood in which they are located.

Comiskey holds 43,000, has an upper-deck that is so high that some fans express fear of the steep angles as well as distress at their distance from home plate. Comiskey is a problem ballpark to the point of embarrassment.

We project that our new type of ballpark would derive 90% of the revenue that the jumbo parks provide in a much smaller, more intimate space. Some of the lost income is in parking rights and could be negotiated. You also would not have as much in-stadium advertising, which many fans find bothersome, anyway.

You have designed an urban ballpark in Chicago for demonstration purposes that you call Armour Field.

It was designed for Chicago, and is fronted on three sides by streets with the fourth side consisting of a park. As described in my book City Baseball Magic, Armour would be symmetrical; 283 feet down the left and right field lines and 423 feet in the power alleys.

Man, those power alleys are deep.

Yes, but I think even the power alleys speak more accurately to the history of the game.

The creation of a Wrigley Field or a Fenway Park type of ballpark is what I believe would work in the Twin Cities. Land is tight in all cities; spatial efficiency is a must. I believe such a park would be a tremendous addition to Minneapolis/St. Paul, and a crucial advance for the game of baseball.

Baseball is in critical need of a restoration to sanity. If Bud Selig can succeed in stabilizing and changing baseball's inequities, and the Twins can remain a viable franchise, Minnesota could be on the cutting edge of fundamental improvement to the heart and soul of the baseball experience. A change that takes us back in time, but allows the game to progress.

I firmly believe that the Twin Cities, and all of Minnesota, would benefit greatly from a small-footprint gem of a ballpark built for the baseball fan and for the public as a whole.

The entire community would derive benefit from a compact urban stadium that had revenue-enhancing features built in: luxury seating, naming rights, etc.

We would have a ballpark that speaks to the truth of the game, outdoors, in the fresh air, under the blue sky on the natural grass.

We should say good-bye to the carpeted concrete and stale environs of the Metrodome. Thank you for the wonderful memories of 1987 and 1991, and good-bye. ◌

TOM TUTTLE'S BEST
MAJOR LEAGUE BALLPARKS

1. Wrigley Field, Chicago

   My hometown park, it's got to be number one for me. Warm and cozy with time and memories on its side. A visit to Wrigley is an experience in the essence of the joy of the game. Packed with personal memories, including my first recollection of a great major league play: Roberto (Clememte) firing a baseball out of the right field corner to nail a base runner at third base. Few amenities, just a great baseball experience.

2. Fenway Park, Boston

   Fenway and Wrigley are very comparable ballparks as far as intimacy and tradition. While Wrigley's seats aren't the greatest, at least they're wider than Fenway's, built for a 1912 behind. The all star game at Fenway was an amazing experience as much for the old Red Sox characters as for the park itself. The Green Monster deserves honor. Nothing beats these two for a genuine baseball experience.

3. Jacob's Field, Cleveland

   From a seat in Jacob's Field it is easy to conjure up a vision of such a ballpark in St. Paul. On the riverfront. A comfortable view of downtown St. Paul would be grand; even downtown Cleveland looks great from the Jake. The city has come a long way from the days when its rivers caught fire, and baseball has palyed a role in the town's renewal.

4. Yankee Stadium, New York

   The history of Yankee Stadium speaks to the observer in a clear voice. It says, "Dimaggio, Ruth, Gehrig, Mantle, Maris and too many more to mention. An appropriate shrine to the greatest teams in baseball history. Very warm despite its neighborhood location in the Bronx.

5. Coors Field, Denver

   Another reminder of what we could do here. A lot of modern amenities (including, believe it or not, a daycare center). But part of the appeal for me is that I used to know Lo-Do, as lower downtown Denver is called. Forget what the economists say, this was a tremendous rejuvenation of an underutilized part of a big city. It's nigh impossible to put a price tag on the value of a ballpark to a city..

6. Camden Yards...another case in point

Smallish, with extraordinary baseball viewing, it services Baltimore, Washington D.C. and even Philadelphia. Not too expensive. A real charmer among the new ballparks. You've got to visit Boog Powell's joint .

15

POLITICS

From "Senate Briefly"

Below are two excerpts from "Senate Briefly," a summary of legislative activity and discussion that is published at the end of each session of the Minnesota state legislature. These excerpts describe the debate over bills related to stadium financing and ownership of the Twins.

Committee on Taxes

Baseball proposals debated

Two bills relating to baseball stadium construction and community ownership of the Minnesota Twins baseball franchise were debated by the Committee on Taxes, Weds., Apr. 8.

S.F. 3081, authored by Sen. Roy Terwilliger (R-Edina), funds a $284 million stadium through a donation of a site worth $50 million, the sale of $138 in revenue bonds, and $96 million in private contributions.

Terwilliger said the idea behind the funding proposal in the bill is sim-

ple. "If you don't use the stadium, you don't pay for it," he said.

The open-air ballpark, as proposed in the bill, seats 40,000, and opens on April 1, 2002. Costs associated with the ballpark include $218.5 million in construction and related costs, $10.9 million in financing costs, $50 million for the site, and $4.5 million for contingencies.

The bill requires Twins ownership to be transferred to a nonprofit foundation and any existing team debt is to be guaranteed by the owner. The owner is to operate the team and absorb annual operating losses, but is to be reimbursed once the foundation sells the team. The bill requires the foundation to sell the team within five years of the date of transfer, offering both class A and class B shares. The class A shares may be sold to one or more new owners, and give the owners the right to operate and control the baseball team. The class B shares may be sold to individuals and offer the right to vote on the team's relocation.

The bill requires an advance deposit of one year's rent to protect against the eventuality of a player's strike, and authorizes Minneapolis and County to exercise the right of eminent domain to acquire a site for the ballpark. The bill also requires the owner and the baseball team to agree to use the ballpark for at least thirty years without an escape clause.

One provision in the bill requires that at least five percent of the tickets in the baseball park will be available at the lower of $5 per ticket, or a price no greater than 25 percent of the highest price seats. Other provisions authorize the Metropolitan Council to impose parking taxes and a two percent income surtax for players and other ballpark employees with incomes over $150,000 a year. The income surtax also applies to visiting players' incomes, based on the number of days the players perform at the baseball park.

The committee adopted an amendment, moved by Sen. Carol Flynn (DFL-Mpls.), deleting the requirement that the Minnesota State Lottery conduct two instant lottery games with sports themes. The net revenues of the games were to be appropriated to the baseball park account after Minnesota environment and natural resources trust fund deductions.

Committee Chair Douglas Johnson (DFL-Tower) questioned whether the level of public support for the project has changed since last year's Minneapolis referendum, when a majority of voters rejected other plans for a ballpark. Sam Grabarski, of the Minneapolis Downtown Council, said that he never viewed the referendum's results as a vote against the ballpark, but against certain funding options. Terwilliger added that the vast majority of people want baseball to stay in Minnesota, but don't want the stadium to be paid for out of the general fund.

Sen. David Knutson (R-Burnsville) said he didn't understand how the committee had the time to adequately hear the proposal one day before adjournment, considering the lack of public notice.

Sen. Arlene Lesewski (R-Marshall) also said that the lack of available public comment was a concern, but that the proposal was much different than last year's, and she would be able to support it.

Sen. Dick Day (R-Owatonna) presented an amendment replacing the language of the bill with language that he said was the same as the Canterbury Downs proposal of the year before, funding a stadium with revenues from slot machines at Canterbury Downs. The amendment failed on a 14-4 roll call vote. Another amendment requiring voter approval, offered by Sen. John Marty (DFL-Roseville), also failed. The amendment prohibited any Minneapolis city department, agency, commission, or board from using over $10 million of city resources for the financing of professional sports facilities without the approval of a majority of votes cast on a ballot question.

S.F. 3081 was recommended to pass and sent to the floor on a 12-11 roll call vote.

S.F. 3106, providing for community ownership of the Minnesota Twins baseball franchise, was also recommended to pass and sent to the floor with little discussion. Authored by Sen. Ellen Anderson (DFL-St. Paul), the bill instructs the governor and the Metropolitan Sports Facilities Commission to attempt to work with the Minnesota Twins to transfer team ownership to a community or non-profit foundation. The bill provides for the ownership of the team through class A and class B stock offerings, and limits certain levels of stock ownership.

Sen. Gen Olson (R-Minnetrista) asked whether the bill assures that there would be a baseball team for the community to buy. Anderson replied that the Pohlads have said that they want baseball to leave a legacy in Minnesota. "This would set the wheels in motion, and the Pohlads would take the next step," said Anderson.

The Senate also engaged in a lengthy discussion on Senate Concurrent Resolution 13, authored by Sen. Roy Terwilliger (R-Edina). Terwilliger said that the resolution is to encourage a diligent effort and sincere and open negotiations with Major League Baseball to keep the Minnesota Twins in Minnesota. He said the resolution acknowledges the value of the Twins and the desire to build a stadium without the use of general fund money. "We want to continue on that effort," Terwilliger said. An amendment was offered by Sen. John Marty (DFL-Roseville) changing the types of funding that should not be used for a new stadium [from] "general fund" to "public," and ask[ing] Major League Baseball to address its problems rather than discuss them. Marty said that the intent of his amendment is to oppose using public money and to ask Major League Baseball to actually fix their problems. The amendment was adopted.

However, discussion soon turned to a bill, also sponsored by Terwilliger, that reached the Senate floor the day before. The bill, S.F. 3081, authorizes the construction of a new open-air baseball stadium and a series of user-fees to pay for it. Sen. Steven Novak (DFL-New Brighton) said "We had a bill here yesterday, but now we have this resolution." and asked why the Senate was not voting on the bill instead. Terwilliger replied that the bill won't pass in the other body, and that the resolution is to encourage discussion in order to find a solution in the 1999 session.

Support for the bill also came from Sen. Dean Johnson (R-Willmar). Johnson said that the bill proposes a 100 percent user-financed stadium and said that the Senate is missing an opportunity by not voting on it. But other Senators raised issues about problems with the bill such as the Twins' management not having agreed to the proposal. Terwilliger reminded members that the resolution was before them, and not the bill. He successfully offered an amendment clarifying that a public stock offering was to ensure local ownership and control of the team. The resolution was adopted on a 61-0 roll call vote.

Mike Osskopp

Mike Osskopp is a radio personality in Hastings, Minn. as well as a Minnesota State Representative from Lake City. He's been involved with the Fellowship of Christian Athletes and claims to be a Twins fan of some duration. He's not optimistic regarding big-league baseball's future in the Twin Cities.

"I think the biggest problem is that, when Carl Pohlad made that 80-some million dollar gift announcement in 1997 and it turned out to be a loan, a lot of people found that to be very misleading. There was a huge loss of faith," Osskopp said.

"In addition, right away Major League Baseball started marching North Carolina businessman Don Beaver all over the country to gain some kind of leverage over teams that were slow to build stadiums, and that was a fraud. North Carolina was not a viable deal and the Twins had nowhere to go. That really looked bad to a lot of people."

Osskopp believes the Twins, management underestimated the Minnesota public's opposition to any type of taxation for new sports facilities.

"It's the same old story: Nobody wants to subsidize millionaires and billionaires with tax dollars. The legislature is not the problem for the Twins, the public is the problem, in that they have clearly stated: "No tax dollars for a ballpark." The St. Paul referendum failure was just a sampling, and they had something to gain from a new baseball facility in their town. I can tell you that statewide, the public is against a taxpayer-funded ballpark."

OK, we've got that. But what about some other sources of revenue, like slot machines at the Canterbury racetrack? Some studies have shown that a few hundred slot machines at Canterbury would largely pick up the public share of a new ballpark. Why are slots at Canterbury not a viable alternative to public funding?

"My feeling is that government should not be in the gaming business," Osskopp said, apparently forgetting for the moment that he heads a government committee that oversees gambling already present in the state. "The Indian casino compacts were negotiated by [then-Attorney General] Skip Humphrey, and there are no closing dates on those compacts. They just keep going, and business is sweet for the tribes right now."

The Indians at Treasure Island are undertaking another big expansion of the casino as we speak, Mike, so why would slots at Canterbury be a big issue? The public appears to favor the racetrack slots idea, and could be accurately polled via a referendum.

"I firmly believe that it is not the job of government to be in the casino business." Osskopp stated again. "It's not the role of the state to own gaming establishments and I don't think the public wants us to go there."

"But if the public were to demand this Canterbury slots idea, it is not beyond the realm of possibility. I just don't see the demand," he said.

Doug Reuter

Representative Doug Reuter doesn't mince words when he talks about the idea of the state building a ballpark for the Minnesota Twins. "There's absolutely no realistic hope of tax money being used to finance any kind of stadium in this state," Reuter said.

"The ballpark malarkey that has been thrown around borders on the insulting. Sports should not be subsidized by government. Where are you going to draw the line if you subsidize Carl Pohlad so he can pay $10 million for a pitcher?

"I don't think we should be subsidizing theaters either," Reuter added, referring to a Guthrie Theater project to be built on a site the Twins had hoped would be used for a riverfront stadium.

I know that's got to add some insult to the Twins already injured feelings. I asked Reuter if he even liked the game of baseball. "I love baseball. I'm [moving] down to Round Rock Texas, and they've got a minor league team that's only about seven miles away from where we will be. I can't wait to get down there and check that out. I think Nolan Ryan (who used to pitch for the Houston Astros and is a Hall of Famer) has a hand in it.

"I love the game of baseball; I used to play the game. And of course, I would never stand in the way of private efforts to bring a new stadium to Minnesota. That's what free enterprise is all about.

"Baseball is way out of control, just way out of control. It needs to be brought back from where ever it is that it has gone to."

Reuter is a conservative Republican who's been involved in human resources in the manufacturing business. He is the inventor of the board game "Sequence" and that's how he made his money, as he explained it to me, and was able to retire and become a politician. He is disgusted with the Republican party and he's leaving the party and the state and moving to Texas.

He also has been the subject of an investigation involving licensing one of his cars in Texas while he is still a Minnesota resident (or sitting in the Minnesota legislature while he's a Texas resident.

Dennis Ozment

Another legislator who feels that baseball and the Twins made empty threats is Dennis Ozment of suburban Rosemount, Minnesota. Ozment also claims to be a baseball fan and thinks there may be a way for the Twins to obtain an new ballpark—just not with tax dollars.

"The legislature won't address tax money for a new baseball facility," Ozment said. "Using taxpayers' dollars for a park is a dead issue. My constituents say, 'If you find a way to build a stadium, I need a barn.'"

But Ozment does not rule out public money being used in the future as a vehicle for a new ballpark; "Public money is a possibility, not tax money. There is a difference."

One source of funds for a ballpark might be lottery revenue, if the Twins could get the issue on the ballot in a referendum. "Should lottery funds be partially earmarked for sports facilities?" might be a sample question. "A referendum of this type, if passed, might give legislators courage," Ozment said. "Of course, opponents will quickly rally against such a proposal, saying that lottery revenue can't be used for sports, it goes to the schools."

Ozment says he opposes using slot machine revenue for sport facilities on principal; he believes that slot gaming at the Canterbury Park horse-racing track would just be the beginning of an expansion of casino gambling in the public sector. "Once Canterbury has them (slots), I don't see how you can stop restaurants and bars throughout the state from demanding equal privileges. I don't believe it would stop with Canterbury, I really don't," Ozment said.

Would the Indians throw some big money at a ballpark for the public relations benefits such a gesture might bring? Not likely.

Then what about the state general fund as a source for funding? That's not using public tax dollars per se.

Ozment tells an interesting story. "Years ago, 50% percent of lottery funds were earmarked for the environmental trust fund and 50% for an economic development fund. Over time, and for whatever reason, that has evolved into 71% "general fund" and 29% environmental trust. The economic development fund, logically, could have been used for projects with a determined public benefit, such as a ballpark. One thing is for certain; lottery funds were never intended to build the general fund."

Left unsaid is the fact that wrestling dime one from the general fund for a sports project would draw loud cries of protest from the left, center and right. The question remains, whatever happened to the state economic development fund, and could it be resurrected? Might it be used for stadium funding for both the Minnesota Twins and the Minnesota Vikings?

Ozment felt the Twins stadium efforts were overweighted with lobbyists from the very beginning of the debate in'97. "Kirby (Puckett) had a positive impact on me and others when he was around. But all the lobbying was a failed effort. You don't use lobbyists to front the project; it's better to bring them on in support. The '91 Twins coming in and talking might have had more success (than the lobbyists). And North Carolina was an empty threat that didn't sit well with a lot of people at the capital. The whole thing has been a public relations 'how not to' study."

16

THE MONEY GAME

Ryan: "The Money's Out of Whack"

Ballplayers in the major leagues make a lot of money. I can remember when the average salary of a big league shortstop first topped a million dollars. Good people sweat blood and guts working all their lives and never earn a million dollars. Of course, the Twins face a consistent battle to keep players in an age when a million dollars is not enough. Good-bye to Pat Meares, the fine shortstop who left for Pittsburgh. Adios to Mike Trombley, a quality reliever (who never gave Terry Ryan an opportunity for a final offer, and who had the temerity to say he was not bitter with the Minnesota Twins after he signed with Boston. Bitter about what? About the Twins giving him an opportunity to become a multi-millionaire?!).

As Will Kenney said: "I'm the fan and I'm bitter. Not that there's any loyalty anymore, but I expected more from a quality guy like Trombley. He's not bitter. Hello!"

Fair-value for Marty Cordova should be a million dollars or less, even in today's market. He'll likely end up with double that amount, and the Twins are wise to let him go; no way they should exercise a $4 million option for a player with his suspect attitude and injuries.

And financially, the Twins probably couldn't keep Cordova even if they wanted to. We're talking about a payroll of less than $17 million for the entire team. About one year's salary for Ken Griffey. When you lose a quality pitcher like Greg Swindell during the 1998 season because of cost, it hurts. It hurts a team mentally. When you basically must surrender a top-shelf closer like Rick Aguilera, a fine pitcher and a better human being, you can bet there is lasting damage. What is it like for the players to know that they are at a consistent and growing disadvantage? Their bosses don't have the bucks and they're probably going down as a team. That's what they know, and that's a burden.

I keep hearing Terry Ryan say "The money's out of whack in this game.

"There's no doubt it's out of whack. You know it. The fans know it. We all know it. Representing the Twins, I have to pay these things. I have to negotiate them. It's not easy."

Runaway Salary Inflation

Just since Ken Griffey, Jr. came into the League in 1989, the average amount of players' salaries carried by each major league team has increased from $12 million to nearly $50 million. Nearly a 500% increase since Junior entered the league. How can one doubt the fact that the money in all of major league sports has become outrageous and is now trending toward the bizarre? Multi-year contracts for mere ballplayers are paying over $100 million. Griffey's salary alone could pay for more than a third of the estimated costs of the proposed St. Paul ballpark. It raises the questions, what does an individual do with $100 million, with $115 million, with $125 million?

When I first learned that the average major league salary was $1 million (not all that long ago, in 1991), it bothered me. When I hear of some of the salaries today I am not alone in feeling repulsed. When I hear a player say he has pursued a better offer in free agency to secure the future of his family, surely he could secure the futures of several families. The money is ridiculous and in many ways is an insult to working Americans.

Of Payrolls and People

P.K. Wrigley, the former owner of the Chicago Cubs, said "Baseball is too much of a sport to be called a business, and too much of a business to be called a sport."

For a long time, Carl Pohlad and the Twins had a lot of chips in the game. That's not the case anymore. The Twins have been reducing their payroll steadily since the end of the 1998 season. In late May of 1999, the Twins decided to trade Rick Aguilera to the Chicago Cubs. General Manager Terry Ryans said, "Three weeks ago we were playing some pretty decent baseball. We were able to use Rick on a pretty regular basis. We were optimistic three weeks ago."

When the Twins eliminated Aguilera from the team, the payroll was reduced by $3.25 million. That's a big cash savings, and teams that are not going to contend are the teams that can afford to get rid of their top relief pitcher.

Manager Tom Kelly seemed resigned to the decision to trade Aguilera. "Terry Ryan had to do what he had to do. I respect that. If I had an argument to make I would make it. But I don't have any bullets."

Paul Molitor said, "[Aguilera] was a

connection to some of the great teams that this franchise has had. It's always frustrating to lose a player of that caliber, and I think the veterans feel the pain more than the young players."

Yes, baseball is a business. A business that has changed dramatically. When Fred Saigh Jr. died at age 94, it was noted that Saigh had been the sole owner of the Saint Louis Cardinals in 1953. That was when tax problems that eventually sent him to prison forced him to sell the ballclub. Groups from Milwaukee and Houston offered as much as $4.5 million to buy the Cardinals and move them. Instead, Saigh accepted $3.75 million from the Busch Family to keep the ballclub in St. Louis. A little more than 45 years ago, one could buy a major league franchise for slightly more than an aging reliever costs today.

Wealth Doesn't Guarantee Happiness: Darryl Strawberry

What about all this wealth in the players' lives? Darryl Strawberry isn't sure extensive wealth contributes to a person's happiness, and his own life has given him knowledge of the pitfalls.

Money gives the player control over what he chooses to experience in his life, Strawberry noted in a brief interview, and if those choices lead to cocaine, that is a real problem.

"I think some professional athletes lose sight of what is important in their lives, and money helps them make that mistake.

"There are people who try to make the fantasy a reality instead of enjoying the fact that they've fulfilled a dream by making the major leagues. It is a problem at the highest levels of all professional sports."

Strawberry has walked some dark valleys in his life, and at that time in the summer of 1998, you could see in his smiling face the amount of growth and spiritual progress he had made. Darryl is a very gentle person in his demeanor when he is working his recovery program. But the full-time requirement of a healthy recovery lifestyle was illustrated when Strawberry relapsed in the winter following the 1998 World Series Championship. And it appears that Darryl faces more recovery challenges in 2000. ◑

17

TOWN BALL

In 1999, the big school state tournament was won by Hastings, which defeated Cretin–Derham Hall en route, stopping Cretin's 66-game winning streak two shy of the national record of 68 set by Archbishop Malloy of Queens, NY from 1963 to 1966.

The 1999 state tournament for small high schools was won by Montgomery-Lonsdale, which defeated Breck High School 15-5 in the tourney final at Dick Putz field in St. Cloud. Montgomery-Lonsdale High School is a merger of two small towns south of the Twin Cities, and the Redbirds won their first baseball state title in bruising fashion due in large part to the Vosejpka cousins.

Brian, Chad, and Brad Vosejpka were key players all year for the Redbird squad, scoring six runs and driving in four in the title game. Montgomery–Lonsdale finished the season 23-1, their only loss coming from a "pretty tough" Bell Plaine team during the regular season, according

to Brian Vosejpka. Brian, who along with cousin Chad captained the Redbirds, said his dad knew when the kids were small that state possibilities loomed, "Dad (Dale Vosejpka) thought we might be special when we got older; we've been playing together for a long time."

Baseball runs in the family of the Vosejpka clan. Dale is a former player who now coaches the Lonsdale town team that the boys play for. Grandfather Fritz is a former player and town team manager himself. Brian loves the town game and at age 18 is in his third year of town ball. He finds the town game fun as well as maturing. "Playing against older guys will make you play tougher. That's gotta help your overall game."

Montgomery has had a better town team of late, finishing fourth in the state a couple of years ago. But Lonsdale is where Brian's loyalty lies; he was the Lonsdale batboy from ages 8 to 13. Currently work is being done to improve the Lonsdale ballfield, so

The author in Miesville, Minnesota

all of the team's games were played away from home in the summer of 1999. Montgomery has a nice field, but, "They play football on the outfield grass, and it takes a pounding," said Brian. "It's funny playing against a lot of my teammates and buddies on the Montgomery team during the summer."

Brian and his teammates were the guests of honor when the Twins sponsored "Redbird Day" at the Metrodome on August 22, 1999. He was hoping the stadium referendum would pass in St. Paul so that the Twins could play outdoors. "We go to the dome once or twice a year, and with outdoor baseball I think we would go more." A lot more? "Probably," Brian said.

It's genuine outdoor baseball when Lonsdale hosts Union Hill in the big annual Fourth of July game. The game, which is followed by the community fireworks display, normally draws a couple thousand fans to Lonsdale. The ballgame and festivities have grown over the years to become a mainstay of the summer season; a great Rice County tradition as American, and as Minnesotan, as baseball itself. "Boy did everybody miss it this year," Brian's dad Dale Vosejpka said. (The game was cancelled due to construction of the new field and grandstands). "We can't wait until the Fourth of July, 2000 gets here. It's going to be one heck of a day."

Todd Warren, Player

Todd Warren is a high quality athlete and a fine town ballplayer. He's a natural ballplayer whose big strides eat up a lot of ground in the outfield and he's also an improving pitcher. Todd's a young guy compared to some of us, but we try not to hold that against him.

"Baseball is a great game for all ages, young and old" Warren said as we sat around talking about our favorite sport one afternoon. "I'm a competitor and I love to play the game, but I know that I would love baseball even if I wasn't playing. It's a part of me.

"In the movie *A League of Their Own* the character played by Tom Hanks says, 'The "hard" about baseball is what makes it so great.' I respect that thought. Baseball is a game that fills one with humility. A ballplayer can be a hero one minute and a big-time goat the next. Even the best guys in the game fail 70% of the time—that's what makes success so rewarding. When you can make a key contribution in the game of baseball there are few things that feel as special, at least for me. 'The hard about baseball is what makes it so great.'

"My family has been exceptional about letting me pursue my passion," Waren continued, "and I think the reason they indulge me is because they know how much joy I obtain from the game. It's give and take of course. But it makes me very proud that my family cheers me on and it's special that my wife Amy gives me her support. When she traveled with our team to Florida to play in the Roy Hobbs tournament, it made the experience all the sweeter. She cares about my love for the game."

Tom Rifkin, Player

Tom Rifkin, a very bright guy who is vice president of a large company, enjoys playing the game as he moves into his 40's for some of the same rea-

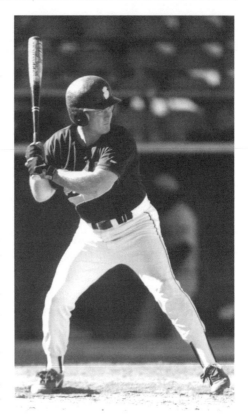

At the plate, in Florida.

sons as a lot of the guys—competition and camaraderie—but he plays for more reasons than those. "If you love the game and you love to play the game then you love to talk about the game. I enjoy baseball conversation and sometimes I find it difficult to talk to people who don't play the game. When you talk to people who are still playing, you can get into the inside baseball stuff a little deeper.

"People who know the game well enough to appreciate the little things tend to be more knowledgeable about what it's like to be in the mix. Talking about baseball, talking about the professional game as well as about the games we play in is enjoyable to me."

Tom grew up in Omaha and has gone to College World Series games for many years. He knows the game and plays a solid left field for the Cavaliers. "Baseball has a couple of sides to it; there's the team stuff, which is primary and most important, but there's also the individual aspect of the games. You get a chance to see if you can still compete, and if you can rise to the occasion as it is demanded. It is interesting to see if you've still got it.

"There's a lot of joy and satisfaction when you succeed. And the challenge, even when you fail, is the essence of the game."

Kevin Lawrence, Player

Kevin Lawrence has played baseball with his brother Scott since they were children, as far back as he can remember. Scott is couple of years older than Kevin, so the boys have sometimes been teammates and sometimes opponents on the field. Kevin and Scott, now into their 40's, hope to play on the same club in senior ball in the summer of 2000.

Commenting on their motivation for staying with baseball, Kevin said, "I still have a lot of fun playing baseball. The game still presents the challenges

that it always has and the satisfaction I receive from the competition and the camaraderie is probably stronger now than it was years ago. It's a lot of fun to play the game with friends, and the special trips that are made to Florida and the like solidify some friendships that I have developed in the game. I know that baseball is a kids game and that we're adults enjoying it for what it is. No money or real prestige is involved in our efforts. Something about it makes the experience incredibly worthwhile for me. I think it is the joy of the game itself."

Like the old days, Kevin's parents still occasionally get a chance to watch him play. And so do his kids.

Steve "Hondo" Handley, Player

Steve "Hondo" Handley has been playing town ball for a long time—for 17 years, he thinks. He played his college ball at the University of St. Thomas, the high-quality academic institution with a very solid Division III baseball program.

The Tommies finished second in the nation in 1999 in D-3, in a program that has come a long way since it fielded the "fairly strong" squads that Steve was a part of in the 1980's. St. Thomas plays good small college baseball and has done so for some time. Steve's favorite Tommy team of memory had 18 wins and only 2 losses in MIAC play, a long-standing record until the Dennis Denning-coached teams of the late 1990's went 19-1 on a couple of occasions.

Steve, who has always been a catcher, started playing town ball for the Columbia Heights, Minnesota team in 1982, when he was just out of high school. He remembers the squad taking a bunch of second-place finishes in the state tourney.

"We were pretty good, with some quality players who knew the game" Handley said. "And we had a pitcher named Jerry Wickman who I think played AAA minor league ball with the Yankees—I'm not certain of that, but I know he played in the high minors—and he was really tough. He was a lefty with great stuff who not only intimidated the other team, but also our guys.

"I was just out of high school, and so was our shortstop, (former Gopher) Mark Hess, and if we made mistakes we would definitely hear about it. We weren't exactly the superstars on the team. Here we are playing for the legendary Columbia Heights town team in key positions at catcher and short, batting 8th and 9th in the order, and the pressure to perform was on!

"I can still hear the bench screaming at me to 'get the bunt down' and Wickman hollering at Hess to 'field the damn ball!' When we won the state tournament in 1986, Jerry was getting by on craftiness more than anything,

and he retired from the team afterward. He was an educator, a teacher of some kind, and a heck of a pitcher. You don't forget guys like that."

More recently, Handley was part of a state championship team with the 1997 Hamel Hawks, an outfit on the western fringe of the Twin Cities that featured a number of former Gopher players who still play for the love of the game, among them Mark Hess and Randy Mosselle from the Columbia Heights team. Hamel, once managed by John Blanchard of N.Y. Yankee fame, has always rubbed the powers that be in Minnesota state amateur baseball the wrong way, partly because they're tough to beat. They have played good baseball in Hamel, behind the roadhouse bar, for many decades. The '97 team had played together for years, some of them having won a title in 1987, and they play well as a unit.

It was Alex, Van Krev, (former Gopher, excellent hitter and out with a broken leg in '97 but still a factor), Hondo, Benny, Kiki, Hess, Flem, Hartman, Joe Mons and a few others who took it all the way in 1997 after a number of close calls, knocking off Cold Spring, Minn. 7-4 in the final. Brian Hartman hit eight home runs in the tournament, including two two-run homers in the championship game.

Handley has now retired as a player and reports that his knees "are killing me. Too much catching, that's a fact." I tell him about Aleve for pain (no side effects) and ask him if he plans to stay around the game.

"Yep, I'm umpiring," Hondo says. "I can stay around the game and I like working with the kids at the high school level."

But Steve, the knees?

"Not so bad. I don't have to go into the full crouch."

I nod in agreement, but in my heart I know that he'd be behind the plate whether his knees hurt or not— and I suspect they hurt plenty. The game has claimed another one. He won't let go of the game that has been such an important piece of his life. Umpiring keeps him close to baseball and that's where he wants to be.

Trip to Florida, October-November, 1999

There's something about playing baseball in Florida that feels just right.

Ever since I first visited the land of grapefruit league ball on a spring trip with my college team, I have dreamed of playing at a major league park in the Sunshine State. At the Roy Hobbs World Series, my dream came true. I've had the opportunity to play shortstop at Hammond Stadium, part of the Lee County Sports Complex in Fort Myers, Florida. It's the springtime baseball home of the Minnesota Twins.

The Roy Hobbs World Series is a big event for both the players and the Fort Myers area. Over 140 teams head south to play in the Over-30, Over-40 and Masters divisions. That's more than 2,500 participants who infuse a great deal of cash into the South Florida area. But while the tournament is a significant source of revenue for the local community and its businesses, money isn't a concern for most of the ballplayers who make the trip. What's most important to them is the opportunity to play serious baseball games in the finest of environments.

"Let's play ball," is the order of every day of World Series week.

The first thing I noticed about Hammond Stadium from a shortstop's perspective was the impeccably manicured turf in the infield, and the dirt where nary a rock was to be found. Very few excuses were built into this infield, which is a luxury not afforded in the picturesque, but frequently lumpy, town ballparks of Minnesota. I watched as Mike, a solid player from Texas who was manning 3rd base for our Minnesota Saints squad, fielded a few fair-hopping ground balls and fired to first. In the beautiful Florida sunshine, in early November, Mike is covering Gary Gaetti's old position and looking good doing it. I'm in the spot where Greg Gagne has spent many a quality afternoon. Life is lovely.

Mike is here to help us out—he's a very strong player with a rocket arm and a powerful bat who plays in an Over-18 league in Texas, while most of us are Over-35 town ballplayers from Minnesota. Mike is in his mid-thirties and is able to keep up with the kids in his league down Texas way. He's something of a ringer among the Minnesota contingent. Our guys played on senior town teams throughout the Twin Cities Metro Area in places like Prior Lake, Minnetonka, Loretto, New Hope, St. Paul, Lexington Park and others.

We have all experienced the joy of summer baseball in the singularly delightful town parks of our home state. And we are all, without exception, thrilled to take our chances on the no-built-in-excuses springtime ball field of the Minnesota Twins.

So is the opposition in our second game, a squad from New Jersey that plays most of its ball back home on a couple of diamonds that recently added lights to accommodate some night games. The difference between their home fields and Hammond stadium probably is greater than that between Hammond and the wonderful town ball fields we play on in Minnesota.

That we would travel to parks around our metro area that were unique in design and atmosphere was a different concept to most urban players I spoke to at the Roy Hobbs.

Having played a couple of years in Chicago, I remember the none-too-flashy fields where we played on the city's north side. A fellow from Cleveland didn't understand the term "Town Ball", and when I explained the concept to him, he seemed surprised that we didn't play in a league-affiliated complex of some kind. I know there are a lot of lovely ball-parks around this grand country of ours, but I feel a sense of gratitude when I reflect on the variety of splendors at our home facilities: From Elko to Young America (A small German heritage town), we've got it great in Minnesota baseball.

Reflections on Town Ball

I was reading a local columnist recently who made the point that tension on a ballclub is not necessarily a bad thing. On good teams, especially at the major league level, there is often some tension among the players. But I think in town ball, teamwork and friendship is essential to a quality club as well as a quality experience.

The best talent doesn't always win in the town game. It seems like the teams that really play together and pull together when the going gets tough are the finest squads. Good teams have players who need and respect each other.

On most quality teams I've been a part of since my youth, there's been a bond, a unity, between the individuals. Rugged individualism, while sometimes a desirable attribute on a big-league club, isn't always an asset on town teams, for whom the weekend recreational experience is primary.

Baseball is a team sport, and even at the top some individualists can go over the edge and be nothing but a distraction. Gary Sheffield didn't help the Los Angeles Dodgers in 1999, and Albert Belle hasn't helped a team in a few years. Baseball is a team sport that requires a team commitment.

Some town teams have played together for a long time, and team members know each other very well. Other teams pick up all star caliber talent and make it happen. That was

A GLOSSARY OF PITCHING

...FASTBALL

Gripped across the seams, or with the seams, the fastball can appear to rise or sink depending on the way it is gripped. Some pitchers can make their fastball move towards either corner of the plate. It is an illusion that a fastball rises. Gravity forces the ball down as it moves to home plate, but the illusion of a rising fastball is created when a ball gripped across the seams falls at a slower rate than a normal pitch.

...CURVEBALL

The curveball, thrown properly, is arguably the most effective pitch in baseball. Joe Mays of the Twins uses his curveball as an "out pitch." The days of the big breaking curveball, a la Sandy Koufax or the Twins own Bert Blyleven, may be going as the slider predominates. The curveball separates good hitters from players who will continue to struggle offensively. A good curveball gets hitters out.

...SLIDER

The slider is thrown much like a fastball with its movement late and lateral. The slider can be created many different ways, says townball pitcher Paul Brogin. His favorite method is to "push" with his right leg and right arm to create the spinning motion. It's difficult to detect that Brogin's slider is not a fastball until it is too late. Sliders that don't slide become line drives.

...KNUCKLEBALL

The knuckleball is a popular pitch among old-timers who want to extend their pitching careers. It takes less stress on the arm to throw a knuckle ball than almost any other pitch. The key to a good knuckleball is to create a lack of rotation on the baseball. A knuckleball that rotates becomes a slow pitch that is probably doomed to being hit extremely hard. A knuckleball needs to float and dance, which it can do when the ball is released with as little spin as possible. A darting knuckleball can be the bane of a catcher's existence.

...CHANGEUP

The changeup is an effective weapon in any pitcher's repertoire, as changing speeds is the name of the game to getting good hitters out in any league, especially in town ball. I am a believer in the old saw "Throw strikes, work fast, change speeds." Changing speeds keeps a hitter off balance, and a changeup, thrown with the same arm motion as a fastball, can be a deadly weapon in pitcher's arsenal. The pitcher's arm motion resembles that of a fast ball delivery, while in fact a slower pitch is en-route to the plate. The "circle change," named for the placement of the forefinger and thumb, is an especially effective type of changeup.

...FORKBALL

An effective forkball is a tremendous tool for any pitcher and is surprisingly common at the town ball level. The forkball is similar to the split-fingered fastball, but involves a tighter grip on the baseball. A properly thrown forkball breaks after the hitter has begun his stride can be a devastating "out pitch." A Jim Wheeler weapon in town ball.

the story with one of our teams in 1999, a team that picked up Jim Wheeler and was something like 25-1 before getting knocked off in the State Tournament finals. Teams that have an aura of togetherness do tend to win, from my experience, though not always. One thing is certain, however: they have more fun on the field. There is encouragement in the face of adversity and genuine friendship. That stuff is important to me as I get older.

A tough play or a muffed chance isn't the end of the world, it can even be a chance to laugh together and show support for a teammate.

Early in our 1999 senior season, there was a play involving one of our guys who was trying to stretch a single into a double. Oscar, a pretty good player who works for Cargill in the Twin Cities, is from Venezuela and he had some wheels. On this particular play, he was motoring around first, headed for second when he started a tremendous slide into second base, with dirt flying and dust filling the air.

There was only one problem. Oscar had come to a dead stop at least 15 feet from second base. The opposing team's second baseman simply had to walk over, or maybe he jogged over, to tag him out.

Needless to say the guys on the bench were doubled over with laughter. One of them turned to me, and said "I'm not sure Oscar has played the game for a while." Oscar is a good man and he was okay with accepting the Fred Merkle award for bonehead play of the year. Both the 1987 and 1991 Twins were major league teams that played with a lot of unity, especially that '87 group.

During the 1999 senior season we played two games on days when the heat index was well over 100 degrees Fahrenheit. People who live in the Twin Cities area will remember a weekend in the end of July when the heat was just unbearable. We had a game at Big Willow when the temperature was 98° and the "misery index" of heat and humidity was 106°.

I suppose a politically correct assessment of Minnesota would find the state to be "climatically challenged." It's one of the few states where the weather warnings can swing from frostbite to heatstroke in little more than a couple of months

When it gets that hot and humid, sweat doesn't evaporate and the body is in danger of overheating. I suppose I shouldn't worry so much about getting hit in the head with a baseball; having a heart attack on one of these ridiculously hot days will probably get me first.

One nice thing about Minnesota weather is that you get to meet a lot of insects. You want bugs? We've got bugs. As a storm approached Big Willow one day, I came under attack at short-stop from black flies that suddenly disappeared around the third inning and were replaced by gnats swarming everywhere in the infield. They were joined by the mosquitoes, and actually it was pretty pathetic out there. Sometimes I'll ask our left fielder, Tom Rifkin, "How are you doing out there?" His constantly shifting body language tells me that he's not doing so good.

Oh well. Rif, as he says, "can take it. It's all part of the deal."

I played on some lousy ballfields in Chicago. They were ballfields, so they were inherently good, but some of the fields at Humboldt Park on the west side of Chicago were really not suitable for sliding. You could end up with a bottle cap permanently imbedded in your knee, or maybe a .22-caliber shell casing.

We used to play a team that called themselves "Manati," after a city in Puerto Rico. It's also the hometown of the Twins young catcher Javier Valentine. One day I told "Javy" that I had played against a baseball team in Chicago with a bunch of guys from Manati, and did he perhaps know any of them. He looked at me and shook his head, and kind of walked away.

Javy has gone a long way beyond the sandlot ball of a Humboldt Park environment. He's in the major leagues and probably didn't know what I was talking about.

As a game was ending in Elko, a blowout in which our Cavalier ballclub had not played well, I was pacing around unhappily out at shortstop. Looking to my right, I watched as a glowing orange sun was slowly melting into the fields that were turning gold in the distance. There was a cardinal sitting on a fence near the opponents' dugout and, in the fading sunlight, I could see his bright red coloring from probably 100 feet away. I thought to myself that the cardinal is truly a fine bird. I was mindful in that moment of God's grace and goodness.

I think a batter sent a ball whizzing by my head a few seconds later, but it was worth it.

It is said that we should gracefully surrender the things of our youth. I will gracefully surrender the joy of playing baseball when that moment comes, but it's not quite here yet, I don't think. Like my friend pitcher, Mark Monson said to me when I asked him why he continued to play the game, "I play the game because I still can. Someday I won't be able to say that."

At some town ballparks you can really feel the encroachment of civilization. Homes, large and small, are closing in on the ball field in Hamel. I don't think the Hamel park could ever be touched, but the view around the park is changing. Driving out to Hamel is no longer the easy shot out highway 55 from Minneapolis that it used to be. It's becoming a tougher hike past mega-movie theaters and blossoming malls that carry all the stuff that we humans think we need. It's progress, and it's not going away, but I hope progress doesn't have to touch things as precious as our town ballparks.

The Minnetonka Cavaliers (my senior town team) have the privilege of playing at a park called "Big Willow" in the Minneapolis suburb of Minnetonka. Big Willow is a fundamentally sound ballpark that the groundskeeper told me one day is described in an amateur baseball publication as "one of the top town amateur ballparks in America." It is exceptionally well maintained, though it lacks the charm of the true town ballparks.

It's a great place to play baseball, though, and we're privileged to have access to it. Big Willow hosted over 200 amateur games in 1999, I was told by a Minnetonka parks manager. The new scoreboard is a nice touch, as well as a nice target for the home run hitters. The left field power alley, where the scoreboard is located, has seen many a Jim Wheeler blast sail into the distance, although I don't recall Wheeler hitting either the scoreboard or a passing train yet. (On Jim Wheeler: Played AA ball for Detroit Tigers. Hit 11 home runs for Cavaliers in 1998. ERA of sub-.200. Best senior player in the state of Minnesota for my money.)

Jim Wheeler is an intense competitor who, it seems to me, would rather win than have fun. Too many botched plays and mistakes behind him, baseball not played the right way, frustrate Jim, but he is a battler. Wheeler pitched a stellar game against eventual Senior State Champion Northfield in 1998, and we had those guys beat. A couple of blown calls by the umpire cost us the game. Isn't that the way it always goes?

Baseball fans who have more than a casual interest in the game's history may recall that in the year 1920, pitcher Carl May of the New York Yankees killed Ray Chapman of the Cleveland Indians by hitting him in the head with a fastball. (Truly ardent fans will recall that Joe Sewell took over at shortstop for the Indians after Chapman's death and was a fixture at the position for a decade.)

I was reminded of Chapman's demise during a town ballgame vs. Edina a couple of years ago, when a big righthander named Brad whizzed one by my head and sent me spinning to the ground. Brad has a tremendous fastball, at least by senior town ball standards. I've got to think that, at that time, Brad was throwing the ball in the mid-80 mph range, although with his size, the speed of his pitches probably seemed faster than they were. He was and is a good pitcher and was probably just backing me off the plate in response to an earlier base hit I'd gotten during the game. Brad is one of those guys who likes to maintain control of home plate.

Anyway, for whatever reason, I thought about that pitch for a few days. Although I had successfully ducked the inside fast ball, just as I have avoided many inside pitches in my baseball life, this one made me stop and think. There are a lot of reasons why I would not like to be beaned on the noggin, prominent among them my realization that all it would take is one to the temple to really ruin my day (or my life). Every ballplayer lives with the danger that the hurled spherical missile possesses when it zips to the plate—and the batter—at high velocity. Thankfully, I will never know if Brad's fastball would have caused me any permanent injury, but for some reason that particular pitch stayed with me for a while.

I don't feel old, but I am considered pretty long in the tooth to be playing a kids game. I don't play the game for any compensation other than the spiritual reward that I derive from baseball. Most people don't realize the quality of some of the pitchers in our league; this isn't softball. Guys do get hurt at the senior level, as they do at all levels of baseball. It was a

moment where I became keenly aware of my baseball mortality. I still had the reflexes to avoid that pitch. I'm going to keep a sharp eye on my reflexes. My playing days will come to an end at some point, and I'd like it to be my choice.

Playing baseball at this time in my life is providing great rewards. I am finding unique moments of peace on the various ball fields of the Twin Cities that I do not find elsewhere in my life, and that serenity comes through no effort of my own. I feel close to God on a baseball diamond. There are so many wonderful moments that touch the spiritual side of who I am.

I don't play for money. It costs me money to play in our league. In middle age I play for joy. I play for the Red-Tailed Hawk circling above the field on a cloudless afternoon in Prior Lake. Or the Great Horned Owl eavesdropping from the big trees along the Minnesota River in Chaska.

I feel like I'm living.

I value a quiet comment of understanding from a teammate during a challenging game situation.

Yes, I'm an older guy with real-world responsibilities and sizable challenges. But on the field, my mind empties. Somehow I'm better for the experience of town baseball, with its

TOM TUTTLE'S
TOP TOWN BALLPARKS

1. Chaska

   A honey of a baseball park. Have to love the fact that Cubs minor league teams played here many years ago. There's always an important game being played in Chaska. Home to a lot of amateur baseball and some tremendous town team battles. Wildlife tends to flourish behind the outfield wall near the banks of the Minnesota River. Once had six robins poking around in the grass behind shortstop; they didn't have a care about being in the way. And they shouldn't.

2. Miesville

   The Miesville Mudhens is a quality town team that plays in a lovely facility just across the street from an establishment called the King's Place. (I think the King may have a pretty good line on the Mudhens—wink-wink.) A Miesville-Red Wing game or a Miesville-Hamel Hawk contest is well worth the inexpensive price of admission. Maybe the most aesthetically pleasing of any town ballpark in the state.

3. Dundas

   Combination of great baseball, a great midseason tournament, and a great bed-and-breakfast make Dundas a great town ball destination. None too shabby a ballclub of late; winners of state championships in 1998 and 1999. They've really been getting it done down in Dundas. The long ball can (and frequently does) end up in the picturesque Cannon River at the Dundas tournament, which is held in mid-summer each year.

4. Big Willow

   The home field for three Minnetonka town ball teams, both open and senior (over 35) squads, as well as for a number of Babe Ruth teams. A beautiful ballpark, well manicured and level, with the best infield of all, measured by the fairest hops and fewest rocks. The new scoreboard adds a lot to the look of the well-maintained town facility.

Big Willow was the site of the National American Legion tournament in 1998, and it is considered by many to be one of the top ten amateur baseball facilities in the country.

5. Northfield

A personal favorite, not least because I have played some of my best baseball on the diamond behind the Malt-O-Meal plant in Northfield, Minnesota. Yes, that Northfield. The home of the Defeat of Jesse James Days, and of Carleton and St. Olaf Colleges. It's surprising and mystifying that more people don't come to games? It's free in Northfield, the play is highquality, and the Archer House Guest House (1876) offers comfortable accommodations. Northfield's ballclub is always tough in over-35 competition.

6. Young America

A special place about two hours west of the Twin cities. Just a charming German town that has a long tradition of good baseball competition. A delightful, old-time ball yard, where the fans come out not caring who the teams are in action. German food is a plus. One of the fans there said, "I think you lead the league in gray hair." I took it as a compliment. I've earned those stripes.

many moments that reveal who we are and what humble satisfaction the game can bring. It's not the big round-trippers that I remember with the greatest fondness (although I recall too few of consequence); rather, it's the sounds of crickets and faraway trains, the hum of a power line and the sight of moths doing their death-dance with the lights, ice-cream-stained kids running for a foul ball. The gentle summer evenings spent in the places where town ball is played. It's the atmosphere and the attitude of the amateur game, and just as I can't have

what Ken Griffey has, neither can he hear the distant hum of engines at Elko Speedway, beyond the right field wall at Elko's gem of a diamond.

The real world doesn't belong in Elko, where they've been playing town baseball for generations. It has no business violating the serenity of the timeless. For a short spell, reality cannot burden me.

Town Ball: For the Love of the Game

When they achieve success at the state tournament, senior town ballplayers don't generally get to share in the adulation reserved for the open division heroes. Still, there might be a few free meals and beverages for a Dundas Duke or a Hamel Hawk when they take the state crown. A supportive town can be a big part of the mix of things that make town ball special.

"It's a tremendous feeling when things are going well and the town is involved," said Minnesota Twins Media Relations Manager Sean Harlin. Harlin is a former town team infielder for Prior Lake, Minnesota. "It's hard to explain how good it can be when a team is thriving. Some folks in town do take care of you. But when things go bad, it does tend to turn around in a hurry. The free beer quickly disappears," pointed out Harlin.

A senior league player like Jim "Big Wheels" Wheeler, who currently plays for the Minnetonka Lakers, could play with the youngsters, and have a good deal of success, despite owning a few more chronological years than the average town ballplayer.

Baseball is not like football, where getting hit by a 250-pound linebacker at age 40 just isn't an option. Baseball is finesse and guile. It requires an artfulness that "Big Wheels" possesses plenty of when he takes the mound. In addition, Wheeler throws a "heavy" ball that hitters tend to pound into the dirt. He throws a kind of split-fingered fastball where the bottom drops out, and almost everything he throws looks like it is sinking or fading. When he needs to rear back and fire, he can still do that, too. Jim Wheeler is a tough pitcher.

On top of his pitching prowess, Wheeler also led the league in home runs a couple of times. He blasted a dozen with us in 1998, and a couple of those were Grand Slams. A lot of good baseball players are not necessarily good athletes, but Jim Wheeler is a good athlete. Everything about Jim, including his demeanor, says, "ballplayer."

Jim spent time in the Detroit Tiger organization, going in as a shortstop. He is a friend of major league player and 1999 All Star Ed Sprague (Pittsburgh).

Sprague has been a solid major leaguer for many years and was a teammate of Paul Molitor in Toronto. Like his friend Sprague, Jim Wheeler still plays the game with intensity. Now in his early 40's, Wheeler has a low tolerance for inadequacy on the field of play.

After a few years with the Minnetonka Cavaliers, during which we seemed to reserve our worst performances for his outings, Wheeler grew frustrated and moved to a new team. He led that squad to an overall record of 27-3 and a second-place finish in the state tournament.

Jim was injured while in the minor leagues, with the Tigers, before he really had a chance to get started.

One can only wonder what might have been if he had stayed healthy.

Jim's not chasing the dream anymore. He's one of us now, playing for the love of the game and the challenge it still presents.

Fellows like Jim Wheeler and I are still enjoying the game of baseball even as our physical prowess wanes. We are pursuing a passion for the game that belies our age. Nonetheless, there are days when it can be very tough.

Many of the guys put in twelve-hour days at their jobs before they arrive at the ballpark to play a night game. We all battle traffic and exhaustion as well as stiffness and the usual range of micro-tears and muscle twinges. Occasional logginess (A feeling both lazy and foggy) is a part of the deal.

It is for the big leaguers, too. Joe Girardi, previously with the Yankees and now with the Cubs, told me that staying mentally sharp is one of the greatest challenges facing him as a ballplayer. "Physically, a player can usually turn it up, if he is healthy. The Yankees are a very strong ballclub mentally. I think in some ways that sets them apart, especially come playoff time," Girardi said.

In senior baseball, we all try to play the best we can. There is no pot of gold rewarding a strong performance, unless the pot of gold is a pitcher of Budweiser.

At the end of the 1999 senior season, I was struggling with the game and questioning my commitment. My shoulder hurt. Tempers were growing short on a team that was fighting itself while striving to get on the right track before the playoffs.

We were playing Chaska. I had worked a long day and it was one of those Minnesota nights where the heat and humidity saturate the air and a continual sweat completely soaks players' uniforms during pre-game warm-ups. You're going to be drenched in perspiration all night, I tell myself, so just relax and deal with it.

It was a night for questioning. Like, just how do these black flies and mosquitoes multiply into the gazillions, anyway?

I was 0 for 2 and I felt soggy as well as loggy. I found myself wondering why I never seem to hit in this beautiful Chaska ballpark, the former home of Chicago Cub farm hands, and a park with a good hitter's backdrop of three tall, full trees in centerfield.

I scolded myself for my persistent daydreaming and bounced around at the edge of the outfield grass to try to liven myself at shortstop. A pop fly lofted toward center, my ball, and I moved back and to the left for the catch. Not a tough play, an easy chance, but enough to bring me around a bit.

We still weren't playing well and were in danger of losing to Chaska, a

1999 Minnetonka Cavaliers Roster

NO.	PLAYER	POSITION	HEIGHT	WEIGHT	BATS	THROWS	BORN	HOMETOWN
1	Abraldes, Oscar	2b, ss	5' 8"	165	R	R	11/21/62	Caracas, Venezuela
2	Euson, Dave	p, c, if, of	5' 9"	170	R	R	04/11/55	Western Springs, IL
3	Lawrence, Kevin	of	6' 2"	195	R	R	03/14/57	Worthington, MN
4	Mellema, Bob	of, 2b	5' 10"	190	B	R	09/04/60	Minneapolis, MN
5	Mossberg, Norm	2b, 3b	5' 8"	185	L	R	12/15/49	Moose Lake, MN
6	Reber, Lee	p, of	6' 1"	200	L	L	03/14/52	Manhattan, KS
7	Johnson, Roger	1b, of, p	5' 10"	185	B	R	07/17/50	Minneapolis, MN
8	Schaller, John	ss, 3b, 2b, p	6' 1"	195	R	R	04/07/53	St. Paul, MN
9	Rifkin, Tom	of	5' 9"	175	R	R	03/09/55	Omaha, NE
10	Finn, Dave	of, if	5' 10"	185	R	R	03/16/49	Minneapolis, MN
11	Tuttle, Tom	2b, ss, of	6' 1"	190	R	R	10/05/57	Evanston, IL
13	Goodman, Roy	c	6' 2"	220	R	R	09/20/66	Asheville, NC
16	Monson, Mark	p, 1b, of	5' 9"	170	L	L	02/01/51	Fargo, ND
23	Warren, Todd	p, of	6' 2"	195	R	R	05/25/63	Fort Dodge, IA
34	Rahm, Mike	p, 3b	5' 7"	185	R	R	08/04/53	Algona, IA
44	Wyatt, Adam	3b, c, of, 1b	6' 1"	255	R	R	11/27/63	St. Petersburg, FL
51	Wyatt, Mike	of, c, 3b	5' 11"	225	R	R	04/25/60	St. Petersburg, FL
77	Nolan, Rick	3b, ss, c, p	5' 7"	170	R	R	09/27/62	Boston, MA

Final 1999 Cavalier Stats

PLAYER	G	AB	Runs	Hits	RBI	AVG.	2B	3B	HR	TB	SLG%	SO	BB
Abraldes, Oscar	15	40	5	10	2	0.250	0	0	0	10	0.250	13	2
Finn, Dave	13	30	2	4	2	0.133	1	0	0	5	0.167	13	2
Goodman, Roy	19	60	19	27	18	0.450	4	1	0	33	0.550	4	7
Johnson, Roger	27	71	18	22	12	0.310	5	0	0	27	0.380	20	13
Lawrence, Kevin	18	45	8	15	6	0.333	3	0	0	18	0.400	13	7
Mellema, Bob	11	32	13	16	9	0.500	3	0	2	25	0.781	8	6
Monson, Mark	27	57	16	16	17	0.281	3	0	0	19	0.333	4	13
Mossberg, Norm	5	10	3	2	0	0.200	0	0	0	2	0.200	0	1
Nolan, Rick	25	71	16	25	13	0.352	6	1	0	33	0.465	9	10
Reber, Lee	21	48	5	13	11	0.271	3	1	0	18	0.375	7	3
Rifkin, Tom	22	61	15	17	7	0.279	2	0	0	19	0.311	7	10
Schaller, John	19	46	14	23	13	0.500	4	0	0	27	0.587	4	4
Steffenhagen, Tom	6	13	1	2	1	0.154	1	0	0	3	0.231	2	0
Tuttle, Tom	22	65	22	27	13	0.415	4	1	0	33	0.508	0	11
Warren, Tod	22	62	11	24	17	0.387	5	1	2	37	0.597	12	6
Wyatt, Adam	15	44	11	13	9	0.295	1	0	0	14	0.318	7	9
Wyatt, Mike	8	23	6	5	6	0.217	2	0	0	7	0.304	7	4
TOTALS	29	778	185	261	156	0.335	47	5	4	330	0.424	130	108

team we should have been able to handle. I contributed my part to a bad inning by muffing a routine ground ball.

Just about everybody on the Cavaliers seemed irritable and short-tempered. I barked at our pitcher, who barked back at me.

"Are we having fun yet?" I thought to myself?

Later, a Chaska batter sent a line drive screaming toward center field. I slid hurriedly to the left, hoping to make a stab at the flying sphere with my glove. I'm a little off-balance, it was dusk and the lights were on, but it was a sticky gloaming along the river bottom.

Where was the ball?

With a lack of grace (no Ray Ordoñez here) the ball struck me just below my normally trustier-than-this Wilson A-2000 mitt.

Thwack! The blow to the top of my wrist re-injured an old wrist-thumb trauma. Crud! It hurt like crazy and I removed myself from the game, walked to the opposing dugout and asked where the nearest urgent care facility might be. I got directions, along with some ice, bid good luck to my teammates and drove myself over to the clinic.

It felt like a perfect time to stop for a couple of quick ones, but for me that was not an option.

I said the Serenity Prayer, and remembered that the game of life is always a challenge.

My entire hand was badly swollen, but the doctor didn't think anything was broken. I tied on a bag of ice and decided to head back to the ballpark.

Ninety minutes had passed since I'd left the field; it was raining and the ball yard is empty. The tower lights were dimming slowly, the way they do when they are first shut down. I sat in our dugout putting on my jacket, which I had left behind.

Three hours before I was soaked in hot a sweat. Now I was feeling a chill. How odd.

Slowly I began to relax in the solitude, watching the rain form puddles in the infield and splash gently off the pitching mound.

I sat in this very special ballpark feeling sorry for myself, and it was time to knock it off.

I became keenly aware of the night and my comfortable aloneness in it. I'm a believer that things are always as they should be at that moment, and that night must have been a part of my journey.

I felt tired. I confronted a lot of maybes. Maybe I'm just too old to be doing this. Maybe I need to allow more time to get ready for a game. Maybe I need to get my eyes tested. Heck, I never really even saw that ball.

I told myself that my attitude is my responsibility, and no one else's. I need to be accountable. I'm reminded again that there comes a time to let go of things in life.

I am reminded of how much I admire Paul Molitor and his dignified retirement; Terry Steinbach's too.

My wrist hurt, but I was okay.

The ballfield and beyond is turning from dark green to black in the fading light. I could hear the rush of trucks at the top of the hill, beyond the grandstands, moving on to somewhere via route 212.

The clouds were moving in odd formations from west to east, and I felt a need to walk with my thoughts. I pulled off my shoes and socks and, still in baseball pants, journey towards the center field fence and the tall trees. I liked the feeling of the wet grass under my bare feet. The rain felt warm again.

I was reminded of an Italian Proverb: "When the game is over, the King and the Pawn go back in the same box." Even someone like Sammy Sosa must remember that.

Shadows and sounds captured my mind. I stood alone, surveying the elegant old ballyard. A movement above, in the center field trees, drew my eye; a big bird decided I was close enough and took off. Must have been an owl. I watched for a moment as he flew silently towards the Minnesota River, into the darkness. I felt at peace, and I knew gratitude. God has been very good to me.

18

A Look Toward the Future

Twins 2000

The Minnesota Twins have an excellent chance to be an aggressive, exciting, non-winning team again in the year 2000. The kids are all right, and if they continue to improve there truly is a nucleus of talent to build on. Some of the Twins players look like real winners; third baseman Corey Koskie is a Canadian who can play the game of baseball with the skill required to be outstanding at this level. Outfielders Jacque Jones, Chad Allen and Torii Hunter have shown occasional brilliance, but all three need to improve on the day-to-day basics to sustain high quality in the major leagues. Jones looks like Willie Mays a lot of the time, with great speed, exceptional defense and great power, while Torii Hunter will need to improve his all-around game to be a regular. Chad Allen looks to be a fine left-fielder and on most days is a Tom Kelly-type ballplayer.

Pitchers Eric Milton and Brad Radke are extremely strong, with Milton an exceptionally strong third-year player who pitched a no-hitter against Anaheim in September. It's almost incredible that Milton is 15-25 for his first two years in the league. He's pitched a lot of good baseball. Brad Radke is still the ace of the staff. His 3.75 ERA ranked fourth in the American League and will make him a very valuable commodity following the 2000 season. Joe Mays and Jason Ryan look like big-leaguers much of the time. The Twins bullpen looked okay last year despite the trade of Rick Aguilera to the Chicago Cubs, but it would have been nice to keep Mike Trombley as a closer. Bob Wells and Eddie Guardado are strong and Hector Carrasco is a solid bullpen specialist.

There's real concern about whether outfielder Matt Lawton will come back strong from his eye injury (Lawton's eye socket was fractured in two places). Matty is a fine major league player and deserves a full recovery from that serious injury. The middle infield, with Christian Guzman playing a solid short and Todd Walker a reasonable second base, is fair. Both offensively and defensively, Walker has to show a lot more consistency. It would be nice to see more of a team attitude as well. Christian Guzman probably needs to have his entire offensive scheme reconstructed, as Paul Molitor has said. But there are signs that Guzman will become a long-term quality major league short-stop. Someone needs to emerge at first base.

Carl Pohlad hates to keep throw-ing money away on this team. But Pohlad, who is as wealthy as or wealthier than many of his fellow owners, will have to spend some money and fill some holes if the team is to be competitive. The Twins absolutely have to acquire a power hitter or two if they want to improve considerably on last year's mark of 63-97 (.394, worst in the major leagues). There are some good ballplayers on the team, but this team definitely needs a few more.

Twins Are a "Good Value" for Fans

In 1998 Mark McGwire broke Roger Maris home run record by almost 15 percentage points. The 1999 average baseball ticket price jumped 9.7% from 1998 according to a study by Team Marketing Report, an organiza-tion based in Chicago that follows sports marketing trends.

Brad Radke: Big money man?

In 1999 the Minnesota Twins had the lowest average ticket price in the major leagues at $8.46 per ticket. The Boston Red Sox had the highest aver-age ticket price in the game at $24.05. Tickets at my old stomping grounds, Wrigley Field, were up over 20% from 1998, with increases across the board from bleachers to box seats. Alas, not included in the *Team Marketing Report*, but of significance to the Cubs rooftop faithful, of which I am a vet-eran member, is the fact that most of the rooftops surrounding Wrigley now require serious coin for admission. Way back when, one just had to know some people and show a friendly smile to "go roof." A 12-pack of beverage usually did not hurt, either.

The average ticket price to watch a major league baseball game increased from $13.59 in 1998 to $14.91 in 1999. Ticket price increases in baseball look better when compared to average ticket prices for other major sports. The average ticket cost is $42.54 in the National Basketball Association, and $42.79 in the National Hockey League.

One can argue that, based on ticket price alone, the Minnesota Twins are the best value in all of the big league sports. The cost for admission to a ballgame is $34.00 less than the average for any of the three other major sports.

Team Marketing Report calculates a "fan cost index" for baseball that reveals the Twins to be a good overall value.

TMR says two beers, four soft drinks, four hot dogs, parking, a couple of game programs and caps plus tickets cost a family of four $97.83 at the Metrodome in '99. The Montreal Expos were the best value at $87.87, but if that same family went to a Yankees game, the same package cost them $166.84.

Minnesota Twins games were the fifth-cheapest to attend among the 30 major league teams in 1999. With just under 40% of all seats priced at $6 or less, the Twins tie with Montreal for the largest percentage of cheap seats available in a major league ballpark.

Strikes, 1994-2001

No one I've spoken to in and around baseball would argue against the assertion that the damage from the 1994 baseball strike was lasting and severe, and certainly no sane baseball person, management or players, would ever want to go there again. Right?

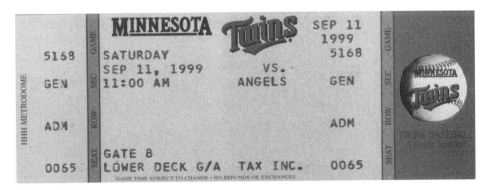

A ticket from Eric Milton's no-hitter

Sport Magazine undertook a survey late in the 1999 season to determine how real the possibility of a work stoppage might be in 2001. The survey polled 95 players, and found that only 29 percent thought a strike unlikely while 45 percent thought a strike possible, and (oh my!) 26 percent thought a strike highly possible.

Some of the players' comments are revealing.

- Sean Casey, Cincinnati Reds: "It's very possible. I don't think baseball can handle another one. I hope that we are all smart enough to figure that out."

- Shawn Green, Seattle Mariners: "Very possible, unfortunately. Salaries have had such ridiculous increases and owners are creating too much of a division between clubs."

- Darren Erstad, fine young Anaheim Angel outfielder who still makes his home in Fargo, North Dakota: "It can't happen. I don't think either side is gonna budge, but baseball cannot withstand another strike."

Amen. Even without a strike, Major League Baseball's future is less than certain. ◐

19

FINAL THOUGHTS

Commissioner Bud Selig and the Strike of 1994

One has to give Bud Selig credit for getting things done, although one can also wonder about *how* he gets things done. A new baseball stadium for Milwaukee looked highly unlikely until Selig essentially willed the ballpark into existence. His forceful (some would say obstinate) personality has been a key to ballpark-building not just in his hometown, but throughout the country: Atlanta, Arizona, Baltimore, Cleveland, Colorado, Detroit, San Francisco, Seattle and Texas (Arlington) sprouted stadiums or gained legislative approval during Selig's term as interim commissioner of baseball.

Selig was also in the driver's seat during the baseball strike that wiped out the 1994 World Series and led to the use of replacement players during 1995 spring training. If you are a fan of interleague play, which began in 1997, then credit Bud Selig. He was the driving force behind both that "experiment" and Milwaukee's realignment to the National League, with the Brewers becoming the first team to change leagues since the turn of the century.

The strike of 1994 was a painful experience for baseball fans and for the game itself. I can recall my anger with players, owners, and Bud Selig. If there was ever a sports work stoppage that could have, and should have, been avoided it was that strike. The price for failing to avert that bitter experience was the alienation of the fan. A neighbor of mine and a fan, Steve Kenn, told me over coffee in my kitchen that, "I don't care if baseball starts up again tomorrow; those idiots have lost me forever." A man of his word, Steve has not been to a major league game since the strike. Where was the like of Kenesaw Mountain Landis (baseball's first commissioner) during those trying times, where leadership seemed lost in a vacuum?

In fairness, the baseball strike of 1994 was hardly all Bud Selig's fault, but his position as both acting baseball commissioner and a team owner clearly created a conflict of interest. The work stoppage happened on his watch as the commissioner of the national pastime. Today he is the full time, permanent commissioner of baseball. As the *Washington Post's* Tom Boswell said when Selig was given that post: "If Bud had been the captain of the Titanic, he'd have survived, blamed the iceberg and been given a bigger ship."

Eric Nelson

Eric Nelson of WCCO-TV was a witness to the effort that Jack Morris made in game seven of that fabulous 1991 fall classic. "Man, it was amazing," Nelson said. "You couldn't have gotten Jack Morris off the mound in extra innings with a tow truck. What a classic game. I remember how the emotions were flowing when Gene Larkin ended it with his hit in the 11th inning. I was standing in the Metrodome with chills running down my spine; people were laughing and crying. It was a tremendous thrill. But you know we've really gone in different directions. Atlanta has been a top team throughout the 1990's, while Minnesota has been a bottom feeder almost since the Twins won that title. It hasn't been a good 1990's for Major League Baseball in Minnesota, but you couldn't have asked for a better start for the decade."

1999 Twins Season Wrap

The Twins held a media luncheon early in December 1999. Those of us

Seeing Stars, and Cents

Baseball Commissioner Bud Selig estimates the 2001 All Star Game will have in excess of a $60 million economic impact on Seattle. Here are the economic impact figures for recent All Star Games, based on information provided by the host cities, using their own studies (numbers are in millions):

Year/Host City	1998/Denver	1997/Cleveland	1996/Philadelphia
Direct Impact	$20.25	$21.0	$32,8
Indirect Impact	$20.25	$16.5	$23.0

Year/Host City	1995/Texas	994/Pittsburgh	1993/Baltimore
Direct Impact	N/A	$26.0	$16,4
Indirect Impact		$18.3	$15.1

gathered at the Nicollet Island Inn, in Minneapolis, hoped to gain some insight into the future of the Minnesota organization from Twins President Jerry Bell as well as from the team's Vice President and General Manager, Terry Ryan.

It was not a raucous get-together by any stretch of the imagination. Most of the assembled press honed in on the stadium referendum defeat in St. Paul and wanted to know what the ballclub was going to do next.

What they heard was not encouraging.

"There is nothing new happening on the stadium front. We've heard 'no' from the politicians and we've heard 'no' from the citizens of St. Paul on November 2nd (the date of the stadium referendum). So there's nothing positive or good to report on the stadium issue," Bell said.

I looked around the room at a full contingent of Twin Cities media, who had just finished a very nice light meal as guests of the Twins. Now, all eyes were on Jerry Bell. They're looking for a miracle, I thought. Maybe phantom developer Socrates Babacas is coming to the rescue.

But there would be no miracles today. Rather, a lot of depressing reality was forthcoming.

"Our only strategy is to get out of the Metrodome." Bell said. "We know we need a new facility. Renovation of the Dome is not an option that the Minnesota Twins are considering."

"There is nothing in the air. There are no plans of any kind to help the Minnesota Twins that the organization is aware of."

Silence, broken only by the quiet clinking of silverware against bone china, fills the room as a collective deep breath is taken.

"We were not able to get the public on board," Bell continued. "We thought we could. Having a positive outlook on the field is a key to getting the public on board. But our payroll is limiting."

There is the catch-22. You need to put a quality ballclub on the field to interest the public in the team, as well as in the concept of a new ballpark, but you need money to build your team into a contender. Money provided by things like suites and club boxes, as well as increased revenue generated by large crowds at a new ballpark. Without new and additional revenue it is impossible to dramatically increase the quality of play.

Terry Ryan seemed stunned by the hard financial facts that he presented.

"Cleveland just gave $14 million to a young Cuban player. Tampa Bay just spent $360,000 on a very young man in the Dominican Republic. They are speculating that they might find a diamond, like Sammy Sosa, in the rough.

"We can't play that game. It used to be that $5,000 would land you that type of quality young Latin player. It wasn't that long ago."

Jerry Bell added, "Twenty-five percent of players currently in the major leagues are foreign-born. That number is higher in the minor leagues. We need a world-wide draft. The lawyers say that could be a problem. Lawyers always see problems, but we need to do it."

A world-wide draft is a priority of commissioner Bud Selig's, and is needed to maintain balance and prevent the big-checkbook teams from getting even farther out of hand. The fat cats of baseball tend to eat all the canaries.

Ryan is a baseball man, and he still believes in his young talent.

"We have some good young pitching in place, and some players who gained valuable experience last year. Joe Mays and Jason Ryan were positives, Eric Milton threw a no-hitter, and he's still a very young major league pitcher.

"We'll have a number of our young guys in spring training camp; Mike Restovich, from Rochester, Minnesota, is 6-4 and has a lot of power. He needs to cut down on his strikeouts, though. Matt LaCroix, at catcher, is promising. Mike Cuddyer, at shortstop, has played well down in Florida...."

Yes, baseball is about hope, it's about springtime, it's about youth. I respect Terry Ryan; budget or no budget, he will never give up. In some ways, perhaps, poverty strengthens the character of those who must live with it. (Which doesn't mean it's ever enjoyable. There were times in 1999 when, as my writer friend Brad Zellar put it, "being at a Twins game at the Metrodome is like going to work, or worse, going to school. The early inning blow-outs are like detention.")

There are a few limited advantages to the Twins' current situation. You really can get to know the young Twins players. Giving interviews and signing autographs are rarely problems for players with uninflated egos, who recognize the privilege of wearing a major league uniform. Also, given some talent and a few breaks, young players may well stick around Minnesota for a while. And for those given to the hope-springs-eternal way of thinking, it's fun to remember that the young Twins players of 1982 grew into the World Series champs of 1987. (Of course, those optimists must also be willfully oblivious to the fact that the current state of checkbook baseball renders a repeat of that situation extremely unlikely.)

There are no baseball questions directed at Terry. The scribes instead persist in asking about the stadium situation. Isn't there something more you want to tell us?

Jerry Bell might as well rip off his tie and yell, "There are no flippin' answers!"

I decided to ask Terry Ryan a baseball question, which he answered. ("When is LaTroy Hawkins going to really step up?" "It better be soon, or we may change his role to relief.") There were no more baseball questions, and then the luncheon was over.

As tables cleared, I sidled up to journalist Larry Fitzgerald. When he saw me he grimaced, and shook his head. "Man, that was depressing. I don't know what I was hoping for when I came here, but now I'm convinced it doesn't look very good," he said.

After giving me some playful grief for "picking on the only brother on the pitching staff," Larry said: "I can see where they may be looking for greener pastures, like the Carolinas. The situation is so flat here, so stagnant, that there's very little to be positive about.

"I didn't hear *anything* that could be described as good news, except for the young players. They do have good young talent. Terry Ryan and Jerry Bell deserve credit for honesty, and you have to feel for those guys."

I believe Twins management has been honest. When Terry Ryan says, "Baseball needs balance, the industry needs competition," and Jerry Bell says, "We're starting to see repetition of the usual suspects in the playoffs," they are stating the obvious truth.

Terry Ryan is a baseball man, not a magician. For Terry to convince even the most devout Minnesota Twins fan that the Twins will be able to compete in 2000 is like trying to shovel Mercury with a pitchfork—darn near impossible.

Deacon Jones: Scout

Deacon Jones is a special assignment scout for the Baltimore Orioles and is currently the only African-American advanced scout in Major League Baseball. Elanis Westbrooks used to do the same job for Colorado, but recently he was reassigned.

I asked Deacon what it was like to be an advance scout in the major leagues.

"The job of an advance scout is to prepare the team to go into baseball battle. We learn everything there is to know about the opposition and we look for opportunities to beat them. By that I mean we look for tendencies a club may exhibit. Who's hot and who's not, both at the plate and on the mound. We look for anything, and we learn just about everything, just like the opposing teams learn just about everything about us."

I asked him what pops into his mind when he thinks about baseball today. He paused to answer between bites of his hot dog.

"Right now what I notice most is that everybody thinks that they're Mark McGwire or Juan Gonzales. Everybody is overswinging, it seems. But these guys know that that's where the money is going, and maybe that's where the game is going. Everybody's gotta be a slugger."

I mentioned to Deacon that in today's world, immediate gratification is primary. The home run is immediate gratification.

Deacon laughed heartily and leaned back in his chair as he rolled his eyes. "Yeah, that's the truth, but I can tell you that not everybody is meant to be a home run hitter and the ones that are not meant to be look pretty foolish attempting to be.

"We're always looking for an edge," Jones said. We also look for trade possibilities who may be available or who may be looking for a way out and we learn contract specifics when it's appropriate."

I suggested to Deacon that, given the Orioles' recent performance woes, he must feel a bit like one of Custer's advance scouts.

Deacon laughed again and winked at me. "We've been underachievers, that's for sure."

Deacon got to talking about the Minnesota Twins with a little prompting.

"The Twins have a great tradition, going back to Killebrew, Oliva and that bunch, right up to 1987 and 1991 with the World Titles. It really hurts to see the lack of fans; one time last year (1999) I was here when the Twins were just home from a road trip and there were only about the 8,000 fans in the place. Of course, Texas was running the Twins out of the Dome at that time. (The Twins lost all 12 games to Texas in 1999.)

"Baseball is a very big shop right now. Somebody may be dropping out. In any other business, you go bankrupt or you get out of the business. That hasn't been the case with baseball to this point.

"I think Middle America is sick of all the money going around in sports. There's a little more tolerance for the excess out on the coasts." He laughs, adding, "Not much more tolerance though.

"People have other ways to spend their money and fans are tired of *money this*, *stadium that* and baseball needs to be careful.

"I know the Twins had some wonderful years in the Metrodome and I can remember Kirby bringing down the house like it was yesterday. As a facility, however, a lot of us don't like to be in the Metrodome. It's no Camden Yards, that's for sure. And I'll tell you something else. From behind homeplate, I frequently can't tell what pitch I just saw—whether it was a sinker or a slider or whatever. I'm not crazy about the lighting in the place or whatever it is that causes my blindness. Other than old age," he chuckles.

Harmon Killebrew

I ran into Harmon Killebrew at Twins Fest, an event that the Twins organization puts on in the Metrodome in February to generate enthusiasm for the coming season. I mentioned to him that I have learned a lot about baseball, and a few things about myself, from watching Paul Molitor during the past couple years. In some ways, Paul has inspired me to look for new edges in my activity as a baseball player and also in some of the challenges facing me as a person. Harmon nodded in agreement.

"Paul has been my favorite player around baseball for some time. I really enjoy him as a player, and always admired the way he played the game. I've watched him play since he was over at the University. I didn't know that Paul was going to have a full career, with all of the injuries that he had to battle early on. But he persevered and has had a Hall of Fame career."

Harmon and I reminisced on Bambi's Bombers: Robin Yount, Jim Gantner and Gordon Thomas, and don't forget Ted Simmons. They were tough, tough players, tough guys on a tough team, and they complemented one another.

"Those guys played the game right," Killebrew said. "Lately there have been a lot of fans expressing appreciation for what we played like back in the 1960's.

"A lot more fans lately are coming up to me, to talk about our teams, than I remember ten years ago. I really believe it's more about *what we were*, how we played the game, than who we are as individuals.

"The fans don't care about a lot of the things that are distracting from the game today."

Harmon is a Hall of Fame player near the top of the all-time home run list; *who he is* speaks volumes. It is powerful to hear him speak on the importance of the fans.

"I don't know if the game today is as satisfying as it used to be for the average fan. A lot of things occurring in baseball are not about the game itself; there are a lot of distractions," Killebrew said.

Harmon is right, of course. Things like John Rocker's racist comments in *Sports Illustrated*, the umpires' failed strike and subsequent dismissal, Pete Rose's gambling problems, stadium pressures and, as always, the huge salaries in baseball distract from the field of play. While those issues really are on the periphery, they tend to become the center of attention.

"Baseball is distracted by all the baloney," Harmon said. He leaned forward across the table and focused on me with his piercing blue eyes.

"What was the 1994 baseball strike about? Why did the players go on strike? Do you know why it happened, what the reasons were?" Killebrew asked. "I'm a former player and I don't understand why that strike occurred. What did they want?"

I guess the players wanted more, I quietly volunteered.

"I guess," Harmon said with a sigh. "But it was a terrible thing for the game and for the fans."

Ah, the fans. No one seems to think too much about the fans anymore.

Let's get this straight: Without the fan there is no Major League Baseball.

The owners are always certain to take care of themselves. The owners may well be happy merely serving the corporate interests, who purchase luxury boxes and suites, but they should not mistake those economic Goliaths for the fan, who is essential to the game.

The players know how to look out for themselves, to the point of *sacrificing a baseball season*. Maybe that's what their agents told them to do. The loss of the 1994 season and World Series was inexcusable.

Baseball may never get back many of the fans lost during that "work stoppage."

The politicians, as usual, like to have their input into the process, and the media (like the umpires) tends to mistakenly believe that their input to the game is critical.

Not so.

Major League Baseball is taking care of the owners, with a former owner as commissioner of the game. The other owners have vested Bud Selig with powers unseen since the days of Landis. He may do some good for the game with that power. It is imperative that he succeed in his efforts.

Meanwhile, the players grow ever more wealthy, while impressing the public little with their rarely expressed gratitude.

The Major League Baseball fan has taken a beating, an undeserved pounding, at the hands of both owners and players. The fan needs to be restored to a proper place at the top of the pecking order. The future of the game depends on it.

Without the fan, this party's over. ◌

My husband Phil and I are loyal baseball fans, and we enjoy traveling together to spring training as well as to different baseball stadiums around the country to watch the game.

I was inspired to take pictures at the Minnesota Twins games when Paul Molitor came "home" to finish his career in Minnesota. I respect Paul immensely for his great passion for the game. I am impressed not only by Paul's great hitting but also by his excellent base running. His athleticism never ceases to amaze me.

Most importantly, I am impressed by Paul's continuous generosity and patience towards the fans and community. The Twins, and especially the young players, are blessed to have Paul continuing on with them as a coach.

It is easy for me to respect Paul Molitor, as well as other players who have a similar respect and appreciation for the great game of baseball.

As a woman (and an injured athlete), the only way I can participate in baseball is through my camera. I watch for unique and genuine moments, like a player blowing a bubble; the picture of Molitor doing just that during his final year is one of my favorites.

I favor moments that show a bit of the kid in every player. I also try to capture highlights of the game, of course, such as when a player like Mark McGwire hits a home run or when Ricky Henderson steals a base. For me, highlights have been photographing every home game during the last year of Paul Molitor's career, capturing his many milestones as well as his final hit. Other special moments were photographing Eric Milton's no-hitter, Mark McGwire's 36th home run of the 70 he hit during the 1998 home run chase, and Paul Molitor's jersey retirement in Milwaukee.

I always try to take pictures with good intentions, and with respect for the players. I try to capture for the viewer both great and simple moments in baseball history. I take great pleasure from a photograph well done.

I would like to thank Tom Tuttle for allowing me to be part of this book journey, my mother for being a wonderful part of my baseball life and the Twins organization for their sup-port regarding my passion for the game. I am grateful to have Major League Baseball here in Minnesota, and I hope it will continue always.

—Sandy Thompson,
photographer and fan